E.T. CULTURE

Duke University Press DURHAM AND LONDON 2005

EDITED BY DEBBORA BATTAGLIA

E.T. CULTURE

Anthropology in Outerspaces

Printed in the United States of America on acid-free paper ♾
Designed by Erin Kirk New
Typeset in Electra and Scala Sans by Tseng Information Systems, Inc.
Library of Congress Cataloging-in-Publication Data appear on the last printed page of this book.

CONTENTS

EDITOR'S NOTE

This book is about how people find and relate to one another around the idea of extraterrestrial life and UFOs. It is also a kind of artifact of that process. Most of those who have contributed chapters first came together at the 2002 annual meeting of the American Anthropological Association, in a session on "The Anthropology of Outerspaces." Inspired by imaginaries of contact with other worlds—which is of course likewise a signature theme of the discipline—our papers gave voice to subjects' questions about what it means to be human in a universe of fabulously different entities and times of swarming informatic flows of unknown origin. While our approaches were methodologically, geopolitically, and even disciplinarily diverse, our presentations on that occasion converged at points where science, magic, and religion flowed into and through one another, unsettling their boundaries and revealing the innerspaces of "alternative" seekers.

The creativity of the moment proved to be contagious. In part owing to the attention of our discussants, Jodi Dean and Susan Harding, scholars in the audience afterwards offered papers of their own for publication in any future volume. Some others who had harbored an interest in extraterrestrial discourse were persuaded to contribute new essays, off-center of their specialty fields, after hearing about the session. As the volume took shape, there emerged the contours of an E.T. orientation toward various forms of visitation—including alien beings, technologies, and uncanny vision—and how these forms engaged primary concepts underpinning anthropological research: host and visitor, home and away, subjectivity and objectivity. Contributors showed how discussions and representations of otherworldly beings express concerns about racial and ethnic differences, the anxieties and fascination associated with modern technologies, and alienation from the inner workings of government.

My opening chapter sketches out the themes of the volume, giving a view of the "galaxies of discourse" that constitute the "E.T. effect" in postmodernity. Purposefully ex-centric, the chapter invites the reader to move at "warp speed" across thematic spaces and to visit topographies in which later chapters dwell more deeply.

Christopher Roth's historical treatment of "Anthropology as Ufology" demonstrates how questions of Darwinian evolution were resisted by the Theosophical movement that, from the late nineteenth century, offered an alternative vision of human racial progress in mystical terms that continue to emerge as common referents of contemporary E.T. and UFO beliefs.

In "Alien Tongues" David Samuels maps adventures of linguistic anthropology in space, from its historic intersection with the impassioned projects of communication with Mars in late-nineteenth-century French salons to the popular cult phenomenon of Klingon language conventions.

Drawing on ethnography from Area 51, site of the first crash narratives of UFOs in the Nevada desert, Susan Lepselter draws us into the lives of those who seek "license" to enter the realms of official culture for which the U.S. government's secret Air Force X base and research zone stand as a reminder of hidden knowledge, and the inscrutable forces of the powers that be.

My chapter on the Raëlian religion's human cloning enterprise, based on its foundational notion that extraterrestrial scientists created life on Earth through advanced cloning technology, is an excursion through the online and offline ethnographic sites of faith-based science in the public sphere.

Tracing the online and offline gaming community of young Yugioh players in Japan, Mimi Ito shows the importance of taking seriously inventive "child's play" as action that subverts the values of mainstream Japanese society in significantly gendered practices, through print, cyber, and physically embodied imagery of alien hybrid entities.

Richard Doyle, venturing farther out, absorbs us in the rhetoric of alien DNA and popular culture "sampling" technologies—of DJs recombining recorded music or the sampling of DNA by replicative science—that challenge us to consider our densely postmodern planetary "mix" of cross-connecting entities alien to their species categories.

Finally, Joseph Dumit grounds alien discourse in the half-joking interpretations of sufferers of diseases not officially recognized by official health care agencies—such as Chronic Fatigue Syndrome—who speak derisively of "Host Planet Rejection Syndrome" in their online chats and of being zapped of strength by off-world agents hidden from view.

This volume, then, itself "samples" cultural sites of off-world agency—interrogating the poetics and politics of power, its visibility and transparency, and the liberation from everyday social constraints that people seek through creative action, in the name of the extraterrestrial. Taken collectively as a collage of creative humanness "designed" here on Terra, it shows that we have much to learn from such de-exoticized subjects' points of view.

Insiders' Voices in Outerspaces

DEBBORA BATTAGLIA

In these pages you are invited to enter the outerspaces of extraterrestrial culture, as a realm of social inquiry. Where this journey leads is perhaps unexpected, especially for the discourse of alien beings and unidentified flying objects. For the fact is that, far from fields of exotic Otherness—the space of technomarvels and weird entities, epic enterprises, and terrors unrecognizable in their "structures of feeling"—we find ourselves instead in the presence of an extraterrestrial uncannily familiar and concrete.[1] It is the image on a cell phone or a backpack, the toy in the window that glows in a child's room, the lead character of a blockbuster film, a teenager dressed for Halloween, the saucer-shaped café on a desert skyline. This deep familiarity is, to quote Gregory Bateson's definition of *information*, the "difference that makes a difference" to how we approach extraterrestrial (E.T.) culture as lived experience. For it connects us to sci-fi as sci-fact and reveals factuality itself to be cultural at the core—and something we may opt to take on faith. Particularly in these insecure times, when information of unknown origin enters our living spaces as a matter of course, and often unbidden, the idea that diversely inhabited worlds contribute in mysterious ways to life's ambiguous messages and contingencies is not so strange.[2] That extraterrestrial life could figure in this socially cosmic mix is something that a third of North Americans believe (Gallop Poll 2000).

Thus, the National Geographic Channel can broadcast *Alien Contact* (2004) to a mainstream television audience already primed to hear that "astronomers and astrophysicists and other real scientists—not just nut cases—believe that extraterrestrial life is not preposterous, not possible, but *probable*" (Heffernan 2004). Notable aerospace engineers, among them the director of the National Investigations Committee on Aerial Phenomena (NICAP Unit-3) and the director of the Mutual UFO Network (MUFON), can produce book-length manuscripts about the close encounters of astronauts and others claiming that "ETs ARE HERE! and have been for thousands of years" (personal communication). While it is not the purpose of this book's contributors to interrogate the truth value of such claims or of the documents circulating as evidence in spheres of public culture, we hope to show that there is much to be learned about what it means to be human at particular historical moments by admitting a *de-exoticized alien* into our ethnoscapes and into the light of anthropology's most searching disciplinary questions.

Galaxies of Discourse

A striking feature of the idea of the extraterrestrial is the extent to which conventionally distinct fields of knowledge cross-connect, collide, or pass through one another under its influence. For "insider" and more detached researchers alike, these *galaxies of discourse* reconfigure how we relate magic, science, and religion in contemporary practice and, often to actors unaware of this, in terms recalling the science spirituality of times putatively more mystical. The "E.T. effect" of social discourse is in this sense deeply cultural and explicitly historical but also intersubjective. Emanating from the outerspaces of cultural imaginaries, it draws us to the horizons of subjects' innerspaces. Whether we train our attention on the idea of the extraterrestrial (aliens) or alien technologies (ufology), on mystical "channels" of communication or "saucerian" visions (as Ryan Cook writes on his AnthroUfology website), each of these homes to places and times right here on Terra (cf. Melucci 1996).[3]

It follows that the extraterrestrial tests anthropology's methodological grounds as well as its reach, requiring a wide variety of available approaches that present "an opportunity to phenomena that . . . would not be 'given a chance' [to appear]" if they were subjected only to the scientific gaze (Latour 2000: 368). "From the Earth native's point of view," as Susan Lepselter cleverly puts it (1997), alien/UFO religions and online and offline communities, and individual seekers of a "truth that is out there," reveal the inner workings of relations enabled, and disabled, by prospecting starward for social connection, with the expectation that this action is reciprocal. Our methods bear witness to this reality for seekers of reflexive contact, and take this as a process worthy of investigating.

Since all of us writing in this volume are anthropologists and/or seasoned ethnographers, our work in one sense or another carries with it the notion of "the field." Classically, this notion calls up images of ethnographic fieldwork and representations of unified "societies" and "cultures," and their "institutions" and "customs" in "out-of-the-way places" (as Anna Tsing has put it [1993]). And, indeed, all of these categorical units of analysis can lend themselves productively to cross-cultural comparison. In the late nineteenth century's Age of Empire, they aided the young field of anthropology in defining itself as a coherent discipline, distinctively positioned to gain new knowledge of complex alien lives—knowledge of its "Others." More to the point, the subjects themselves participated in this, creating their own Others in their self-definitional identity politics.

Yet E.T. culture—being both of this world and out of it, and, more importantly, being shaped in respect of alien "differences not yet otherness" (Agamben 1999: 126)—subverts us/them categories. To the extent that alternative knowledge networks and communities chart their life courses by means of the occlusions and silences of dominant culture authorities and gaps in walls of knowledge, forming identity by contrast to official culture produces social entities that are inherently "spacey." It follows that any anthropological project that orients itself to local "models of and models for" the social actions of coherent cultures and bounded societies—Clifford Geertz's profound formulation—is unlikely to hold for the subjectivities we encounter here. For theirs is a fluid sociality of *contact consciousness in an alien key*;[4] making and finding rules of order wherever they find themselves mutually engaged—in, say, conspiracy theories or science futurism or abduction scenarios or plans to build an embassy for welcoming E.T. Taken together such sites of social action do not require the encompassing value of a coherent cultural system of belief in order to do the work subjects ask of them. Such subjects abide, suffer, and thrive in a historically contingent social. They orient themselves to the flickering light of mortal prophets, social gatherings of shifting membership, and an eclectic range of material touchstones. One might say that they markedly anticipated anthropology's move out of Empire's shadow, and into critical perspective on Empire's master narratives.

Wherever we turn in history, the movements of these seekers across their distinctive ethnoscapes show the traces of the social insecurity that we associate with "liquid modernity" (to borrow Zygmunt Bauman's phrase) but also traces of hope for a brighter future for humanity than it is managing to produce on its own. A requirement of writing culture in congruence with such space-time topologies, which are from the start complexly, even holographically multisited, is that we keep sight of the fact that for subjects the validity of being "elsewhere" is a given.[5] So, too, is the validity of being "elsewhen," whether in the "lost time" of an abduction experience, "in the beginning" of a religious philosophy of alien Creationism, or in the event time of a pilgrimage to the historical *faith sites* of contact and exchange: to Roswell, New Mexico, where *everyone knows* that the first "flying saucer" crashed on an Independence Day weekend in 1947; or to the "mother of all crop circles," created by unidentified artists in the grain fields of southern England in 2001. The diversity and numerical growth in the "contact zones" of E.T. culture, which include UFO theme museums, archives and collections of ufological artifacts, talk radio airspace, archaeological sites, television documentaries, Web logs, and so forth, defy us to ignore—as Jodi Dean has observed—that we are living in an "alien age" wherein "the ideal and the material repeatedly cross-cut their separation" (Karen Sykes's comment on the network theory of Bruno Latour [2003: 157]).[6] As indicated by the limits of our disciplinary technologies, and by our many anthropological approach routes, out of literary, linguistic, social and cultural theory, history, and science studies, it is our willingness to observe an "ethics of dissensus" (Ziarek 2001) that in the end will determine how successful we are in writing E.T. culture and, too, in realizing our potential for discursive articulation among ourselves as scholars.[7]

In sum, our search for models sufficient to writing E.T. culture leads us to the interstitial coordinates that people wonder by. Their dedicated leaps of faith, their brave hypothesis making, are the reality with which we must converge as anthropological writers.[8] This is perhaps why, as one who tends to plunge into my ethnographic fieldwork, I could read Dan Barry's "Close Encounters" in the *New York Times Magazine* and feel at home in the sensibility and social process he describes.

> One summer evening, our parents piled us into the station wagon for a "very special" 70-mile trip to a place in New Jersey called Wanaque—where, kids, spaceships have supposedly been hovering over a reservoir. I never thought how strange this mission was, how odd that my family half-expected to see an alien spaceship that night. We had been reared on the general premise that it was arrogant to think that humans were the only intelligent beings in the universe. (2004: 132)

The E.T. effect. In an abstract sense it acts upon the social like Latour's proposition: "an offer made by an entity to relate to another under a certain perspective" (2000: 372). Unlike (linguistic and optical) metaphors, which hold that interpretative bias interferes with accuracy, the proposition finds its value in the notion that "The more activity there is, and the more intermediaries there are, the *better* the chance to articulate meaningful propositions" (375). Accordingly "each entity," as Stafford notes further, "is forced to pay attention to the other, and, in so doing, both diverge from their customary paths to venture into territory which, although it appears foreign from each of their unique vantage points, nonetheless belongs to an interdependent existence" (1999: 183). This process is at the armature of what I would call an *anthropological model of visits*—a model of inquiry that calls forth the structures of feeling in the proposition.

Less simple than it may appear, such a model challenges us to reevaluate our attachments to and detachments from place, as a cultural ethics of visitation. On the one hand, it acknowledges the problematic of departures, enjoining us to *honor the disconnect*, even as our focus shifts to the work we more commonly undertake as anthropologists of interrogating contact and the problematic of connecting across differences. Too, our "rites of return," as Vincent Crapanzano has termed them and as we know from studies of what James Clifford terms "diasporic consciousness," point to the importance of understanding what time "offworld" can do to our experience of "home." The prime-time television miniseries *The 4400* (which was airing in the United States as I sat down to write this essay) is based on what might be called the reintegration narratives of abductees returned to Earth after different lengths of time out of historical time—a journey understood by television critics as an allegory of life-worlds rendered unrecognizable by the trauma of the 9/11 terrorist attacks.

Overall, then, this volume might be understood as an exploratory project in two registers: a project of reflexive contact involving subjects and alien entities and subjects and cultural researchers in boundary negotiations and exchanges at the sites of E.T. culture. Partly because of this structural affinity, the two sets of relations can productively engage one another in their departures from the more usual grounds of authority for recognizing modalities of humanness. But, too, since the metaphysical is not essential to such mutually supplemental acts of reflexivity,[9] they can, taken together, raise a common, and profound, question regarding who claims the status of "host" and who "visitor" in this discursive realm.[10] In this matter, which is centrally about where, how, and when "home" might be found, anthropology can pose useful questions in the company of scholars who have engaged alien/UFO beliefs out of religion, political theory, and science culture.[11] We do so in anticipation that our questions will yield new knowledge that will supplement and destabilize prior knowledge, acting back on this, and constructively reveal gaps and insufficiencies (see Battaglia 1995; and "For Those Who Are Not Afraid of the Future" in this volume), and new itineraries of critical inquiry.

But fundamentally, if we are doing our work properly, our questions in this volume will acknowledge subjects' own concerning what it is to be human. They will consider, on the one hand, our openness to foreignness within the social spaces we know or have thought we understood as home and, on the other hand, our ability to make sense of everyday lives in which we sometimes seem foreign to ourselves. They will ask who our ancestors are and where they came from; who we are and are not; what throws this knowledge into doubt; and who or what moves us to act, to make choices—that is, where agency is located.

Indeed, agency as an anthropological issue is vastly complexified by E.T. culture. Is it located within us as individual or relational persons or in the space between us? Or in an author or a figure of authority, such as the prophet of a UFO religion or a charismatic writer or interpreter of theosophical texts? Is it contained in a shamanic healer's body or in whomever or whatever possesses it? Or an extraterrestrial scientist/creator's experiment of life on Earth? Or alien technologies: spacecraft, robotic entities, computers that have arrived at their own agendas? Or is agency in the images that act on us? In the popular scenarios of cultural imaginaries of contact, abduction, or colonization and invasion and their imaging technologies: cameras, sonar, FLIR sensors, telepathy? In a Web master's vision or the ether of online chats between ufological researchers or members of "plugged in" cult religions and fan culture networks? Perhaps agency resides in the events that give rise to dissociative states. For that matter, who or what dictates what counts as evidence, and truth, and for whom?

The essays in this volume suggest all of these and also make the argument that extraterrestrial discourse cannot be dismissed as pseudoscience before we know precisely what of social and material consequence to a heterogeneous life on Earth we are dismissing: what the extra in extraterrestrial is and what a view of *globalization as planetization* is doing for and to the creativity of social life.[12]

"The Powers-That-Be"

Not surprisingly, authority, authorship, and authorization will figure centrally in these pages, in reference to questions about sources of power and access to knowledge.[13] In a positive vein, the idea of an alien knowledge source can inspire bold efforts of translation across differences, carrying the promise of more closely articulated social exchange (see especially David Samuels's essay in this volume). In a negative vein, alien powers can call up a common nemesis: the opaque and inaccessible "powers that be" (Jodi Dean's great notion, drawn from conspiracy theory [1998]), who guard access to knowledge.

Recent anthropology has raised questions about this domain's invisibility or transparency and produced groundbreaking collections that emphasize the tyranny of the one (Marcus 1999; West and Sanders 2003) or the other (Strathern 2000). Refusing to write the culture concept out of the picture, these collections focus much-needed attention on operations of modernity and postmodernity that would seem to warrant anxiety from the subject's point of view. In the main, this anxiety is focused on a truth that is "out there," to cite the signature theme of conspiracy studies, but hidden and controlled by an absolutely powerful few—to disastrous effect for future life on Earth. Whether such authorities are the scientific establishment's "vigilante skeptics" (Collins and Pinch 1982: 155), the corrupt moral police of world religions, the government's military-industrial complex, or academic tenure and promotion committees, the victimage and rewards for subjects who challenge them are in some sense shared by all Earth dwellers.

From this perspective, it is not inappropriate to construct their, and our, concerns in terms of boundary maintenance and the barriers to resources that bodies, the body politic, and celestial bodies need in order to be viable and flourish. In this volume, for example, Susan Lepselter accompanies folks who are traveling through the American Southwest, compulsively seeking official access not to the government's restricted zone of Area 51 in Nevada, or to Roswell's fabled UFO crash site, but to the desert highway's seemingly boundless fields of entrepreneurial dreams. All that is missing is a driver's license. And for the license seekers all that comes between them and their dream of legitimate travel is encrypted, perhaps, in a bar code, and controlled by the issuing authorities of the Nevada licensing bureau. Denied access in another sense, the subjects of Joseph Dumit's essay seek official recognition of their "unmarked" diseases, including chronic fatigue syndrome (CFS), which is key to the realm of insurable disease categories and medical diagnostic codes devised by the powers that be. Barred from this, CFS sufferers—victims of "host planet rejection syndrome" (as Dumit refers to it)—have recourse only to the abject domain of extraterrestrial etiology.

Meanwhile, it is the opposite of this abjection, namely, the release from constraining structures of globalized economies that cyberlocales offer the online communities of youth culture "aliens" in Japan (Mizuko Ito's ethnography), the promise of context-liberated lives in a cyberinformatic age that is figured in the trope of "alien DNA" (Richard Doyle's analysis), and release from the limitations of human reproduction that is embodied in the Raëlians' "Baby Eve"—the first media-cloned baby to be delivered by a flesh-and-blood new religious movement (my essay's theme). Often such sites of optimism recover earlier ages' hard faith in science, such as Theosophy's creationist science reaction to nineteenth-century Darwinian theory (as Christopher Roth discusses in his essay); or the late-nineteenth-century fixation on the science of communication with beings on other planets and on Martians' engineering skills (discussed in David Samuels's essay). Under interrogation here are both the hope and the anxiety of the E.T. effect and the strange social hybrids that it spawns.

The phenomenon of "optimistic apocalypticism" explored by Susan Harding and Kathleen Stewart (2003) makes the case in point.[14] From their studies of present-day New Age healing (Stewart's ethnography) and the ufological prophesy of the Heaven's Gate movement (Harding's text-based analysis), we come to understand both movements in terms of their negotiations of polarized cultural values in which "future events, which are fixed in the known, determine the shape, the content, and the significance of present events and actions" (Harding and Stewart 2003: 270).[15] Further, we are shown how this is fundamental to the E.T. effect in modernity, which is likely to be as tyrannical as liberating, as terrifying as reassuring, and as violent as conserving of Earth's resources and viable and diverse societies.

In sum, as you enter these pages, you will travel "back to the future" of many of the social issues and assumptions that have marked discourses of the "occult" or "paranormal" or "pseudoscience"[16] which have led anthropology to debate issues of science, magic, and religion since its formative years as a discipline.[17] But you will also travel in the opposite direction, toward a new mission for anthropology in recognizing planetized persons' intellectual, spiritual, and popular culture cross-connections. And, as if you were traveling round a bending universe, you may find an unexpected relation to the self you thought you knew along the way.

E.T.: "Foreigners to Ourselves"

> For years Cathy Land was plagued by an unsettling sense of being "visited." When she realized what was happening, she turned to God to end her abduction experiences.—Andy Butcher (2001: 52)

> I entirely forgot that I was a scientist by profession when I began my manuscript of *Passport to Magonia*. My only guide has been the persistent feeling that science had offered no answer to some basic needs in our hearts.—Jacques Vallee (1993: xi)

> Another ex-member [of the Heaven's Gate "cult"] captured the openness of the metaphysical seeker when he explained that the "willing suspension of disbelief" is an essential part of any genuine spiritual quest.—Robert Balch and David Taylor (1977: 853)

I have proposed that the idea of the extraterrestrial is shaped in response to inadequacies of cultural models for explaining lived experience—or, more exactly, the parameters of lived experience. Where E.T. culture recognizes a marked ambiguity, contingency, and power structures of unknown origin and dimensions, other explanatory systems might find miracles, spirit possession, and the like. It is when attempts to comprehend social worlds draw us off our common maps of connection with other earthly beings, when we move out of sight of our internal and external structures for making sense of our relations, that we enter worlds apart. Entering these worlds is one thing when it is we who are going there, together, for example, as a member of a UFO movement or minority religious or therapeutic community or network. It is another thing when we are alone, in our own mortal skins. The "God of the Gaps,"[18] as theologians derisively label divine intervention invoked to explain whatever science cannot, could be E.T.—a foreignness appropriate to lived experience beyond comprehension and our zones of comfort and visibility. Or, as put to me by John Mack, pioneering psychoanalyst of abduction experiencers, "Call it ET or anything you like. What we are really dealing with is epistemological shock."

Virginia Aronson, a researcher of "celestial healing" experiences, relates the following observations of an E.T. believer, Connie Isele, who when she wrote them was a student of psychology in Colorado and a survivor of a serious car accident. While her car was sailing off a bridge, Isele experienced "a rip in time and space" in which extraterrestrials intervened to save her life and later watched over her recovery. Many years after the "little miracle" of waking from a coma and after extensive therapeutic bodywork, she describes herself as "living like a normal human being" except that:

> Lately, I have noticed that E.T communication often comes through to my consciousness in the form of my own thoughts. With everything mingled together, I am not sure which thoughts are truly my own. I believe that all my thoughts are *mine*, but may be formed due to previous discussions and agreements that I am not aware of consciously. Occasionally, I find myself feeling very odd. I call this condition "la-la land," requiring much more concentration than normal. I may feel dizzy, my own voice sounding odd and distorted. Everything feels slower, my surroundings sharper and brighter, yet somehow distorted. *Reality* seems distorted, in sense and shape. *I feel as if I am inside a fish bowl, looking out at a world I don't quite understand.* (1999: 79, emphasis in final sentence mine)

Remove the reference to E.T. from Connie Isele's account and "la-la land" could as well be a description of intensive care unit psychosis from a patient's point of view. For that matter, many of us can relate to the fishbowl effect as a feature of the postmodern condition. There is no shortage in any earthly society of explanatory models for dissociative states or unexplained phenomena and an array of sanctioned responses to them. For the devils within, or the malevolent effects of witches, sorcerers, or angry ancestors, we can turn to the exorcisms, offerings, and other sacrifices of spirit mediums and priests or to the healing hand of God or Jesus or the Virgin Mary. Connie Isele could have credited angels with saving her life or her doctors or nurses or an online religious community's prayers or the healing energy of her children's love and care. So, while we return to the question of what the *extra* in extraterrestrial is doing for and to her narrative, what it expresses, it is its social consequences we must determine.

I want to use this question to raise two significant problems we encounter in approaching the extraterrestrial as a matter of either "teratology" or "paranoia,"[19] that is, an abomination of sociality or psychology, respectively.[20] The first requires that Connie Isele's experience not be exiled to a discourse that is worlds apart from more commonplace expressions of helplessness and absence of support. Subjects in an E.T. state of mind are not in the grip of some *excessive* knowledge that renders them monsters to themselves. Neither are they wholly "mirroring" the social problems that gave rise to their precarious situation. Rather, la-la land—where one goes in a state of *partial disconnect* from oneself as others see one—is an uncanny realm of *disturbance* of a mirroring everyday habitus.[21] The E.T. realm is not "other" than earthly but acts back on and unsettles assumptions about commonplace brands of knowledge.

A paradoxical consequence for subjects such as Connie Isele is a fresh appreciation of human life *in an expanded sense of its possible affinities*—frightening and/or fulfilling. Again, from this perspective, extraterrestrial encounters reveal themselves as ways of thinking about the unexpected or contingent rather than in and of themselves uncanny, which is my second point.

Julia Kristeva captures this "prospective, fragmentary, 'subjective'" everyday mode of being, which is "more than demonstrative or didactic" in describing how:

> Foreignness, an uncanny one, creeps into the tranquility of reason itself, and, without being restricted to madness, beauty, or faith anymore than to ethnicity or race, irrigates our very speaking-being, estranged by other logics, including the heterogeneity of biology. . . . Henceforth, we know that we are foreigners to ourselves, and it is with the help of that sole support that we can attempt to live with others. (1991: 169–70)

This creeping sense, this *intimate foreignness* "within reason" (as Marcus [1999] puts it)—in other terms, the idea of the extraterrestrial—can relieve us from the duty to maintain either homogeneity or connection across all our different contexts of social action, the freedom to part company with normative social structures. Further, it can support, strangely but quite pragmatically, our creative leaps into hypothesis—into the gaps of comprehension that are requisite for imagining new forms of relationality and new ways of knowing—and thus of agency and empowerment.

The anthropologist Roy Willis writes this about a paranormal experience in Egypt, which he visited thirty-seven years after being "struck down" by polio.

> Sitting near the imposing fourth-century obelisk erected by the Christian patriarch Theophilus, I became aware of a voice that sounded, paradoxically, as if it were coming both from immensely far away and from deep inside me. The speech was flowing, powerful and beautiful as a river of liquid silver and, although the words were in English, it was being translated, by some mechanism that also looked "silvery," from an unknown tongue. What was said was arresting. I was, it seemed, "guiltless and free." . . . Then, the mysterious sentence: "After long exile the King has come home." Finally, at about fifteen degrees above the horizon to the (I think) north of where I sat, I saw the most unexpected and astonishing object: a silver-gold cylinder tapered and rounded at both ends, with two rows of nine square windows running along its central part. These windows were glowing with an amber light as if illuminated from within and the whole object, which was very beautiful, was slowly turning on its axis. After a few moments this vision, which was startlingly clear, faded and I returned to ordinary reality. . . . Afterwards I felt as one reborn, made anew. (1999: 6–7)

While it is an alien device that transmits its liberating message to Willis, and a glowing spaceship that hovers in his memory, what "arrests" his narrative is the return from exile of the king. A characteristic feature of the biomyths of prophets' lives through time and across cultures, this event of mythical return carries with it a "charter" (as Bronislaw Malinowski theorized myth's function) to transform, positively, the lives of others. Willis writes humbly of discovering his own paranormal healing powers before this event, without linking the "deep strangeness" of that discovery either to his vision in Egypt or to the spiritual practices he knows as a traditional ethnographer of a sub-Saharan African people. Indeed, it may be so culturally natural for anthropologists to draw comparisons between alien communication and the trance states of healers in exotic locations, or spirit mediums who inhabit the "channeling zones" "betwixt and between" seen and unseen worlds (see Brown 1997, 1999), that the connections seem hardly worth noting. Yet, if we are to recover diverse senses of the alien in different historical moments and modalities of social exchange, we must examine such an interlocution as we would any other, which is to say as a situated knowledge practice.

Recently John Mack was taken to task on this point by Jodi Dean. Her searing critique (2003) is directed at a grant that Mack received for a cross-cultural study of shamanic healing trances, which he sought to apply to the experiences recounted by abductees. Accepting that trance performances are culturally specific (e.g., Desjarlais 1992), whatever else they may be for subjects, it is difficult for an anthropologist to accept where this particular line of research might have been headed. However, the critique of healing-linked abduction from insider researchers, and in particular the author of *Intruders* (1987), Budd Hopkins, is impassioned along other lines. For Hopkins, casting abduction as anything but dangerous participates in an alien "deceit." To approach abduction as a liberating out-of-body experience is to take the path of mass suicide cults liberated once and for all from their earthly bodies: abduction (not to be confused with benign contact) is categorically detrimental to human well-being. A Heaven's Gate Internet "poster" would appear to make the point when it states: "You *can't* simply be a good 'Christian,' die, and go to the *true* Kingdom of Heaven. You can only become a *new creature*. . . . That *birthing* requires that you become *dead* to all *humanness* . . . totally under the care of your 'new family' " (accessed March 10, 1994, www.heavensgate.com).

Following the vein of more conventional theories of trauma, while some subjects may come to reframe an abduction event as illuminating, what we should take as a fundamental reality is that they have been traumatized (or retraumatized) and are open to repeat "intrusions." From this point of view, imagistic, fragmented abduction recollections—the term Dean argues should be substituted for narratives given the absence of narrative sequencing in "recovered" memories—are struggles with all too human situations of helplessness that are inextricably linked to abusive conditions or relations with powerful human others. In this volume, Joseph Dumit makes that point for chronic fatigue syndrome sufferers who seek explanations for their symptoms in the realm of the extraterrestrial: whatever else, CFS is located within a system of politicized medical culture. The situation —including feelings of paranoia—in which CFS sufferers find themselves is consistent with their estrangement from reliable individual somatic or social supports. The system and its implementation, not the individual psyche alone, are dysfunctional.

This debate prompts us to revisit Richard Hofstadter's famous essay, "The Paranoid Style in American Politics" (1965; also Marcus 1999), in which he argues for a "higher paranoid scholarship" that entails "A careful accumulation of facts, or at least what appear to be facts, and to marshal these facts toward an overwhelming 'proof' of a particular conspiracy that is to be established. In fact, the paranoid mentality is far more coherent than the real world since it leaves no room for mistakes, failures, or ambiguities." Of special interest here: "What distinguishes the paranoid style is not, then, the absence of verifiable facts . . . but rather the curious leap in imagination that is always made at some critical point in the recital of events" (reprinted in Marcus 1999: 1). An interesting point about Hofstadter's discourse is that the "leap of imagination" characteristic of paranoid ideation is likewise an element of scientific hypothesis making and other forms of creative action (as I discuss later). In fact, the use of the term *paranoid* arguably precludes process-level comparison with other operations of imagination and the alternative value of these for making new connections, including new social relational connections—for example, connecting with others who are investigating governmental secrecy. As regards the extraterrestrial, contemporary discourse privileges the affective force and cultural and historical thematic of fear over optimistic imaginaries and social strategies of hope. In short, the construct of paranoia, or even the less charged "anxiety," while training our attention on opaque technologies of power that are important to confront, should not preclude a *constructive* value for mistakes, failures, and ambiguities as spurs to creative action.

The debate over whether aliens' plans for humankind are destructive or constructive is a displacement of the same logic and the same "problematic of gaps." In public culture, both positive and negative relations to the alien are significant themes. Big budget films such as E.T.: *The Extra-Terrestrial*, *Contact*, and A.I.: *Artificial Intelligence* make the point for the "good alien" and *Independence Day*, *Signs*, and *The Matrix* for the "bad"—to mention only a small sample of the films that alien/UFO believers consume avidly and critically.

Meanwhile for "insiders," these positive and negative positions on alien contact have been distilled in dense descriptive accounts of contact and (since the mid-1960s) abduction (e.g., Pritchard et al. 1994), in which persons relate experiences of profound deterritorialization. Unlike Connie Isele's rescue scenarios, exchanges in this domain may produce embodied artifacts: emblematically, the part human, part alien "babies in bottles"[22] and fully developed "Greys," who move among us unrecognizably, their motivations and powers unknown. John Mack again represents the side of optimism in *Passport to the Cosmos* (1999), arguing that aliens' hybrid "project," placed within the larger context of our ecological crisis, is to "fulfill our responsibility for the care of Earth . . . as a kind of intervention, sometimes harsh, that may have the purpose of bringing about change in the ways of human kind" (110–12). Again, he is arguing against Hopkins, for whom the essence of abduction is a nefarious hybridization project. In these terms, Greys embody a dangerous, essentially racial, program. They threaten our species purity and that of the body politic—as Mary Douglas would have put it in her classic *Purity and Danger* ([1966] 1978), or Georg Simmel writing in "The Stranger" of the traveler half-expected to seduce, steal from, and abandon his host (n.23). In this light, the "imag*en*ation" (Dyck 1998) of cross-species exchange expresses the *mobility anxiety* of those most firmly attached to their species identity and its status privileges.

Race in Space: "Future Talk Is Ordering Talk"

I have proposed that the extraterrestrial as it emerges in this book does not submit to borders, or require Otherness, so much as it "comes-going" (Weber 2001: 51) through fields of possible, but in no sense guaranteed, discursive connection. Otherness is the enemy of this potential. And no case makes the point more clearly than that of the alien as a figure of racialized difference—a "Star-Trekking" ethnic.

Christopher Roth's essay explores the theme of alien encounter as an interplanetary, "interracial drama" focused on alien physical forms in light of understandings and paradigms of physical anthropology. Through this lens, "ufology as anthropology" is "all about race, and has more to do with terrestrial racial schemes and social and cultural constructs than most UFO believers are aware."

When *Space Is the Place* (the title of John Szwed's fine ethnobiography of jazz performance artist Sun Ra) that draws people into relations with others, virtual homelands open to the displaced and marginalized of Earth. Indeed, as we shall see, relocated to space, race exerts a strong gravitational pull on an anthropological model of visits. Too, it highlights critical turning points in the historical discourse of the extraterrestrial. Here I indicate some racial themes of three: the age of empire, the nuclear age, and the post–cold war era—"alien ages" all—from the perspective of race relations.

A wellspring of any genealogy of race in space is the mid- to late-nineteenth-century imaginary of the Theosophists: occult practitioners who attributed to science a mystical creationism and influence on the order of the universe in contradistinction to Darwin's. This order presented a racialized progress narrative of the species ordered as a series of events in time and space. Carried to the far shores of North America under the influence of Madame Blavatsky's charismatic visions of "Anthropogenesis," most modern UFO/alien religions could trace their descent in species terms to Theosophy's narratives of "root races." From the first race, the Self-Born of the Moon, the races surface and submerge until the last one emerges: humans capable of surviving severe environmental trauma without the aid of extraterrestrial eugenic engineering.

But the major turning point for extraterrestrial discourse came with the first nuclear age, in which almond-eyed aliens remaindered from the "yellow peril" captured the postwar, specifically post-Hiroshima, imagination, often in the hues of ash. Loose in the desert near Roswell after 1947, these desubjectified entities were this period's arch ethnics,[23] articulating the ambivalence toward a now-victimized foreign presence. As such they introduced the risk of not merely "passing" within U.S. society, with racial consequences for the worse, but of unsettling the national conscience. American society, in particular, would have difficulty recognizing itself within the warm circle of the family of man from this time onward.

It was not until the 1960s–80s, as gender and sexual boundaries were being challenged and crossed on various social fronts, that race identity would emerge as anxiety over species miscegenation in widely disseminated accounts of alien abduction and their corollary discourse of Greys.[24] One atypical but sensational account was the abduction narrative of the mixed-race couple Betty and Barney Hill in 1961. Living testimony to the myth of racial purity, their story would travel into covertly racist scenarios of miscegenation, including the terrifying but transcendent plotline of Whitley Strieber's best-selling book, *Communion: A True Story* (1987).[25] Expert therapeutic interventions within the new abduction genre were not far behind, leading commentator Luise White to caution: "UFO abduction narratives are sort of alien ethnography reconfigured by the hypnotist. The images of race and culture that obsess abductees are often turned into the linear symptoms of alien abduction by the experts" (1994: 25). This problem of racialized abduction politics points to a concern that subjects, being oblivious to themselves and desubjectified,[26] can only enter recovery by handing over their agency to the psychotherapeutic interlocutors who convey their accounts—not always accurately or in the patient's voice. More to the point, psychotherapists can document testimony of abduction experiences without publicly addressing racism. An important shift would therefore need to occur before abduction could engage race in mutually legitimate terms. To begin with, abduction would need to go public, and in the late 1980s John Mack would take it there, using his position in psychiatry at the Harvard Medical School to draw media attention to the abduction accounts of a large number of clients whose psyches were demonstrably healthy and by all diagnostic criteria, otherwise normal. Abductees would also need to be visibly organized, as happened with the formation of abductee support groups during this period. The effect on racialized fears of this shift from the dark "hold" of psychopathology into the light of a free press and community action, was to liberate the politics of race to express its kinship with the alien condition of social abjection.

At this time, black pride was appropriating space for race outside the abduction genre entering the public sphere not only through the printed word and image but also through political demonstrations and expressive culture. While new religious movements such as the United Nuwaubian Nation of Moors wove Egyptian "roots" themes into elaborate Afro-futurist visions (Gabriel 2003), the stage of popular culture belonged to "Sonny" Sun Ra and his Arkestra band. A brilliant interpreter of the racialist themes of the time, Sun Ra responded as follows to an invitation, in 1968, to comment on the international "race for space":

> According to my research, the governments of this world have conspired to destroy the nations of black people. . . . The consequence though has been that there now exists a separate kind of human being, the American Black man. And I should say that he doesn't belong on this Earth. . . . But here in America there are also Black people who have given up nothing, who couldn't give up anything

> because they live in harmony with the Creator of the cosmos. And they will always be a source of difficulty for every nation on this planet, because they've no other ruler than the Creator of the cosmos and they're faithful only to him.

Sun Ra's ethnographer, John Szwed, goes on to comment:

> Here . . . space was both a metaphor of exclusion and of reterritorialization, of claiming the "outside" as one's own, of tying a revised and corrected past to a claimed future. Space was also a metaphor which transvalues the dominant terms so that they become aberrant, a minority position, while the terms of the outside, the beyond, the margins, become standard. (1997: 140)

Adding his own poetics to these themes, Joe Goncalves writes in a review of the Arkestra band's first West Coast appearance that they offered:

> What we never had for so long, space, outer space. Or no space at all. Squeezes so tight. From the slaveship to the shack to the tenement. No space to really move. . . . Sun Ra & Co. herald Space to Come, Freedom, to move, to live again as ourselves. Expansion. And *future talk is ordering talk*. . . . When we hear a brother say, "A nigger ain't never *been* shit, a nigger ain't never *going* to be shit," we know he has no knowledge of his past, and no past = no future. Sun Ra is future/ALTER/ what's coming. (Szwed 1997: 140–41, emphasis mine)

Recent descendants of Afro-futurist rhetoric have recovered the abduction idiom as captivity narratives. In films such as John Sayles's *The Brother from Another Planet* (1986), a voiceless African American slave-alien joins "brothers" and "sisters" who have escaped captivity on their host planet, healing and repairing a Harlem afflicted by drug lords operating from the city's White South. And in academic terms, we can read today that:

> African Americans, in a very real sense, are the descendants of alien abductees; they inhabit a sci-fi nightmare in which unseen but no less impassible force fields of intolerance frustrate their movements; official histories undo what has been done; and technology is too often brought to bear on black bodies. (Dery, quoted in Williams 2001, courtesy of Stefan Helmreich in an e-mail conversation)

The outerspaces of Sun Ra's artistic and intellectual productivity were shared by others of his time in other cultural locations as a realm of subversive political potential. In the early 1970s his career began to take off in a "blur of travel" that took him, among other places that had received him energetically before this, to the Fête de l'Humanité, a festival supported by the Communist Party, on September 9, 1973, in Paris (he and his orchestra were already well known there as "enfants terribles" who took to "childlike partying on stage").

Intriguingly, on December 13, 1973, an artist in another mode would have a "fantastic encounter" with aliens in the French countryside and conceive the idea of a new religious movement in France based on the alternative anthropological truth that extraterrestrial scientists—not God and not the path of Darwinian evolution—created mankind by cloning human beings "in their own image." Claude Vorhilon, a young sports car journalist and singer-songwriter who was doing reasonably well on the Parisian cabaret circuit and Radio No. 1 before this, would from this time on know himself as the prophet Raël, founder of the long-lived Raëlian movement.[27]

Raël would eventually elaborate his vision to embrace a futurology of clonehood on planets far from Earth, where clones of evolved human beings destroyed in the apocalypse of a nuclear war could enjoy lives of sensual pleasure, administered to by beauties of all blends of races and genders and freed by robots to enjoy unlimited creative pursuit of the arts and the sciences. In his vision of a radical "geniocracy," Raël displaced the racialized enslavement that is implicitly central in eugenic-centered cloning discourse, onto robotic utility machines.[28] But by 2002 space was again being depicted by Raëlians as a welcoming environment for racial and ethnic minorities (fig. 1), as the movement courted African members.

Nuclear and Networked

> Why didn't someone tell me the Cold War was over? We're already forgetting Gorbachev and here I am, pumped up and ready to push the button. Let the missiles fly, man. Blast me to oblivion. I'm Madame Strangelove . . . a victim of radiation and alien invasion wars. . . . I'm timing Doomsday, or at least I'm timing the minutes I'm still breathing . . . waiting for radioactive clouds to fall to the ground in the form of rain. . . . Buy me. Sell me. I deserve it.
> —Susan Smith Nash (1996: 173)

It is worth dwelling longer on the cultural environment of the cold war, which gave birth to modern ufology—the technological wing of the E.T. imaginary.[29] Indeed, since the early days of the first nuclear age, public de-

FIG. 1. Brother from another planet. (From *Apocalypse International* 56, no. 126 [winter 2002]: 7.

bate concerning nuclear technology's potential for bringing both progress and apocalyptic doom has been a staple of ufological discourse. In particular, themes that emerged in the seminal "age of dualism" (from the bombing of Hiroshima to the 1960s),[30] cannot be overemphasized as orientors of extraterrestrial communities. On the one hand, nuclear energy promised a utopian world of respite from human labor (while at the same time engaging in the parallel play of a productive future for mankind). On the other hand, this same energy brought in its wake a dystopic narrative of the "runaway" machine entity: "a Frankenstein's monster that might turn on its Creator" (Gamson and Modigliani 1989: 20).

Such was the ethos of post–World War II public culture when in 1947 the pilot of a small aircraft reported the first fleeting glimpse of an unidentified flying object—later to be described by a journalist as the signature "saucer." The sighting was followed almost immediately by stories of a UFO crash near Roswell, New Mexico. The U.S. government would move quickly to investigate the site, cordoning off the area and in effect enshrining (or incarcerating) its mysterious remnants.

In a chapter in *Wetwares* (2003) entitled "Sympathy for the Alien," Richard Doyle offers an image of these official cold warriors seeking to contain the idea of uninvited extraterrestrial guests. As Doyle notes, the indeterminacy of the discourse of extraterrestriality, the runaway "replication and propagation of the rumors," disturbed early UFO investigative panels more than these objects' possible existence. It followed that attention turned to the problem of managing the untrackable speed of contagious abduction rhetoric and the sense that something of "us" was being "leaked" or "stolen" by the aliens invisibly stealing in. At the same time, these investigative panels were concerned by what Doyle calls "info-clog": a blockage of narrative density that placed the normalizing flow of sociality at risk, no less than the racing rumor mill.

If, as Gamson and Modigliani (1989) argue, we are currently living in an "age of insecurity" in which conspiracy has displaced trust—a time in which the means of access to the knowledge and apparatuses of production of the conditions of our own biosocial lives are not transparent to us—the discourse of the extraterrestrial should overwhelmingly reflect our "close encounters" with these fears. Malcolm Bull could be writing of such fears in *Seeing Things Hidden*: "If something is hidden from you, it is not because truth has eluded you and is unattainable, but because truth is flirting with you, simultaneously offering and withholding, or keeping herself from you while giving herself to others in your presence" (1999: 19). However, *E.T. Culture* complicates the picture on one level by suggesting that the phenomenon of *visibility anxiety* is inextricably linked to the phenomenon already alluded to as *mobility anxiety*, both technological (information is being generated too fast to get a handle on it) and social (people come and go too fast for any community to arrange its status system). The idea of secret technological knowledge relates directly to the apprehension of the inaccessibility of the sources of social "license" that Lepselter (in this volume) recognizes as a problem of social status mobility for her fellow travelers in ufology. A version of this kind of mobility anxiety surfaces in the distressed abductee recollections of "lost time" that proliferated in the 1980s, in which persons spoke of being absent to themselves, at least partially (for memories of abduction are often "recovered" piecemeal), and absent for who knows how long.

In addition, each of these phenomena would appear to enter into a dialectic of presence and absence with its opposite value: visibility optimism and mobility optimism, respectively. The case of the media blitz of the Raëlian religion's claim to have cloned Baby Eve, just as the Creators cloned the first humans, shows how powerful this phenomenon is. (Even an established "new religious movement" needs visibility and new membership.)

The fact that sequences of digital information and publicity images—texts, music, DNA—can be liberated from corporate control and sent into who knows what spaces of play is of concern not only to corporate management and guardians of official narratives. As with the "sampling" of music or image sequences—the technique of removing them from their contexts for grafting as information into other contexts—the mobility of "alien DNA" articulates the problem of a "movable" and "removable script" of ourselves exteriorized to a site we cannot control (citing Doyle in this volume). Identity theft as pleasure theft. Jodi Dean's discussion (1998) of Žižek's idea of "the theft of pleasure" in relation to abduction narratives is important to consider in this regard. Dean quotes Žižek's contention that "What we conceal by imputing to the Other the theft of enjoyment is the traumatic fact that we never possessed what was allegedly stolen from us: the lack ('castration') is original" (174). Accordingly, she posits that the abduction narrative, which thematizes passivity, "functions to conceal the fact that our agency was an illusion, just like our security and certainty" (174) and "exposes the alien as that which reminds us that nothing is completely other (and everything is somewhat other), that the very border between 'like' and 'unlike' is illusory" (175). It is easy to lose sight of such complexities of agency and accountability when we are focusing on categories of culture, zones of power, and the like; less easy to do so when we are focusing on senses of self and place in their social contingency. Basically, cultural categories have histories; like Greys, they can shape-shift, disappear, or move around at unnatural speeds. They may be purposefully made ambiguous or otherwise manipulated by both the "powers that be" and those seeking to evade them. And, as the values attached to them change, persons find themselves now on one side and now on another of some line of judgment without knowing how they got there (e.g., the prophet Raël is described as both a dangerous "cult leader" and "Our Favorite Prophet" in the *New York Times Magazine*). Sampling from this perspective "disappears" information not by means of a systematic cover-up but by wink-of-the-eye absconding, revealing gaps in our understandings of who actually controls redistribution. And, as George Marcus observes (1999), this informational "excision" can happen fast—faster than a speeding spacecraft, faster than the click of a computer mouse or an invading virus.

It is, as Ito's ethnography of Yugioh fan culture (in this volume) would suggest, the speed of history on the flow. The otherworldly heroes and demons of Yugioh comic (*manga*) and *anime* television networking spawns dressed-for-play fans in the flesh and in cyberlocales that "juxtapose old technologies with new and integrate the fantastic with everyday social dramas." In offline card game competitions and playing card markets, the alien is (re)produced by multiple creators at multiple performance sites in a public space that resists territorialization. Such a "playful appropriation of texts and images for their own ends" and its sustained momentum in what might be called the *devotional mode of the cult alien* are predicated on the context-transgressive nature of images under the influence of commercialized planetization, on the one hand, and the cultural ownership to which the idea of the alien submits in its contexts of social use, on the other. Like the human genome, the popular life of the Yugioh world is related to, as Doyle puts it in reference to the science visionary Kary Mullis, "less as a 'book of life' to be 'read' than as a program to be hacked—in his case, to be extracted and copied."

This image of deterritorialization and reterritorialization, which in one form or another is a staple of E.T. culture, is likewise a feature of the creative disarray of digital media—its openness to sampling and being sampled—as a condition of new formations of social connection. Whether this process promotes or elides social relationships is of course another question (see Lister et al. 2003).

Human creativity displaced to realms of the extraterrestrial opens up a distance on the self that permits for some believers "ways out" of humanity's seemingly inexorable drive toward self-destruction. To the extent that we keep faith in the inherent creativity of action, as Hans Joas (1996) has argued, the critical distance on the self in postmodernity and the "alien self" (or its counterpart, the "alien within") resist the abdication of agency and the "suggestive apparatus" of a mechanistic society that renders the individual "an extension of itself" (Melley 2000: 31, citing Ellus). As we remind ourselves over and over again in our popular films, for example, machines, alien or otherwise, cannot know the *desire* for a fully engaged relationality, even accepting that human and nonhuman agency "can be continuously transformed into one another . . . and emergently productive of one another" (Pickering 1999: 374).[31]

It is at this juncture that we as anthropologists must scrutinize the notion of the "soul in the machine" or, to spin a phrase from Brown's ethnography of "pseudo-science" healers, the "technomancer of the soul" (1999: 151).[32] For subjects, cyborg relationality is conducive to social flourishing only within a situated ethics of *human* relationality and humane action. Currently, machines do not have a plan for humans independent of the plans the species devises for itself. Turn the tables and ascribe intentionality to machines or their programs and we are left with a circumscribed, mechanical, goal-oriented network model of social life—again connection passing for relationality.

This is the problematic that the film version of *Contact* would seek to transcend in a kind of E.T. coming of age story for *technoscience spirituality*—by which I mean hard faith in technoscience future (see my essay in this volume). The film climaxes with the partnership of former enemies: a (cross-gendered and, in the case of the characters representing them, cross-dressed) science and religion, reconciled to their differences by a technoscientific "miracle." In the final scene, we see the female rocket scientist and the humanistic male evangelist holding hands on the steps of the U.S. Capitol Building before throngs of the grateful.

Of course, long before *Contact* (1997), the imagined consequences of intimate faith-science and human-machine articulations were documented as public issues in an impressive genealogy of artificial intelligence and cyborg films, ranging from the sad to the catastrophic. One "apical ancestor" is certainly the rogue computer Hal, whose independent agenda in *2001: A Space Odyssey* left humanity lost in space or, if you will, "lost in translation" (as Geertz phrases the hazards for anthropological practice). Hal spawned a seemingly inexhaustible line of box office descendants—morphing into machines and programs that give the appearance or even evidence of being (to cite the corporate slogan of *Blade-Runner's* replicant manufacturers) "more human than humans" (see Bukatman 1997; and Battaglia 2001) in their complementary capacities as agents, both moral (*The Terminator*) and utterly amoral (Agent Smith of *The Matrix*). Both *Bicentennial Man* and *A.I.: Artificial Intelligence* put the matter plainly (the latter is recognized by the Raëlian movement as the first popular film to more or less "get" the alien-human ancestral connection): what machines want is an "author function" or, in films that place the emphasis less on human consciousness and more on meaningful social relationships, a "co-author function."

As I have indicated, these scenarios exist only in *our* dreams and nightmares, however intentionally or accidentally the author function may land on machines' creators or controllers. Neither do machines seek an identity and life trajectory distinct from those of the humans they might otherwise resemble (though such is certainly part of our cultural imaginary).[33] It is intriguing to recognize the possibility of a role for a temporally emergent material agency (Pickering 1999: 374)—say, the "free spirited" UFOs beheld by Susan Lepselter in the company of her traveling companions as they look toward a previously familiar horizon in Nevada (in this volume). However, even the MIT robots that as I write are entering into haptic exchanges with humans, responding not only to the voices but to the touch of human dance partners, do not as yet take the lead. The machine emerges in the "real time" of the scientist; the reverse is not the case.

The situation becomes significantly more complicated, however, when the ego-based criterion of intentionality is replaced with the criterion of interrelationality. Among "alien/UFO believers," to travel life's "-scapes" in a state of legitimacy and in "real time" has a felt urgency precisely because a shared social reality cannot, in their terms, be taken for granted. What Foucault, in his role of futurologist, grasped as the problem of a social context in which "The Death of the Author" is even imaginable is a context many UFO believers (not unlike other alternative spiritualists) call home—here, now: "I think that, as our society changes, the author-function will disappear. . . . All discourses, whatever their status, form, value and whatever the treatment to which they will be subjected, would then develop in the anonymity of a murmur. . . . The result will be an indifference: 'What difference does it make who is speaking?' " (Foucault 1979: 160, quoted in Gusterson 2003: 302). It is proper that I should lift this quotation not from the "original source" but from Hugh Gusterson's important study of authorship's official erasure in the mazes of the Livermore laboratory, a site of the birth of the nuclear age. For arguably more significant than a lifetime of scientific work vanished by authorities without trace of author's identities, is the U.S. government's denial of license to circulate scientific knowledge, credited or otherwise, in the public sphere—as Gusterson appreciates, to "disappear" such knowledge from the historical record.

This scenario resonates to ethnographies that show how actors recover their agency—and resist erasure of the official record—in the wake of programmatic nuclear displacement. Lawrence Carucci's *Nuclear Nativity* (1997), for example, analyzes rituals that enact an inversion of Harding's and Stewart's "optimistic apocalypticism" in the ethnographic thick description of displaced Micronesians' complex scripts of cultural renewal, reinvention, and Christian/traditional religious hybridization *in the wake of* the holocaust of the U.S. program of nuclear testing in the Pacific.

The theme of hope as an experiential and analytic category, both situated and contingent, is theorized in a reflexive anthropological thought piece by Vincent Crapanzano (2003: 3–32) that could have been a postscript to Carucci's ethnography. While optimism and faith in the creativity of action are currently less evident in popular culture E.T. imagery and texts than are horror stories (even while characters such as Agent Mulder of *The X-Files* claim a place for them in televisual history), we have ample evidence that alongside a "healthy paranoia" hope has a value for human sociality that the discourse of extraterrestriality locates—and may even activate.

Overall, the articulation of anxiety and optimism in the social discourse of technoscience spirituality puts a restraining order both on scenarios of technology-produced alienation and of transcendental humanism. Sven Birkets writes that "One day soon we will conduct our public and private lives within networks so dense, among so many channels of instantaneous information, that it will make almost no sense to speak of the differentiated self" (quoted in Melley 2000: 31). What Birkets imagines is a process of connecting across contexts so intense and time warped that it covers for the work of relationality. The cart of connection *becomes* the horse of social relating; singular acts of connection are taken for social exchange. This is "endgame" insofar as subjectivity becomes so absorbed in technoscience that its difference from information is a matter of indifference to subjects. The danger from this perspective is of ceding human agency to nonvisible forces as the body's heterogeneous material enmeshments are given over to commodifying forces, for the greater benefit of the few. (Clonaid's Internet enterprise fulfills the promise of network in these terms.) In contrast, technoscience spirituality can be reduced neither to commerce nor to negative applications, since in a larger sense it embraces both "life as we know it" and "life as it could be" (Christopher Langton, cited in Helmreich 2001: 612). If, as Sun Ra's reviewer stated it, "future talk is ordering talk," then we can expect more artistic genre fusions and hybrid cult religions, "not without a note of optimism." In his illuminating ethnography of artificial life scientists in New Mexico (2001), Stefan Helmreich notes that just as scientists have come to appreciate the "third culture" of public culture that crosscuts science and humanities discourses, new bridges can be imagined from here to realms of the spiritual, and from these bridges leaps of faith across all these chasms. Such leaps are risky, of course. But they also enliven a situated futurology and humanistic hypothesis making in a "secular modernity" that is showing itself to be less secular by the moment (see especially de Vries 2001).

In all of the scenarios just considered, failure of critical models to "mind the gap" (Baudrillard 1988) between what we can imagine doing and making and being and what we do, make, or are in the material world can lead to underappreciation of human capacities for constructive and destructive action. This is precisely what the messages of benevolent aliens since the dawn of the nuclear age have been credited with calling to our attention. As David Samuels's and my own essay on Raëlians note in this volume, it is no historical accident that in *The Day the Earth Stood Still* Klaatu, the first alien undercover agent/ethnographer in popular cinematic history, sets about saving humans from themselves by "passing" among them and observing with growing alarm their irrational, belligerent tendencies. It is not until he sheds his human guise to emerge as an alien prophet from his gleaming flying saucer—dressed in the same formal white suit that the contemporary prophet Rael dons for publicity photos against the backdrop of an exact replica of Klaatu's flying saucer, which is also an exact replica of the saucer that transported Rael to higher consciousness and other planets—that Klaatu's warning is taken seriously by a select audience of "the greatest scientists on Earth."

The nuclear nightmare Klaatu envisions has a corollary in the horror of *The Matrix*. In the wake of apocalypse, sentient human bodies imagine themselves to be free agents, while in physical reality they exist as living food for an alien intelligence that controls the apparatuses of their delusional contentment within a corporate, "cubicled" habitus. Humans, as any cult site on the Internet will tell you with or without reference to Baudrillard, have become "simulacra" of themselves.

But *The Matrix's* heroic Neo is guided in "hacking into" this condition.

And the fact that he can arrive at consciousness of his alienated situation of false security offers hope that he will be able to recognize the possibility of experiencing the real thing: meaningful relationships with others similarly awakened to the consequences of their desubjectification and what Heidegger terms the "enframement" of Earth's resources as consumables. In this scenario of recovering self-authorship through the agency of relations with others similarly disabled and struggling toward social engagement, acts of liberation are their own reward, recognition aside. But the reward is not sufficient as such until it is supplemented by a sense of mission and the salvation that comes from freeing others similarly trapped in postmodernity's imaginary of fulfillment (cf. Biagioli 2003).

In *The Matrix* trilogy, what humans are freed to is a romantic "state of nature" and tribal sensuality: the subversive underground society outside *The Matrix* teams with a heterogeneous, physical social life—the counterpart of the densely creolized *Blade-Runner* underworld, where, for example, the fittest survive but they don't have a life in any meaningful sense empowered.

"Aliens-R-Us": Kinship at the Crossroads

Taking up a description of the planets in a solar system described by the astrologer John Herschel in 1833, Marilyn Strathern observes, in her provocatively titled "Emergent Kinship" (2003), Herschel's rhetorical displacement of a "weak sense of analogy (they look alike) by a strong sense of affinity between them (their orbits are related to one another)." It is in this latter sense, she argues, that one can find "resonances of kinship": "For English speakers, a 'peculiarity of knowing in kinship terms is that information about origins . . . constitutes what [people] know about themselves. Facts about birth imply parentage, and people who find things out about their ancestry, and thus about their relations with others, acquire identity by that very discovery" (179). *Discovery* is the term I am interested in here. For if one's ancestor is "discovered" to be an extraterrestrial being, or in its further declension one's offspring is (always, of course, partially), the relations one discovers, whether by identification or contrast, may create affinity, *but they cannot do without analogy*. Any identity as an alien/UFO insider relies strongly on one's recognition of the family features of the discourse.

And these are remarkably homogeneous. E.T. culture is "pulled to-

FIG. 2. Contactee drawing of E.T. (From Bryan 1995, cover, *Close Encounters of the Fourth Kind*.)

gether" by formal analogies, reduced to slogans and icons. The touchstones that convey a sense of a unified cultural field are embodied in emblematic forms (humanoid aliens and flying saucers) and categories of inscription (crop circles and ancient signs).

Recall, if you can bear to one more time, the generic image of the extraterresetrial, which one can find anywhere and everywhere (e.g., fig. 2). It seems that this image has been with us since before we can remember—and for good reason. When Theosophy disseminated its resistance to Darwinian theory in the nineteenth century, its "strongest influence" was its genericization: its interrogation of the "species concept" as a *social* fact of human history (see Roth in this volume; and Hoon Song, in press). The visibly genericized alien of the contemporary public domains is perhaps Theosophy's purest survival, a veritable stem cell of *humanness itself*, embodying the ambivalent capacity to express itself in favor of human survival and against it. And the same is true for cult religions of the extraterrestrial. The very "weakness" or vagueness of resemblance of the genericized alien of these cultural imaginaries is its strength as an icon for generating new anthropologies of the body politic and fantasies of and for insider E.T. communities of the future. To return to Jodi Dean's contagious imagery: "Alien images and alien copies and copies of aliens appear unpredictably and unannounced in places they shouldn't, in places we can't understand, in multiple, contradictory, alien places . . . infiltrating American popular culture [and providing] icons through which to access the new conditions of democratic politics at the millennium" (1998: 5).

Paradoxically, the alien's replicability extends a kind of invitation to resist the gravitational pull of the genetic family's imprimatur and bloodline and to seek out new *terrestrial* associations with like-minded others. Predicated on principles of counterspeciation, this imaginary recasts any myth of human origin as a project of interplanetary exchange, as open to genetic engineering (alien or human and with all its attendant ethical issues) as to mutation, recombination, and random drift. In this imaginary, the notion that truly has no place is a fixed and essential Otherness, pure and simple. "It is really laughable," Darwin wrote to his friend Joseph Hooker, "to see what different ideas predominate in various naturalists' minds when they speak of 'species.'" He continues: "In some, resemblance is everything and descent of little weight—in some resemblance seems to go for nothing, and Creation the reigning idea . . . *it all comes, I believe, from trying to define the indefinable*" (December 23, 1856; in Darwin 1887: 2:88, emphasis mine). Export these musings to the idea of an ancestral relation to the alien—"looking upward, not downward for the missing link" (perhaps our creators are a "race of Superintelligent dinosaurs") and to "a *living example* and not a stony fossil," as David Barclay imagines doing (quoted in Kossy 2001: 37–39)—and the extraterrestrial as Other might better be understood with the rest of us as *entities in (be)coming*, our bodies, as in an X-*Files* episode that examines the body of an alien, a "fantastic space" for contemplating what is for anthropology an elementary triad of human belonging expressed in idioms of blood (descent), relationality (alliance), and hosting (place). The truth, as Badley observes, is not "out there so much as in there—or rather, here, there, and everywhere" (1996: 149).[34]

It requires only a minor displacement to appreciate the irony of "aliens sprouting everywhere" as generic alien products (stickers on backpacks and so on)—"rendering a networked ubiquity within a citational network . . . in popular culture contexts—out of context of narrative terrains of meaning" erasing history (as Doyle comments in these pages and Dean does elsewhere [1998]). (Corporately assisted) replication stands in for (unnatural) reproduction. The mediatized emergence of a generic "E.T. currency" in popular images, texts, and "product" is our cue to rethink production, redistribution, and consumption within its force field, to think beyond globalization—or even "glocalization"—to planetization. And when we do so what we find, or can no longer avoid, is a notion of "life" not observant of the rules of maintaining permanent boundaries between nature and culture. We find "nature seconded . . . and invoked in the service of culture," as Franklin, Lury, and Stacey describe it so well (2000). Similarly, for "fabrication," Stefan Helmreich writes: "Artificial Life is a deliberate oxymoron, meant to edge us toward considering the possibility that 'life' might not be an exclusively 'natural' object or process; new forms of life might come into being, for example, in silico, with genomes built in the binary code of zeroes and ones" (2001: 613, noting Farmer and Belin). Within this consciousness, space is created for new forms of social life to play out across the borders of the virtual and the material. The online/offline Yugioh tournament play makes the point, as do the "cyberathletes" whose gaming skills earn them corporate sponsorship for professional circuit tournaments of outer-space computer strategy competitions in hotel conference rooms across the globe (Brandon Bongar, personal communication). And David Samuels (in this volume) tells of the emergence of the wholly original *Star Trek* language of Klingon and its lived expression for Klingon fans at conventions that take them where no day job ever could (as Greenwald writes in *Future Perfect*, "speaking Klingon means never having to say you're sorry" [1998: 168]).

Of course, it should come as no surprise that the notion of community cannot withstand its deconstruction by the online/offline networks of seekers defining themselves by their alien ability from orthodox science or religion or mainstream society. Whether in play or in religious or political action, or by more accidental convergences, the point of coming together—to play or watch Yugioh games, to speak Klingon, to perform their love of alien ancestors—is the sense they share that in any other terms the world eludes their secure purchase on it. Zygmund Bauman reminds us in more pragmatic language that the future is the "natural habitat" of the notion of community, not the present day. Furthermore, community brings to this future a "'feel' that is invariably good" (2002: 4–5), promising a security and serenity that is only knowable in contrast to friction and that only a fantasist could expect it to deliver without the sacrifice of freedom. So, while it is not beyond the capacity of the community ideal to extend an open invitation to its secure spaces—to present itself as host to those who would find themselves and one another in its terms—participants in E.T. culture who seek identity in such terms are central only to themselves. Functionally, they are *communities in disconnect*. It follows that their participants are often not beholden to any (other) nation or offer their uncritical allegiance to the rhetoric of nationness or any such persuasion of belonging. Where outerspaces are places of both persecution and liberation, community becomes a project for the *bricoleur* (Barkun 1998: 442, crediting the anthropologist Richard Werbner [1989]).

This presents a real problem for the idea of a community "pragmatically constructed from many starting points" toward the goal of social equilibrium (Laclau 1996: 114) since "community" in such terms presumes a world system unbending to the E.T. effect, that is, it requires placing an *impractical* value on coherence.[35] In this regard, E.T. "planetizers" are weirdly akin to Bauman's "new elite" and the "secession of the successful," whose world

> is not defined by any locality: it is truly and fully extraterrestrial. Extraterrestriality alone is guaranteed to be a community-free zone . . . where togetherness is understood as sameness. . . . There is a very narrow, if any interface between the "territory of extraterrestriality" and the lands in which its various outposts and half-way inns happen to be physically located. (2002: 54–58)

In short, the good faith notion of Bauman's "warm circle" of community, while in effect a "virtual actuality," may be the best that modernity can offer those who abide in alternative culture outerspaces.

On a Final Note

These pages suggest how the idea of the extraterrestrial can attune us to insiders' voices in outerspaces and, too, guide our critical inquiry of the reach and range of anthropological theory and methods, productively destabilizing prior knowledge of the field. While I could have focused entirely on "differences not yet otherness," I have instead tried to expose otherness (though not a sense of the foreign) as misleading for the planetized and familiar discourse of the alien. As more cross-cultural ethnography emerges, it will make this point, I believe, in no uncertain terms (Cook 2004; Lepselter 2005). Some of the lives we encounter here have been rough going for actors and for that matter, and properly, not all that easy for their ethnographers and ethnohistorians to document. The collage of essays in this volume seeks to bear witness to the complexity of cross-cultural exchanges generally speaking, and in strict accord with the subjectivities it considers, so as to make a case for questioning more broadly and sampling freely the rich diversity of approaches to a situated futurology. It is a project both terrifying and hopeful beyond belief.

Notes

I could not have attempted this project without the support of Mount Holyoke College and Ken Wissoker's unflagging faith. For comments on the essay I am grateful to Jodi Dean and Kathleen Stewart and to each one of the authors in the volume. I owe a special debt of gratitude to Alberto Sandoval for his insightful guidance and patient reading of earlier drafts. Stefan Helmreich's observations on the project's theoretical turning points were extremely useful at just the right moment, as was Kevin McCaffrey's uncannily pertinent input. Of course, all errors and oversights are entirely my own.

1. For more on this important concept, see R. Williams 1977.

2. See especially Weldes et al. 1999.

3. I borrow Anna Tsing's phrase to particular purpose, since her study argues that folks living on Indonesia's "peripheries" are peripheral only vis-à-vis the dominant culture and state structures, while their unique cultural practices are central from local actors' points of view.

4. The collected essays in George Marcus's anthology *Technoscientific Imaginaries* (1995) are a close agnostic cousin.

5. For intriguing thoughts on holographic models and related matters of social scale, I would direct you to Karen Sykes's review essay of the network theories of Marilyn Strathern, Roy Wagner, and Bruno Latour (2003).

6. The concept of the contact zone, which James Clifford (1997) introduced for the public spaces of museums, refers here to an environment of contact possibilities in the social universe.

7. A very few exemplary volumes that are anthropologically engaged are Biagioli 1999; E. Keller 1995; Latour and Woolgar 1986; Martin 1997; Nader 1996; and Strum and Fedigan 2000. Emily Martin, for example, notes two possible models: one, the string figure proposed by Donna Haraway for understanding how cultural configurations are formed in exchanges in the material world (1997:138; see also

Haraway 1996); and another the image of the rhizome, extrapolated from Giles Deleuze for tracing surface extensions of connected processes (Martin 1997) and more recently applied as an ecological model for a feminist ethics of flourishing (Fernandez 2001). Too, both Marilyn Strathern and Roy Wagner explore a "holographic" model of the complex relations of diverse entities in the world wherein "every part [contains] information about the whole and information about the whole [is] enfolded into each part. It is a holographic effect to imagine one can make connections anywhere" (Strathern 1995: 17–18; see also Strathern 1999; and Wagner 2001), calling attention to issues of scale in social relations.

8. For critical discussion of this "three-cornered constellation," which has fueled anthropological debate since Malinowski first suggested that Trobriand Islanders could be no less rational and no more magical in their thinking than Western scientists, see Nader 1996b.

9. The position I am taking on the metaphysical is contrary to that of Levinas, who asserts "the necessity of the metaphysical gaze of the Other in registering, and creating the futures of the self" and speaks of "the alterity of each face (the presentation of the Other in excess of the idea of the Other in me)" (quoted in Bhatt 1997: 30). One could argue that reduction to the generic—as it were, the stem cell arrived at from the differentiated cell of identity—and not excess alone, is at work here.

10. I was moved to raise this question while reading Derrida on "the host." He writes in *Acts of Religion*: "Who dares to say welcome" and thus "to insinuate that one is at home here . . . given all the claims to 'home' one might imagine oneself, and others, making?" (2002: 356). This question is central to an anthropological model of visits and is particularly apt for religious movements, such as that of the Raëlians, which culturally elaborate hosting—raising money for an embassy for human-alien exchange on Earth and welcoming human-alien sexual intercourse. But hosting is not always a matter of "saying welcome," which comes as no surprise to anyone who has seen films made after 1980 in which aliens inhabit subjects' bodies and may even subsume their hosts' subjectivity (as in *The Astronaut's Wife*). Such hosting as victimage and hostile takeover is a central topic in contemporary abduction recollections in which alien seed is implanted in human bodies. Of course, anthropologists understand this scenario from studying demon possessions that demand exorcism.

11. For anthologies, see Lewis 1995; Partridge 2003; Dean's well-theorized study (1998); and Denzler's (2001) and Lieb's (1998) well-researched works from religious studies.

12. I am reminded here and elsewhere in this essay of Laura Nader's quotation of Robert Young (1972) regarding the difficulties "of distinguishing science from

pseudo-science and from the political, economic and ideological contexts" of its practice (1996b: 262).

13. Whereas qualitative methods and questions about human-alien contact are part of UFO/alien studies that derive from religious studies, sociology, and political science and are employed by interpreters of science fiction and the "text artifacts" of popular culture and the arts, anthropology has rarely engaged either E.T. insiders' diverse understandings, histories, practices, and subjectivities or the topic of how these relate to anthropology's own disciplinary practice.

14. Fieldwork with UFO communities is emerging across the globe, but most publications are North America based.

15. In her study of Calvary Chapel, Kathleen Stewart captures the sense of "optimistic apocalypticism" as "optimistic because it signals the fulfillment of Bible prophecy, the rapture, the Second Coming of Christ" (Harding and Stewart 2003: 267).

16. Hexham and Poewe (1997) refer to this realm as Supernature, although, as the following pages show, culture's impact on nature is more complex than this category label implies. All such categories are in a sense a response to what Hudson Hoagland, President Emeritus of the Worcester Foundation for Experimental Biology, refers to as "the basic difficulty inherent in any investigation of phenomena such as those of psychic research or of UFO's," for "it is impossible for science ever to prove a universal negative" (1969: 1).

17. It is common in the literature of "UFO religion" to reference the British anthropologist E. E. Evans-Pritchard, who while working among the Azande of East Africa concluded that to engage subjects and to understand their ordering of everyday village life required "a leap of the imagination" into the realm of witchcraft belief. One had to accept the reality of witchcraft for the Azande, and learn its cultural logic, as a matter of everyday lived experience (Hexham 1997: 439). Since Evans-Pritchard's time, anthropology has included the logic of feeling and experience in its inquiries, while recognizing that gaining knowledge of another is an intersubjective process in which the anthropologist's position as a subject must be taken into account. Understanding this direction of disciplinary growth is important, since it does not allow us to ignore subject-object relations in their reflexivity.

18. This phenomenon is well described in an *Atlantic Monthly* article by Paul Davies (2003).

19. Alberto Sandoval-Sanchez's discussion of *travesti* in the context of the Efrain Barradas interpretation of the term in reference to a coming of age genre points to some interesting issues for New World Order discourse (Sandoval-Sanchez 2003:12).

20. But, as I discuss in the text, exorcism is not the only solution, or even the

best one, for individual subjects, whom Judith Herman (1992) would say require a safe environment, guided mourning, and *reintegration* of their fundamentally *relational* traumatic experiences in order to recover a sense of agency in their social lives.

21. I wish to acknowledge my debt here to Marilyn Strathern's brilliant *Partial Connections* (1991).

22. For a rich discussion of fetal imaging and fetus collections outside the secret zone of Area 51, see Lynn Morgan and Meredith Michaels's introduction to *Fetal Subjects, Feminist Positions* (1999).

23. An extrapolation of the negative scenario allows us to appreciate Alan Kraut's summary of the devastating diseases borne by Old World travelers in their "first encounters" with New World subjects, in which we read that "the breath of other people killed them" (1994: 10). As we follow that breath through its many displacements, we could be following an extraterrestrial contact narrative that ends up in New York City's immigrant settings among sufferers too culturally self-stigmatizing, too distrustful of Western medicine, and too passport vulnerable to seek medical assistance for diseases such as lead poisoning and tuberculosis. The diseases of modernity that Kraut documents—diseases of "first contact"—are explained in terms of work conditions, for example, "painter's disease" for lead poisoning. In social settings where a person is what he or she does, persons are reduced to their diseases in their own eyes and in the eyes of invisible, untranslatable, and powerful Others. *Contact*, too, refers to sites of material toxins or germs rather than to the conditions of social exchange and power asymmetries that generated them. And the process is reciprocal: aliens carry diseases back to human sources that no longer recognize themselves in the disease.

24. According to a report by the project manager of the MUFON Abduction Transcription Project, the 250 abductee cases examined from the 1940s onward indicate a wide range of skin tones in "cool" colors (mainly hyphenated ones such as "blue-green") and specifically indicate the gestation of "hybrid-beings" in "test tube" settings "attested to by numerous subjects shown rows of aquarium-like tanks, filled in liquid, in which partially formed fetuses were floating" (Wright 1996: 11).

25. A journalist notes in an interview with Strieber "an intense and well-informed ability to visualize scenarios in the immediate future based upon well-known trends in technology and society." Hence Strieber's vision of "neotony": the extraction of a human-alien fetus from "less dominant" human species from a woman's womb and its development outside the womb toward the "more dominant" species. "It may be," Strieber comments, "that the human species is the womb of the angels. . . . Then we would literally be the receptacle out of which the future is flowing" (Conroy 1989: 354–55).

26. Agamben offers insight on the value of testimony in the context of Ausch-

witz—a topic not irrelevant here, though not one this essay can address. He writes: "At a certain point, it became clear that testimony contained at its core an essential lacuna; in other words, the survivors bore witness to something it is impossible to bear witness to. As a consequence, commenting on survivors' testimony necessarily meant interrogating this lacuna or, more precisely, attempting to listen to it. Listening to something absent." He adds that the goal is "a newly orienting ethical cartography" (1999: 13).

27. See especially the writings of Susan Palmer (1994, 1995, 1997a, 1997b, 2004; Palmer and Hardman 1999) and Chryssides (2003) and my essay later in this volume.

28. Elsewhere (Battaglia 2001) I develop an argument for relating clones and replicants to race and gender in popular cinema.

29. It is interesting to note that UFO sightings in eastern Europe and Russia also increased after the collapse of communism. See Ramet 1998.

30. Gamson and Modigliani's rendering of the historicity of public reception to nuclear power draws an important parallel narrative to ufology's.

31. A recent symposium at the San Francisco Exploratorium on techno-organism hybridizations demonstrated an interactive connection—and even an exchange of information in some exhibits—though in no instance did the "partial life" entity initiate the exchange. Perhaps as fascinating was the cross-disciplinarity of the event as a form of parallel fusion play.

32. As Young (1972) states (quoted in Nader 1996a: 262), the difficulties of "distinguishing science from pseudo-science and from the political, economic and ideological contexts" are increasingly significant.

33. Donna Haraway's "A Manifesto for Cyborgs" (in Haraway 2004), which launched cyborg anthropology as a force within the discipline, is where reading on this topic begins. It includes a feminist genealogy of "monsters," from the individual automaton to the mechanical, biological, robotic, and cyborg-relational entity.

34. Badley goes on to note that this is appropriate to a world open less to "invasion" than "pervasion" (she credits Vivian Sobshack).

35. To take a particularly well-documented example, there was no love lost between the "spoon bender" researchers in Bath, England, whose scientific experiments were rigorously designed but who suffered the wrath of "vigilante skeptics" of the science establishment and the early demise (from their view) of their experiments. The "thick description" ethnography in defense of their project, written in the scientistic language in which the Bath scientists were trained by their enemies, is a model of its type (Collins and Pinch 1982).

Ufology as Anthropology: Race, Extraterrestrials, and the Occult

CHRISTOPHER F. ROTH

> Everything was puzzling for those early explorers. . . . Pierre Martyr quotes descriptions of monstrous beasts: snakes like crocodiles; animals with the body of an ox and a proboscis like that of the elephant; four-legged fish with ox-heads, their backs studded with thousands of warts and tortoise-like shells, as well as man-eating tyburons. But these, after all, are only boas, tapirs, manatees or hippopotamuses and sharks . . . In that happy age, everything was still possible, as it is again today, no doubt, thanks to flying saucers!—Claude Lévi-Strauss ([1955] 1984: 76)

Colonialism was the midwife of anthropology. European exploration and conquest of the world outside Europe in the eighteenth and nineteenth centuries spurred a desire to collect and describe and understand a biological and geographical diversity of the planet that had only been wondered about or filtered through implausible legends. This included the study of human diversity, of race. In the beginning, this diversity was understood through unapologetically Western paradigms: biblical creation and eschatology, the theory of the humors, assumptions about climate and biology, Christian themes of divinity and hierarchy, and European folklore about vampires and devils. Today physical anthropology has become a harder science, employing concepts from genetics, statistics, and ecology that anthropology's precursors could not have imagined. In turn, anthropology's beginnings have themselves been made the object of anthropological contemplation, itself a form of folklore, of a piece with the social order that produced it, the same order of phenomenon as the beliefs and customs of the non-Europeans anthropology initially tried to understand.

Ufology, too—the study of and interest in unidentified flying objects and extraterrestrial visitors—is a discipline that has tried to understand racial diversity. Ufologists do not always call it "human" diversity, but then the earliest European anthropologists were not sure that all speaking bipeds outside Europe were human either. Ufology also has had to monitor its own folkloric and religious assumptions and strive for more scientific objectivity, hampered by the fact that the wider society, including academia, regards ufology's very premise as folklore. That premise is that some kind of intelligences, with forms that resemble those of humans, are interacting with humanity on a clandestine basis. Unlike the naturalists who accompanied the great European explorers on their expeditions, ufologists are in the position of responding to specimens that are coming to us. In fact, these specimens, the aliens, seem themselves to be anthropologists of a sort—and, to be fair, they might in fact prefer to call themselves zoologists, even entomologists, as they abduct frightened bipedal mammals from our towns and cities and examine, tag, and release them. Just as Europe's early explorer-anthropologists contemplated and debated the position of "savages" in a divine social order at the same time that they were operating through scientific and governmental institutions that were in the business of imposing that order on a global scale, so, in the same way, are Earth's UFO investigators in the odd position of trying to answer the question of how aliens fit into a cosmic order of intelligent races that also includes human races. I say odd because ufologists tell us that the spotty evidence we have to go on as to what this cosmic order might be is reports of encounters that seem to be the unfolding of an interplanetary, interracial drama, our role in which can only be guessed at, though most such guesses are not particularly encouraging.

Given such structural affinities, we should not be surprised to find that ufology and anthropology share intellectual roots: scientific and pseudoscientific discourses whose commingling confounds boundaries between official and unofficial science, science and religion, anthropology and zoology, and historiography and prophecy. As a sociocultural anthropologist and someone who has immersed himself in UFO communities in several parts of the United States, I have constantly been in a position to notice this crosspollination. Never, when I tell someone I meet at a UFO interest group meeting that I am an anthropologist, is there the remotest wonder that I am therefore attracted to the topic.

Introduction

To explore the relationship between ufology and anthropology requires combining ethnography with intellectual history. Ufological communities, such as American ufology, which I focus on here, are not bounded communities that can be delimited demographically or geographically in a manner that permits their analysis to be coextensive with traditionally defined ethnographic projects. "Experiencers" of UFOs (abductees and contactees), enthusiasts, and researchers compose networks of individuals geographically dispersed and united mainly by discourses rooted in the published UFO literature, video media, and now the Internet. They communicate as individuals, in local groups, through organizations such as the Mutual UFO Network (MUFON), and in online communities. To the extent that such a subculture has a "heritage," it is to be found in the canonical UFO sightings and events dating from the mid–twentieth century and the canonical texts that record and interpret those events. This literature has its own pedigree, of which most UFO enthusiasts are unaware. Its nineteenth-century origins are in occultism and the human sciences, evolving discourses that continue to intersect with ufology. Any exploration of the spread of these ideas must note their slow leakage from academia and occult institutions such as the Theosophical Society into loosely dispersed networks of autodidacts such as the ufological community. In this discursive space, older scientific and theological paradigms, however discredited they might be in contemporary academia, mix and combine with images from popular culture and the assumptions and belief structures that make up the worldview—including especially racial conceptions—that UFO enthusiasts share with their fellow citizens.

Ufology and academic social science intersect at various points. The "ancient astronaut" literature has been responding to developments in academic archaeology for more than half a century. Millennial flying-saucer religions have been investigated by social psychologists and scholars of religion (Festinger, Riecken, and Schachter 1956; Balch and Taylor 1977; Balch 1982; Lewis 1995; Denzler 2001). Ufologists turn to folklore studies (such as Evans-Wentz 1911) to demonstrate the universality of something resembling the UFO experience (Vallee 1969a; Conroy 1989: 302–44), while sympathetic folklorists have fitted UFO reports into a "legend" paradigm (Rojcewicz 1987; Bullard 1987, 1989). Ufology has its own school of thought, referred to as the "psychosocial hypothesis," which explores the limits of the social and psychological embeddedness of UFO imagery and beliefs. Each of these intertwinings of traditions of thought deserves a separate study of the type attempted here. What I concentrate on now, however, is a particular line of thinking in ufology that has been continually informed by academic human sciences: the attempt to understand alien physical forms in light of understandings and paradigms in physical anthropology—a discipline that I will treat as, even in its high-academic form, emergent from and responding to folk thought and embedded in political, social, and popular-cultural discourses. Put simply, ufology is in one sense all about race, and it has more to do with terrestrial racial schemes as social and cultural constructs than most UFO believers are aware.

Cultural and physical anthropologists have attended to the social and political contexts of nineteenth- and early-twentieth-century physical anthropology and how its understanding of human variation reflected and supported social and political structures in Europe and America. But, as twentieth-century anthropology shed the race concept and cultural and social anthropologists began to dominate the discipline and separate their project from physical anthropology, the older anthropological discourses that had legitimized a hierarchical racial and class order did not vanish. Those "disproven" paradigms persist in scientific creationism, racist anthropology, and other pseudo sciences. Donna Kossy (2001) provides a model for an intellectual history of such pseudo science (see also Kafton-Minkel 1989; Godwin 1992). Her work is essentially the dark underbelly of George Stocking's work on the history of academic anthropology. Ufology, despite its deep intellectual roots, is one less well-studied reservoir of such discredited ideas. I decline, as Stocking does (1968), to distinguish science and pseudo science, instead treating both as shifting folk categories (like the concepts "disproven" and "discredited" themselves), which, if applied analytically, would deny the historical contextualizability of institutionalized knowledge. Instead, I trace the rise of anthropological concepts and their diffusion into what became the ufological community, a community whose members by necessity have always been embedded in and responding to the socially constructed ethnoscapes of the larger society.

There is, in one sense, no organic folk culture of ufology distinct from a more official or intellectual discourse of it. Those interested in UFOs have always been avid autodidacts of religion, history, biology, physics, anthropology, and the occult. At a typical UFO interest group meeting in any American city, one can hear debates about social psychology, interdimensional physics, and the ethnography of shamanism. But there might be not a degree holder among them, and the names dropped are far more likely to include Carl Jung, Terence McKenna, Stephen Hawking, Immanuel Velikovsky, and Julian Jaynes than Freud, Marx, Boas, or Lévi-Strauss. Their ideas are more likely to echo the essentialisms of Müller, Eliade, and Castañeda than the relativism and social constructivism that characterize most academic thinking in the humanities and social sciences today. Any ethnography of the belief structure of ufology must, then, also be an intellectual history, responding to social and historical shifts in a tighter feedback loop than is the case with the mainstream developments in any academic discipline.

Ufology, explicitly or implicitly, is about the dissolution of boundaries—the boundaries between science and esotericism, fact and intuition, human and alien, and past and future. But as these boundaries blur others harden, including some already socially and culturally constituted by the wider society. What follows is a genealogy of some of the thought structures that diffused from anthropology to ufology during the twentieth century.

Ufology's Beginnings

A series of rapid stages following the Second World War led to the establishment of the ufological paradigm as we know it today. In the late 1940s, reports of strange aircraft were of wide interest, but the suggestion that they involved contact with nonhuman intelligence was explored mainly in pulp science fiction. In the 1950s, esoteric teachers on the fringes of American society seized on the flying-saucer topic as self-styled "contactees" and commanded wide audiences but little respect or credibility. In the 1960s, the idea of humans interacting with aliens began, at least theoretically, to acquire scientific respectability. By then, the reports were not explicitly ideological or religious, and the thought structures and historical sequences that had structured science fiction and contactee narratives—all racially inflected through the terms and understandings of esoteric anthropologies—persisted in a more subtle, though still determinate, form, this time in the charged atmosphere of the American racial landscape. It is this progression that I will trace here.

Although anomalous "airships" were reported in large numbers in the 1890s and most writers date the beginning of the UFO age to a series of events in 1947—the Kenneth Arnold sighting, the Maury Island Incident, the Roswell Incident—it was not until the early 1950s that anything that could be characterized as a UFO subculture or a flying-saucer movement came into being. Indeed, extraterrestrial explanations for UFO sightings did not even dominate public discourse on UFOs for the first few years after 1947 (Gross 1988).

But in the 1950s a cadre of self-described UFO contactees began reporting journeys and conversations with the "space brothers," the pilots of the mysterious flying saucers that so many were seeing in the sky. The key contactees—George Adamski, Truman Bethurum, Daniel Fry, Orfeo Angelucci, Frank Stranges, Gabriel Green, George Hunt Williamson, and others—grabbed public attention from more sober-minded investigators of the sightings and, most importantly, established ideologies, narratives, terminologies, and positionings with respect to other discourses, all of which continue to shape ufology to the present day. Admittedly, this particular pedigree of ufology is an embarrassment to investigators of sightings and landings who imposed a forensic seriousness on the saucer topic in the 1960s and to the abduction investigators who have dominated ufology since the 1980s. For these "serious" investigators, the space brother movement is religion, while the investigation of sightings is science (Dean 1998: 40–41). But we will see that such disavowals and distinctions belie vigorous continuities in ideology, worldview, and language. The disavowal derives in part from the split in the 1950s UFO movement between the subjects of the encounters and the purveyors of the explanations (Keel 1975). The 1950s contactees were both, while serious investigators did not pretend to offer definitive answers to the flying-saucer mystery. When, in the early 1970s and afterward, "serious" ufologists such as Jacques Vallee and John Keel began offering fully formed hypotheses, they relied more than they would admit on the milieu and mindset the contactees had brought about.

The explanations the contactees offered, and even the structure of their encounters with the space brothers, can be understood primarily in terms of the Theosophically based worldviews of which some explicitly partook and some versions of which much of their disparate audiences already accepted (Denzler 2001: 46). To understand that occult milieu, which was and remains the crucible of ufological thought, one must understand Theosophy and its role in a vernacular anthropology that countered a scientific discourse that had become separated from the foundational rationales of European and American society. Although few people did or do accept strict Theosophical tenets, and its principles and terminologies remain mostly impenetrable, Theosophy nonetheless created, reflected, and reinforced assumptions and beliefs that continue to permeate strains of Western thought that run afoul of both mainstream science and mainstream Christianity. These strains are where ufology lives.

Evolutionism to Theosophy

Theosophy, which was founded in the 1870s in England and the United States and reached its period of strongest influence in the 1890s, was in large part a reaction against Darwinism, and against scientism and rationalism in general, but it hardly resembled the scientific creationism that came to dominate anti-Darwinian thought in twentieth-century Britain and America. Stocking (1968) describes the shifting landscape of academic positions that characterized the transition from biblical creationism to Darwinian evolutionism, a landscape that defies the categories of "science" and "pseudo science," even when one focuses only on academic debates. Stocking reads this intellectual history through a debate between monogenism and polygenism, which predated the publication of Darwin's *Origin of Species* in 1859. Polygenism validated the British "commonsense" folk view of human physical variation, which held that there are biologically distinct races, some superior to others. This suggestion was heretical both to late-eighteenth-century biblical creationism and to the emerging position that humanity probably descended from primate stock.

In this light, Theosophist racial theory was one in a panoply of responses to Darwinism and monogenism in the late nineteenth century.

This diversity is in fact reflected in the kaleidoscope of nonacademic scientific traditions still in play today (Kossy 2001: 77). In particular, Theosophy rejected Darwinian evolution's implication that hierarchies in creation, such as human dominance over animals, were random or illusory. Theosophists nonetheless also absorbed new findings in astronomy, geology, archaeology, philology, and comparative religion—in which their founder Helena Petrovna Blavatsky was unusually well versed—findings that, alongside Darwinism, were threatening to displace academic biblical creationism in what has been called the "death of Adam" (Greene 1959). Theosophy is a mystically based worldview that infuses with divinity the revolutionary findings in science while retaining the sense of order and progress in the universe—almost akin to a medieval theory of correspondences—that Christianity was feared to be surrendering to science. In rejecting the idea that all creation was of common stock, differentiating randomly and without direction or an overarching meaning, Blavatsky shared the concerns of Pierre Teilhard de Chardin, a Jesuit paleontologist, who, noting the phased evolutionary periods in the fossil record that we now call punctuated equilibrium, developed a theory of autonomously directed biological and spiritual evolution guided not by programmatic divine intervention but by immanent cosmic principles. With an ultimately nontheistic view of evolution, Theosophy imposes order, direction, and hierarchy on anthropology, geography, and history.

Theosophy is a revealed religion that is based on texts and messages delivered to Blavatsky and her circle by discarnate Ascended Masters, usually multiply reincarnated Tibetan lamas. Theosophical ideas continued to shape occult movements throughout the twentieth century. Most of the vocabulary of the New Age—auras, astral projection, chakras, spirit guides, gurus, the Age of Aquarius—can be traced directly to Theosophical writers. This is equally true of occult treatment of race and difference, of human history, progress, and evolution, and of the supernatural geographies—interdimensional, subterranean, and extraterrestrial—on which a racial schema could be laid out. For its synthesis of science and religion, Theosophy drew on Eastern religions, which in Blavatsky's day linguistics, archaeology, and greater communication with the literate civilizations of the Far East were making available to westerners for the first time. The core of Theosophical thought is contained in Blavatsky's *Isis Unveiled* (1877) and especially *The Secret Doctrine* ([1888] 1938), the latter purportedly based on the "Stanzas of Dzyan," an apocryphal text. Blavatsky relied on obscure kabbalistic, Masonic, gnostic, and orientalist sources, but her views on race grew out of a combination of these and Victorian anthropology and philology.

Human origins and physical variation dominate the second volume of *The Secret Doctrine*, "Anthropogenesis." Here we read of the (not yet completed) history of humanity as a succession of seven "Root-Races," corresponding to seven continents, some sunken, some yet to rise. The ethereal First Root-Race arrived from the moon to people a continent called the Imperishable Sacred Land (Blavatsky [1888] 1938, 3:35–58). The Third Root-Race lived on Lemuria—here borrowing geology's term for the protocontinent approximating present-day South Asia. The Lemurians, Blavatsky wrote, were the first to have humanoid bodies and sexual dimorphism. They mated not only with one another but with "she-animals," resulting in a mongrel race of low-browed cretins. Theosophy traces modern anthropoid apes to these Lemurian mongrels (Scott-Elliot [1925] 1962: 94). Purebred Lemurians learned agriculture, weaving, and other technologies from "Serpents of Wisdom and Dragons" (Blavatsky [1888] 1938, 3:219) from Venus (a planet whose inhabitants had by then evolved, ahead of us, to a state of divinity). Venusians helped the Lemurians, just "as we possibly, long ages hence, may similarly be called to give a helping hand to the beings struggling up to manhood on the Jupiter or the Saturn chain" (Scott-Elliot [1925] 1962: 99). These extraterrestrials also established the ancient Egyptian civilization (Fuller 1988: 212), as well as the whole tradition of occult lodges (Rosicrucians, Freemasons, and so on) that pass on secret knowledge today (Blavatsky [1888] 1938, 3:129–221; Scott-Elliot [1925] 1962: 106–7). Each of these elements emerges again in standard scenarios in ufology and in the subdiscipline of "ancient astronaut" historiography.

Survivors of Lemuria's catastrophic sinking, about eighteen million years ago according to *The Secret Doctrine*, became the Fourth Root-Race, which peopled Atlantis, the lost continent familiar to all occultists (Scott-Elliot [1925] 1962). The fifth race, the Aryans, spread from the Gobi Desert and Tibet to South Asia and Europe (Blavatsky [1888] 1938, 3:15–352; Campbell 1980: 44–45; Godwin 1992: 19–20; Kossy 2001: 7–8). The Anglo-Saxons, an Aryan subrace, dominated the world in the Victorian period as part of a divinely ordained sequence.

With the Aryans, Blavatsky's chronology begins to overlap scenarios developed by nineteenth-century historians and ethnologists. Specifically, Blavatsky drew on the work of F. Max Müller, the Sanskritist who championed the classification of language stocks as a method for sorting out the genealogies of races. Müller had turned to language structure, using a hierarchy of morphological systems to postulate the increasing or decreasing (evolving or degenerating) sophistication of civilizations and languages as they branched off from the parent stock. This lapsarianism defied western European common sense in privileging the revealed religions of India, not Judeo-Christian ones, as the original connection with the divine.

Blavatsky—unlike Müller, her affinity was also racial—linked modern groups with the seven Root-Races: Lemurians with black Africans and Dravidians (Scott-Elliot [1925] 1962: 92); Atlanteans with Mongols and Mesoamericans; and Aryans with Semites, Europeans, and others. There was and is agreement in Theosophy that two of the seven races were yet to come or were beginning to emerge. European dominance is, in Theosophical belief, currently waning as part of a divinely ordained evolutionary sequence. Most thinking on this subject was taken up by Blavatsky's followers after her death. Following Blavatsky, Annie Besant in 1909 identified the seven subraces of the (currently dominant) Fifth Root-Race as including North Indian Aryans, westward-migrating Aryans, Iranians, Celts, and the then cresting Teutonic (A.K.A.. Anglo-Saxon) race (Besant 1910: 212). These races overlap, and superseded races can still remain strong and vital, but it is in the emerging sixth subrace of the Fifth Root-Race that we can find harbingers of the Sixth Root-Race. That great shift, Theosophists argued, would involve severe environmental changes, just as continental sinkings and climatic change accompanied the passing of the baton from one Root-Race to the other in the past. Such evolution was to occur independently, without either eugenic engineering or further extraterrestrial intervention, but the larger process was implacable (Besant and Leadbeater 1947; Wauchope 1962: 121–23).

American Occultism and the Shaver Mystery

After the First World War, Theosophy's currency waned. In America, where the attention of this history has settled, a Theosophist splinter group established itself at Point Loma, California, near the site where C. W. Leadbeater, a disciple of Blavatsky, predicted the emergence of the Coming Race (Tillett 1982: 164). But by the 1940s it was only one of a panoply of alternative religions available to those who found both mainstream religion and mainstream science lacking in satisfactory answers. In the fertile ground of the occultist subculture, it is not surprising that the first reports of "flying saucers" and "flying disks" in the 1940s were taken seriously (see Heard 1950). While news reports in 1947 focused on possible military origins of the craft (Gross 1988), occultists looked to their own rich lore for answers. Two pairs emerge as founding figures in the 1940s and 1950s, around whom occult scenarios for the origins of the saucers coalesced. George Adamski and George Hunt Williamson are familiar to saucer historians as founders of the space brother movement. Setting the stage for them, however, were Richard Shaver and Ray Palmer, who led the first attempts to fit saucer sightings into a coherent occult schema.

Shaver was an amateur artist prominent in the radical labor movement of 1920s and 1930s Detroit. After his brother, Taylor Shaver, an author of boys' adventure fiction, died at the age of thirty in 1934 under what Richard felt were suspicious circumstances connected with their political activities, he entered an alcoholic decline and was institutionalized for paranoid delusions. He spent much of the next few years as an itinerant laborer throughout the United States (Pobst 1989). In 1943, Shaver cofounded much of UFO lore in accidental collaboration with Raymond Palmer, whom John Keel, one of the more perspicacious and skeptical observers of the flying-saucer phenomenon, considers, as a result, "the man who invented flying saucers" (1989). Palmer published the pulp science-fiction magazine *Amazing Stories*, as well as, later, the popular nonfiction occult magazine *Fate*, still in print today. By the early 1940s, pulp science fiction had run its course and faced competition from comic books for its male teenaged readership. Palmer was looking for a way to spice up sales when a letter arrived from one Richard Shaver containing a purported key to an ancient occult "Mantong Alphabet," based on the principle that "There is a basic universal meaning to every sound" (Palmer 1975: 43). Shaver's biographer puts it kindly when pointing out that the alphabet "runs counter to every accepted notion of history and the origin of language" (Pobst 1989: 22), though in its own way it echoes Müller's concept, via Blavatsky, of discoverable resonances of a perfect ancestral mother tongue. *Amazing Stories* published the alphabet on its letters page to test readers' response. "Many hundreds of readers' letters came in," Palmer recalled, "and the net result was a query to Richard S. Shaver asking him where he got his Alphabet. The answer was in the form of a 10,000 word 'manuscript' entitled 'A Warning to Future Man'" (Palmer 1975: 36; see also Kafton-Minkel 1989: 136–37).

In it, Shaver asserted that Earth was first peopled by a race of extraterrestrial Titans. Making their home on Atlantis, they created "robot races" to serve them, but an increasing bombardment of lethal solar rays, which truncated the Titans' originally Methuselah-like life spans, drove them to build and inhabit a network of caves, which honeycomb the Earth today. Failing to escape the solar rays even there, the Titans migrated to another star, but there was not enough room on their rockets for all of the robot races, who were left behind. Some of these returned to the surface as they adapted to the changed atmosphere; these are humanity's ancestors. Others stayed underground; they survive today in two groups: the Deros, who de-evolved into a race of evil "midgetlike idiots," and a smaller population of Teros who continue to resist them. Most wars, plagues, and other ills are caused by Deros wielding the machines abandoned by the Titans, which fire fiendish "stim" rays. These stim rays are also used to broadcast voices into surface-dwellers' heads—which is how Shaver learned of this complex history (Shaver 1975: 48–66; Kafton-Minkel 1989: 136–39; Keel 1989: 140–41).

Palmer reworked "A Warning to Future Man" as "I Remember Lemuria!" and published it in the March 1945 issue of *Amazing Stories*. He altered "the 'factual' basis of Mr. Shaver's manuscript" in only one instance.

> I could not bring myself to believe that Mr. Shaver had really gotten his Alphabet, and his Warning to Future Man, and all the "science" he propounded, from actual caves in the Earth, and actual people living there. Instead, I translated his thought-records into "racial memory," and felt sure this would be more believable to my readers, and a reasonable and actual explanation for what was going on in Mr. Shaver's mind—which is where I felt it really was going on. (Palmer 1975: 38)

Much of Shaver's worldview is derived from Theosophy. The stim rays are modeled on the vril rays wielded by subsurface dwellers in the 1871 proto-science-fiction novel *The Coming Race* by Edward Bulwer Lytton, a

Rosicrucian. That novel was a direct influence on Blavatsky, who used the title phrase to describe the Sixth Root-Race (Kafton-Minkel 1989: 262). Shaver read Bulwer Lytton (Pobst 1989: 19), and the term *Tero*, which he etymologized according to the Mantong Alphabet, was actually probably derived from *Teros*, which meant "protective psychic energy" in Theosophical texts (Godwin 1992: 104). Shaver's stories of extraterrestrials, Atlantis, and Lemuria betray a familiarity with Theosophical ideas, as does Palmer's concept of racial memory.

The response to "I Remember Lemuria!" was overwhelming. Soon whole issues of *Amazing Stories* were devoted to the Shaver Mystery. The September 1946 issue featured flying-saucer-like ships on its cover and a Shaver piece, "Earth Slaves to Space," about extraterrestrials who abduct humans into their spaceship (Keel 1989: 141–42). *Amazing Stories*' circulation jumped to a quarter million, and thousands testified to their own Lemurian memories, encounters with Deros and Teros, and sightings of Dero and Tero craft (Kafton-Minkel 1989: 137; Keel 1989: 141). Palmer called Shaver "one of the most brilliant men I have ever met" (1975: 40), but it would be hard for anyone to dispute his original diagnosis that the Deros and Teros were figments of his imagination (38). As Keel writes:

> Palmer had accidentally tapped a huge, previously unrecognized audience. Nearly every community has at least one person who complains constantly to the local police that someone—usually a neighbor—is aiming a terrible ray gun at their house or apartment. This ray, they claim, is ruining their health, causing their plants to die, turning their bread moldy, making their hair and teeth fall out, and broadcasting voices into their heads. Psychiatrists are very familiar with these "ray" victims and relate their problem with paranoid-schizophrenia. . . . They are a distrustful lot . . . and very suspicious of everyone, including the government and all figures of authority. In earlier times, they thought they were hearing voices of God and/or the Devil. Today they often blame the CIA or space beings for their woes. . . . Ray Palmer unintentionally gave thousands of these people focus to their lives. (1989: 140)

Then, on June 24, 1947, Kenneth Arnold, a pilot, reported seeing crescent-shaped craft skipping along in the air over Mount Rainier in Washington, "like a saucer would if you skipped it across the water" (Arnold and Palmer 1952: 11), and a reporter mangled his description to produce the catchphrase *flying saucer*. Palmer, by now fancying himself an investigator, contacted Arnold for details and enlisted his help later that year to investigate a dramatic sighting of a sputtering, listing, doughnut-shaped craft that hovered near Tacoma, Washington (20–21ff.), which became known as the Maury Island Incident. The prime witness, it turned out, was a dock operator who had once written a letter to *Amazing Stories* describing his encounters with stim-shooting Dero spaceships in Burma and Kashmir during the Second World War (Keel 1989: 141, Thomas 1999: 31–33, 40, 82). Science fiction and nonfiction were by now hopelessly blurred, and by the end of 1947 the modern age of UFO investigation was under way.

George Adamski and Orthon

Quite separately from Arnold and Palmer's gumshoeing or Shaver's jottings, by the early 1950s some were claiming to have contacted the flying saucers' pilots. Peter Washington (1993) sees some of these UFO contactees as among the most direct continuations of Theosophical belief (380–81). But contactees as overtly Theosophist as, for instance, George King or Eduard "Billy" Meier decades later are the exception rather than the rule. For the most part, occultism has been an oblique influence, as was the case with Adamski, and Williamson, who segregated, even hid, their Theosophical doctrines from their more UFO-oriented readership. Adamski's narratives and theories unite quasi Theosophy, anthropology, and a new model for the relationships between experiences and investigation and between humans and extraterrestrials.

Adamski, "philosopher, student, researcher, saucer researcher" (Leslie and Adamski 1953: 171), was a Polish immigrant who also claimed "Egyptian" ancestry and began his career as an esoteric writer, the author of the explicitly Theosophical *Questions and Answers by the Royal Order of Tibet*. Arriving in the 1920s in California, he settled on the slopes of Mount Palomar (near the Hale Observatory), where he acquired an informal following as an esoteric teacher (Flammonde 1971: 52–54).

But Adamski's innovation was to claim face-to-face contact with extraterrestrials. His lectures on UFOs and an article in *Fate* (Flammonde 1971: 55) attracted local saucer enthusiasts, including a "Dr." George Hunt Williamson and his wife Betty and one Alfred C. Bailey, a chiropractic-school dropout and railway conductor (Williamson and Bailey 1954: 35–36), and his wife, who attended Adamski's next attempt to flag down and establish contact with saucer pilots (Leslie and Adamski 1953: 185–86). Picnicking with the Williamsons and Baileys near Blythe, California, on November 20, 1952, Adamski photographed a silvery, cigar-shaped craft hovering above them (188–89). Then he was approached by a long-haired man who emerged from a landed saucer dispatched from this "mother ship" (200). His name, Adamski learned later, was Orthon. Here we get the first real account in the literature of an encountered alien. The creature was

> about five feet six . . . round faced with an extremely high forehead; large, but calm, grey-green eyes, slightly aslant at the outer corners; with slightly higher cheek bones than an Occidental, but not so high as an Indian or an Oriental; a finely chiselled nose, not conspicuously large. . . . As nearly as I can describe his skin the colouring would be an even, medium-colored suntan. And it did not look to me as though he had ever had to shave, for there was no more hair on his face than on a child's. (195)

The most unusual thing about Orthon was his androgyny. When they shook hands,

> The flesh of his hand to the touch of mine was like a baby's. . . . His hands were slender, with long tapering fingers like the beautiful hands of a woman. In fact, in different clothing, he could easily have passed for an unusually beautiful woman; yet he definitely was a man. . . . His hair was sandy in color and hung in beautiful waves to his shoulders, glistening more beautifully than any woman's I have ever seen. And I remember a passing thought of how Earth women would enjoy having such beautiful hair as this man had. (195)

Everything about the description of this "first" extraterrestrial was to prove a durable model, not only for other 1950s space brothers, but for reports stretching to the present day, of gentle, androgynous, humanlike beings resembling a mixture of Nordic and "Oriental" (which could imply Semitic as well as South or East Asian) features (see Sanderson 1967: 165). Although these human-looking types have been eclipsed by the "Grey" types that now dominate ufological imagery, they are still with us; since the 1980s, ufologists have called them Nordics (often pronounced "Nordiques," with an accent on the second syllable). Orthon, in fact, resembled no one so much as the Himalayan Ascended Masters in the Theosophical literature, who "combined their handsome Indian looks with suspiciously pale skin and European features" (Washington 1993: 166). In the classic nineteenth-century ethnologist's sense, Orthon was a true Aryan, a spiritually advanced, androgynous, and physiognomically Orient-tinged Nordic.

Orthon told Adamski that his fellow Venusians, as well as those from other planets visiting Earth, were worried about radiation from atomic bomb tests leaking into space (Washington 1993: 198–99). He explained that spacemen do not visit populated areas because "there would be a tremendous amount of fear . . . and probably the visitors would be torn to pieces by the Earth people, if such public landings were attempted" (202). Every aspect of the meeting with Orthon has continued to echo throughout the contactee and abductee literature.

Adamski sent an account of the event to a British publisher, who coincidentally was looking for a way to package a slim manuscript it had received from an Irish nobleman (Moseley and Pflock 2002: 27) named Desmond Leslie, which explained various archaeological mysteries in terms of the Venusian visitation scenarios in Blavatsky's *Secret Doctrine*. This coincidence led to the publication of *Flying Saucers Have Landed* (Leslie and Adamski 1953). With this book, two now-vast literatures were launched: that of alien contact and that of the ancient astronaut theory.

The following spring, the first Interplanetary Spacecraft Convention was held at Giant Rock, California. Already Adamski shared the podium with other "contactees," including George Van Tassel, Orfeo Angelucci, Truman Bethurum, and Daniel Fry, as well as Williamson and the author of the first book on the Roswell, New Mexico, crash, the Hollywood journalist and professional con man Frank Scully (Flammonde 1971: 63). Fry was a military engineer at the White Sands Proving Ground in New Mexico; his Martian contact, Alan (with the accent on the second syllable), was descended from refugees to Mars from a human colony in the Himalayas after a Lemurian-Atlantean war, following Shaver's take on Theosophical history (Fry 1966; Flammonde 1971: 71–73). Bethurum's abductor was Captain Aura Rhanes, an olive-skinned, brown-eyed woman from the planet Clarion, whom, like the other contacts, he met in an impromptu desert saucer landing. Rhanes, like Alan, warned of the evils of pollution and war and unchecked technological leaps in general (Bethurum 1954). What is striking is how rapidly so many details of the contactee phenomenon became established in this initial period, roughly 1953 to 1959.

In the 1950s, the contactees were regarded as a lunatic fringe by those who increasingly wanted to study UFOs scientifically and had no patience for reports of contact with the saucers' pilots, even when it was agreed that those saucers were probably piloted. By the 1960s, this distinction would gradually erode, and, as we will see, investigators by the 1980s devoted themselves primarily to contacts and abductions. With that shift, what had been the 1950s contactee discourses began to color ufology as a whole, despite the fact that by that time Adamski and his contemporaries had been rejected as frauds. It is important, then, to locate socially and institutionally some of the key figures in the development of interstellar racial schemata in the 1950s contactee movement.

Not surprisingly, a pivotal role in the early contactee movement belonged to an anthropologist—or at least a self-styled one—George Hunt Williamson, mentioned previously as having witnessed Adamski's first contact. He was involved around that time in an esoteric society called Soulcraft, whose founder, William Dudley Pelley, had been the most prominent pro-Nazi activist in the United States from the rise of Hitler through the attack on Pearl Harbor. Pelley had organized the paramilitary Silver Shirts organization, modeled on Hitler's Brown Shirts, whose membership overlapped heavily with that of the I AM Religious Activity (Vallee 1979: 192–93), a direct Theosophical offshoot (still in existence), which adds, to the usual Tibetan adepts, more thoroughly Anglo-Saxon Ascended (or reincarnated) Masters such as King Arthur and George Washington (Kinney 1989: 27–28). In 1936, Pelley ran for president on the Christian Party ticket, with German Nazi funding and an anti-Semitic platform. "The time has come for an American Hitler and a pogrom," he stated in one campaign speech (Kossy 2001: 12). President Franklin Roosevelt interned Pelley for sedition in 1942. Paroled in 1950, he immediately founded Soulcraft, and Williamson was among his first associates.

James Moseley, who met and interviewed all of the contactees in the 1950s and later published exposés of both Williamson (Aharon 1957; Moseley and Mann 1959; Robinson 1963) and Adamski (Moseley and Pflock 2002: 333–52), writes that Williamson was "deeply interested in anthropology and, he claimed, possessed extensive knowledge of the ways of various tribes of Plains Indians, acquired by years of living among them"

(62), though his curriculum vitae was riddled with fabrications and phony degrees (Moseley and Mann 1959; Robinson 1963). More or less simultaneously with the publication of *Flying Saucers Have Landed*, Williamson and another witness to the Orthon landing, Alfred Bailey, published an account of communications from interplanetary civilizations, *The Saucers Speak!*. Williamson claims in the book to have conducted "anthropological field-work amongst the Chippewa Indians" of northern Minnesota (Williamson and Bailey 1953: 28), but, after reading news reports of flying saucers and reading Donald Keyhoe's *Flying Saucers Are Real* (1950), he "now collected my legends and so-called myths in a more serious manner" (Williamson and Bailey 1953: 30). Williamson asserts, as most ufologists and contactees would today, that many myths and legends throughout the world are records of interactions with interplanetary visitors.

The Saucers Speak! is the first detailed published message from extraterrestrials. The bulk of it transcribes messages—through automatic writing, the Ouija board, and ham radio—from saucer pilots sternly warning Earthlings either to join a political and spiritual confederation of planetary civilizations or to risk self-annihilation through war, atomic testing, and other evils. "You are a dead civilization," "Nah-9" of the "Solar X" group warns bluntly. "We want your cooperation. Time is limited" (Williamson and Bailey 1953: 44). With only occasional references to a deity, these extraterrestrials mostly invoke evolutionary hierarchies à la Blavatsky: "Do not think of us as Gods," Ponnar from the planet Hatonn advises the Williamsons and Baileys. "We are men like yourselves. We are only far ahead of you in progression" (77). But Nah-9 also warns that imperialist aliens from Orion had less benevolent designs on Earth (57).

Later, Palmer published Williamson's solo effort, *Other Tongues—Other Flesh* (1953), which, like the more widely read Leslie and Adamski volume, was divided between an account of the 1952 contact and a more historical and mythological section. Here for the first time extraterrestrial races are fitted into a Theosophical scheme of racial hierarchy. Williamson claims that humanity began with ancient breeding between advanced extraterrestrials from Sirius and Earth's indigenous apes. Other chimeras bred in this period disappeared in the Deluge. The task today, Williamson argues, is to sort out the purer from the mongrel races, for humanity today is made up of an array of different alien-animal or "angel and beast" combinations, with different races visiting Earth all the time and interbreeding and going unnoticed among us. Some of this quotes directly Pelley's own Blavatsky-influenced book *Star Guests* (1950), which conveyed information, received through automatic writing, about early evolution.

Williamson, performing an esoteric exegesis of pictographs embedded in Orthon's Mojave Desert boot print, reveals that there are three main alien races visiting Earth today. The first are the "Migrants," angelic beings trying to guide humanity toward its highest potential. Venusians such as Orthon were presumably among these. The second are the "Harvesters," who visit Earth in flying saucers, preparing for a new age by exterminating the "evil children" of the planet. The third are the "Intruders," the conquering forces from Orion referred to by Nah-9. The Intruders from Orion were cast-off souls, "slop" and "waste" (1953: 383), and his description of how to recognize Orion folk in human society draws directly on 1930s-style anti-Semitic boilerplate of the kind that Pelley shouted in his rallies.

> People of Orion are not our kind of people, they do not belong in our Confederation. They interrupt and are unruly. At present time there is a small group of people on Earth working for Orion. These people are sometimes small in stature with strange, oriental type eyes. Their faces are thin and they possess weak bodies. They come among you to disperse all things not in keeping with their own ideas; they upset our plans. They run amuck and we avoid them. They prey on the unsuspecting; they are talkative; they astound intellects with their words of magnificence. While their wisdom may have merit, it is materialistic, and not of pure aspiration towards the Father. We have our own men who watch over these pirates of Creation. They have their own Council and the Orion Confederation; but they know little through their own ingenuity for they are the Universal parasites! Disturbers, negative; soon they will be eradicated. (386–87)

Later Williamson claimed that this fifth column aimed to "come to Earth and eliminate all life forms on it and then land and use our planet as a great storehouse of natural resources" (1959: 223). But they would fail because "these forces have had their day under the sun and that day has been 500,000 years of continuing decadence. Their sun is about to set, and their day is done. Their power is momentary now as the Earth prepares for its Graduation Day, its Purification Day" (226).

This message was echoed in a founding text of an I AM Religious Activity offshoot called Summit Lighthouse or Church Universal and Triumphant, a more militant and UFO-oriented Ascended Master fellowship.

Mark Prophet, Summit Lighthouse's founder, identifies a counterfeit race on Earth, not born of God.

> Needless to say, these human automatons are the chaff and their final end can come through only one process: transmutation. For this is the only approved method whereby the wicked shall be removed from the face of the earth.
>
> In the Bible these soulless beings are referred to throughout as "the wicked," for they have seen to it that all the more specific descriptions of their race have been removed—lest mankind discover them and rise in righteous indignation against their overlords. And thus the death of John the Baptist and that of Jesus the Christ were brought about by the counterfeit race.
>
> Today, as always, they occupy positions of authority and financial power. They have gained control of the destiny of empires. . . . The injudicious use of taxation exerted by their direction has placed an unconscionable yoke upon the neck of humanity.
>
> Their control of entertainment media and the trends of youth toward dissonant art forms and discordant music has perverted noble attitudes and spawned a race of delinquent rebels. (1965: 11214)

Although such explicit anti-Semitism has always been on the fringes even of the UFO movement, it is impossible to ignore its formative effect on the UFO discourse. It is not the fascist political orientation of the old contactees that marginalizes them today; in fact, it is striking how many UFO enthusiasts will, off the record and after some theatrical dissembling, allow, for example, that Jews probably do control the media. This has been especially true since the 1990s, when the Internet facilitated a convergence between ufological and conspiracy-theory discourses that is now nearly total.[1] Rather, modern believers are put off only by the lack of verisimilitude in the 1950s reports: the rosiness of the Venusian (and other) messages, the beings' too human appearance, and the rapid obsolescence of their scientific pronouncements.

Nonetheless, the 1950s contactees quietly shaped ufological discourses. For one thing, we can see in contactees' writings some of the shifts from an Old World theosophy (broadly defined), with its orientation toward South Asian civilizations and esoteric mystery religions and its obsession with the place of the Anglo-Saxon in world politics and history, to a New World occultism focused on futuristic technology; a more generalized valorization of the tribal, with less emphasis on the East and more on the Americas;

and a preoccupation, always present and rarely acknowledged, with comprehending the role of America in the world and the meanings and values of different components of the American ethnoscape. These shifts can be read in and on alien bodies, since so much of American racial discourse is inscribed on bodies and in folk racial classifications.

Williamson's vision of the physically weak, materialistic aliens infiltrating our society is a durable image, even though these particular beings—like Shaver's Deros, whom they resemble—were never reported, photographed, or encountered face-to-face during the early contactee period. They were invoked only as a specter. It was instead the soft-skinned, long-haired Nordic space brothers who were stepping out of the saucers to interact with humans directly. In effect, the "slop and waste" beings from Orion were not so much aliens as a secret society within humanity, hidden in plain sight. This concept of demonic intruders among us, infiltrating our social institutions, moving in next door, originates in anti-Semitic conspiracy theories dating even to the Middle Ages (Trachtenberg 1943), and, as we will see, some features of the image of the abducting Greys stem directly from components of these scenarios.

Nonhuman Alien Imagery

Two images are important for seeing the shift from Aryans to Greys that began to accelerate by the 1960s. First are the Martians in H. G. Wells's 1898 novel *The War of the Worlds*: technologically invincible, coldheartedly bent on conquest, and yet so physically vulnerable that tiny terrestrial microbes fell them on the brink of world conquest. Second, we can mention the dead pilots from the Roswell crash. In the first Roswell book, Scully's *Behind the Flying Saucers* (1950), the alien corpses are not long-haired Aryan-featured Venusians but "little fellows . . . in all respects perfectly normal human beings," except for unusually perfect teeth (133), a "lack of beards" (though "some had a fine growth resembling peach fuzz") (24), and their stature (a little more than three feet tall) (22). They were, according to Scully, "perfectly normal in their development. The only trouble was that their skin seemed to be charred a very dark chocolate color" as a result of the crash (129). The pilots' fully human morphology in these initial reports is significant, since descriptions of their (always hidden) bodies changed as the UFO mythos did: by the late 1980s, the corpses in Hangar 18 were popularly represented as more or less standard Greys (see, e.g., Beckley 1989).

I want to connect these two images, Wells's and Scully's, with the idea of the human-looking but slightly ethnic invaders of Williamson's warnings. The Roswell aliens were "men" in nearly every respect except their size, their indiscernible ethnic look due to the charred skin, and the fact that their piloting skills were (apparently) unsuited to Earth's conditions, just as Wells's aliens were vulnerable to Earth's pathogens. Like Williamson's space Jews, with dastardly but quixotic designs, the Roswell and *War of the Worlds* aliens were ultimately paper tigers, poor pilots and all bluster, weaklings who did not fully appreciate their own vulnerability. In this, there is an affinity with the muscular condescension in much anti-Semitic propaganda.

I am hardly arguing that Wells's and Scully's aliens were as metaphorically Jewish as Williamson's Orion races. But some larger symbolic associations in European and American culture inform both sets of images: the idea of a vulnerable, decrepit race, fancying itself privileged ("chosen"), which preys, or attempts to prey, on more healthy decent folk. But to indulge that argument fully we need first to understand the Greys and explore the emergence of that image, which has become by now the central racial image in ufology.

It is not until the 1960s that we find U.S. sightings of UFO pilots that are not of the thoroughly human-looking type. The idea that aliens might look human became the old, discredited view, just as we smile at the American-English-speaking Caucasians that populate every galaxy in the old *Star Trek* series. Moseley interviewed Scully on this point in the early 1950s and "asked him how he accounted for his little spacemen and Adamski's big ones looking so much like Earth people. After all, conditions on other planets were much different than those here. A practicing Catholic, he offered an argument I'd already heard from several saucerers, among them Adamski and Williamson: since God made Earthmen in his own image, and since he also made the creatures on other planets, it follows that they look similar to us. 'It would not be like God to make a monster. Besides, what does science really know about conditions on other planets?' (Scully didn't have much use for science.)" (Moseley and Pflock 2002: 79).

In fact, when the origins of Adamski's Venusians and other space brothers were speculated on at all, the answers were usually some form of Blavatsky's: that Earth's indigenous apes were jump-started in their evolution by either direct physical breeding with or metempsychotic spiritual infusion by extraterrestrials. This thesis is in fact the mainstay of all ancient astronaut scenarios (Kossy 2001: 1–43; Sanderson 1967: 207–16; Sitchin 1976), and of course it dodges the question of why terrestrial apes and extraterrestrial humanoids were so similar to begin with. Pelley, for example, theorized that present-day terrestrial races as well as spiritual visitors among us today trace their ancestry to various permutations of interbreeding and directed evolution among indigenous apes, other animals, visitors from Sirius, and angelic "Christ People" (1950: 101–3)—most, coincidentally, already being upright bipeds.

Now, however, in the 1960s came reports of what would soon be called "little men" sightings. The more scientifically minded ufologists only gradually acknowledged that there was an emerging consistent pattern to "reliable" reports (unlike, say, those of Adamski et al.) of "UFO occupants." Jacques Vallee wrote in the late 1960s:

> Interest in landing reports is rapidly rising among the public and among UFO students. Several factors contribute to the development of this interest. First of all, the recent wave, with its maximum in July-August 1965, has confronted us with a remarkable number of incidents in this category, thus forcing many to accept the reality of accounts they had previously denounced as hoaxes. (1969b: 27)

A typical such encounter involved a witness who accidentally stumbles on a landed saucer, with a "little man" either taking soil samples or servicing the craft; on realizing he has been seen, the creature climbs back in the ship and flies away.

Amid the bewildering variety of creatures in 1960s reports—robots, little gremlins, elves, and, especially in European and South American reports, hairy dwarves (Bullard 1987 Lorenzen and Lorenzen 1976)—there was nonetheless a statistical tendency for the beings to be short, large headed, and hairless, with not at all prominent mouths and noses. There was nothing of the Aryan Venusian about them. As one collator of these reports summarized it:

> Comparatively few people have claimed that they were both close enough and calm enough when they encountered the pygmy types to make any detailed observations, but those who have reported more than generalities have certainly given us some things to think about . . . Here, we find a strong indication of the

> head being disproportionately large; the eyes large; and the mouth slit-like; the ears range all the way from "not apparent" to fantastic structures like those of some bats that can be folded at will. In only one case that I know of have the hands been said to differ markedly from ours. . . . The feet are often said to be "like stumps" but are seldom seen, as the little creatures have usually been observed standing in grass or other ground cover. (Sanderson 1967: 147; see also Lorenzen 1969; and Denzler 2001: 47)

"Skin color," this study continues, "has been said to range from 'very dark,' whatever that may mean, to very white, and bluish, or bluish-green" (Sanderson 1967: 149). Most features of this pattern became more solidified after 1966, with the publication of the first reported American UFO abduction, the 1961 experience of Betty and Barney Hill.

Betty and Barney Hill

If it is significant that the 1950s contactee movement was founded by white supremacist theosophists in the aftermath of the Second World War, it is also not surprising that the abduction phenomenon began with the suppressed trauma of a mixed-race couple during the civil rights era. Whereas the 1950s contactees sought to reerect a toppled racial order on a shifting cold war geopolitical landscape, the Hills' story grasps for a position from which white and black Americans can ponder, resolve, and transcend racial divisions. Like the 1960s themselves, the Hill abduction was terrifying, but with a note of optimism.

Keel has pointed out that "Contactees remained in disgrace in the U.S. until 1966 when John Fuller published the story of Betty and Barney Hill" (1975: 885)—though modern saucer jargon now classifies them as abductees, as opposed to noncoerced contactees. In many ways, indeed, the Hill abduction put figures from the little men sightings into a contactee narrative but in a form palatable to more scientifically minded members of the UFO community, partly because the Hills were unwilling and confused, in contrast to the suspiciously confident and coherent ideological pronouncements of Adamski and other gurus (Denzler 2001: 58). While Adamski and Williamson purveyed specific racial ideologies, for example, and while each contactee had a political agenda, the Hills were passive victims of interstellar racial dynamics that they little understood.

In brief, Barney Hill, a black postal employee, and his wife Betty, a white social worker, were returning from a driving trip to Quebec on their way to their home in Portsmouth, New Hampshire, on the night of September 19, 1961, when they were distracted by an odd light in the sky and then by uniformed men at what seemed to be a roadblock. They arrived home inexplicably later than they had planned and with distressing memory gaps. Barney reported the sighting to a nearby air force base (not mentioning the roadblock), after which they tried to put the incident out of their minds. But gnawing facts such as scuff marks on the tops of Barney's shoes, unusual marks on their car, the amnesia, and disturbing nightmares caused them to question whether there had not been more to their superficially uneventful sighting. Betty wrote to the National Investigative Committee on Aerial Phenomena (NICAP), the most prominent UFO organization of its day, and was put in touch with Donald Keyhoe, the country's most prominent ufologist. The committee sent two investigators, who suggested that regressive hypnosis could pierce the amnesia. By then Betty had devoured every book on UFOs in her local library. Eventually the Hills were regressed by Benjamin Simon, an army psychiatrist. What emerged were memories of an abduction from their car into a spaceship by entities far stranger than those first recalled, a medical examination that included a "pregnancy test" on Betty and an extended conversation with the crew's leader on the extent and purpose of the aliens' presence.

Simon elicited and compiled the story in fits and starts, drawing on notes Betty had made of vivid dreams she had had after the incident, the details of which were discussed with Barney at the time and collaboratively redefined as true memories sharpened through further hypnosis. This much-criticized methodology has since become nearly universal in ufological research. In 1966, a locally renowned UFO author, John Fuller, published the Hills' full story, first in *Look* magazine and then in a book, *The Interrupted Journey* (1966). Thus, a template was created that contained nearly all the elements of what came to be known as a typical alien abduction.

To say that *The Interrupted Journey* has racial overtones is a bit like saying that *Moby-Dick* has nautical overtones. It is fundamentally a book about race and not only insofar as a mixed-race couple becomes the focus of an epochal confrontation between humanity and an extraterrestrial race, with sharp hints of an interest in interbreeding. Jodi Dean has discussed how, oddly, Fuller attempts to bury racial aspects in the Hills' lives (1998: 55, 164–65). But race erupts throughout the narrative nonetheless.

Any difficulties in being a mixed-race couple in 1961 is belied by the consciously mundane scene Fuller sets at the beginning of his narrative to contrast with the horror that follows: Betty and Barney stopping at a diner in northern New Hampshire on their way home from a vacation in Montreal. Already, though, the geography in which they are moving suggests transgression and liminality: boundaries of all types are constantly crossed, with a density and structure that are almost literary or mythical. Barney describes wonderment at the presence of "Negroes in Montreal" (1966: 72), recounts difficulties with a non-English-speaking gas station attendant (72), and was tickled to tune in French-language radio (124). After clearing U.S. customs out of Quebec, they enter a new border region within America, "a section of the state," Fuller writes, "that is said to have threatened to secede not only from Vermont, but from the United States as well" (4). Their encounter will occur in the White Mountains, near a town called Indian Head. Their attempt to reach the comfort and safety of home will be resisted by a slowing down of time and their inability to pull free of these border zones.

Just past another border, that between Vermont and New Hampshire, they stop at the diner. The waitress reacts negatively to the fact that they are a mixed couple, but Fuller tries to assure us that, "Regardless of what attention their mixed marriage drew in public places, they were no longer self-conscious about it" (1966: 4). The encounter with the waitress is given a more menacing mood when it is described in Barney's own voice under hypnosis two years later. Once in the diner

> There is a dark-skinned woman in there, I think, dark by Caucasian standards, and I wonder—is she a light-skinned Negro, or is she Indian, or is she white?—and she waits on us and she is not very friendly, and I notice this, and others are there and they are looking at me and Betty, and they seem to be friendly or pleased, but this dark-skinned woman doesn't. I wonder then more so—is she Negro and wonder if I—if she is wondering if I know she is Negro and is passing for white. (73)

This attention to social detail and vigilant assessment of the safety of different social situations and the racial identities of different people is surely an African American survival strategy. Even by those standards, Barney's preoccupations with hybridity and hostility are obsessive. For Fuller, however, the recovered memories get interesting only later that night, as the

Hills, in their car, begin to see lights in the sky and hear strange beeping noises.

Barney's descriptions of the men at the roadblock are shot through with racial imagery. His first glimpse, through binoculars aimed at the saucer's windows, is of a face like "a red-headed Irishman," an impression he attributes to the fact that "Irish are usually hostile to Negroes." Next to the "Irishman," staring directly at Barney, is a less friendly alien who looks "like a German Nazi" with "a black scarf around his neck" (87). But they have eyes that are "slanted! But not like a Chinese" (88). "I've never seen eyes slanted like that," he adds (91); they are hypnotic eyes, "telling me, 'Don't be afraid' " (96). They have uniforms that put him as much in mind of the hats and jackets of Canadian hoodlums that unnerved him on the Montreal trip as they do of military uniforms (113–14). The Hills and their hypnotist consistently refer to their abductors as "men," "strangers," and "pilots," and Barney goes so far as to say "it did not seem that they had different faces from white men" (120).

But, though Barney's initial descriptions are mostly of menacing Caucasians, during one hypnotic session he draws what we can call the first illustration of a typical late-twentieth-century alien abductor, with bald head, large slanted eyes wrapping around the side of the head, vestigial nose, and lipless, expressionless mouth (143). He clarified these impressions later: "The men had rather odd-shaped heads, with a large cranium, diminishing in size as it got toward the chin. And the eyes continued around to the sides of their heads, so that it appeared that they could see several degrees beyond the lateral extent of our vision. This was startling to me." The mouth "was much like when you draw one horizontal line with a short perpendicular line on each end. This horizontal line would represent the lips without the muscle that we have. And it would part slightly as they made this mumumumming sound . . . Also, I didn't notice any proboscis, there just seemed to be two slits that represented the nostrils" (260).

Betty saw and remembered more, especially through her initial dreams, which were later clarified as real memories. Her descriptions of the "men" are less "alien" than Barney's. They were between five feet and five feet four inches tall: "Their chests are larger than ours; their noses were larger (longer) than the average size although I have seen people with noses like theirs—like Jimmy Durante's. Hair and eyes were very dark, possibly black. . . . They were very human in their appearance, not frightening. . . .

They seemed to be very relaxed, friendly, in a professional way" (296–97). Betty says only, "I had the feeling they were more like cats' eyes" (264). Her claim that the crew looked reassuringly human contrasts with her description of their skin tone: "Their complexions were of a gray tone; like a gray paint with a black base; their lips were of a bluish tint" (296), and "The surface of their skin seemed to be a bluish gray, but probably whiter than that" (264). Barney called the skin "grayish, almost metallic looking" (260).

Despite their disagreement on hair and noses, the points where Betty and Barney agreed—gray skin, unusual eyes, vestigial mouth, and cool demeanor—came to be typical of the Grey alien image now firmly lodged not only in the narrow world of UFO lore but, since the 1990s, in American mass culture. But the Hills cannot stop returning to an attempt to classify the crewmen by human ethnicity: "I keep thinking that the crew members are Oriental, Asiatic"—only shorter (271). "In a sense," Betty recalled, "they looked like mongoloids, because I was comparing them with a case I had been working with, a specific mongoloid child—the sort of round face and broad forehead, along with a certain type of coarseness" (264).

In a convergence of themes that is almost dizzying, Barney invokes academic anthropology to clarify his description.

> Betty and I went to hear a lecture one time by Dr. Carleton S. Coon of the Department of Anthropology at Harvard, and he showed a slide of a group of people who lived around the Magellan Straits. We both had quite a reaction when we saw it, because this group of Indians, who lived in an extremely cold atmosphere high in the mountains where there was little oxygen, bore a considerably close resemblance to what I'm trying to describe. And the professor was telling us how this group of people had, in the course of many generations, shown considerable physiological changes to adapt to the climate. They had Oriental sort of eyes, but the eye socket gave an appearance of being much larger than it was, because nature had developed a roll of fat around the eye and also around the mouth. So it looked as if the mouth had no opening and as if they had practically no nose. They were quite similar, in a general way, to the men I'm trying to describe. (260)

Coon was in fact the last of the racist evolutionists in academic anthropology in the United States, a virulent segregationist as well as a dabbler in paranormal topics such as the yeti, and by the 1960s he was an embarrassment to his discipline and Harvard (Jackson 2001). By the time of the Hills' abduction he was completing his magnum opus, *The Origins of Races* (1962), which was perhaps the last academic publication to follow the nineteenth-century practice of juxtaposing photos of Hottentots, Australian Aborigines, and Indians with head shots of lemurs, orangutans, and gorillas. Coon's was a polygenist argument, a variant on Vogt's ultimately, which held that the threshold to *Homo sapiens* had been crossed five separate times by five separate hominid populations, the ancestors of today's five races. Not only had the Hills been exposed to the routine racist practices of 1950s and 1960s America, but they had been directly exposed to raw, nineteenth-century racist anthropology halfheartedly repackaged for modern scientific sensibilities.

The Hills were struggling to identify their abductors' race, just as Barney had fretted over the ethnicity of the waitress in the diner—hence the theories that Barney and Betty spin out in their descriptions. Were the crewmen Nazis? white hoodlums? Irishmen? Chinese? South American Indians? Italian Americans like Jimmy Durante? And if they were none of these but something else, then how can their physical appearance enable categorization? If, as the Hills gradually came to feel sure, these were extraterrestrials, what would extraterrestrials look like? Would they be physiologically adapted to a colder, less oxygenated atmosphere, like the Straits of Magellan natives, but with those features more exaggerated? Would they be more evolved humans? And, if so, what would that look like? The descriptions of extraterrestrials in reports cannot be dissociated from attempts to understand what an extraterrestrial should look like.

***Communion* and the Birth of a Subculture**

After the publication of *The Interrupted Journey*, the abduction phenomenon took off slowly. For one thing, more attention was suddenly paid to an earlier, dubious report from South America concerning Antônio Villas-Boas, a Brazilian farmer who was seduced aboard a flying saucer by a redheaded alien who then used sign language to indicate that their offspring would be born and raised "up there" (Creighton 1969). Two dockworkers in Pascagoula, Mississippi, reported an abduction by clawed robotlike creatures in 1973, and Travis Walton, who went missing for five days in 1975 following a UFO sighting, told the story of his abduction to a still largely unbelieving ufological establishment. The year 1979 saw the publication of the story of Betty Andreasson, a Massachusetts housewife, who reported ongoing encounters with squat, large-headed, cavernous-eyed creatures who invaded her home, examined her, and fed her religious imagery and messages. Andreasson, a devout Christian, called them "angels" (Fowler 1979).

The real explosion in the abduction phenomenon came only in 1987 with the publication of *Communion: A True Story*, by Whitley Strieber, a horror novelist known for tales of supernatural predators such as *The Wolfen*. *Communion* is a highly personal narrative of coming to grips with a consciousness-shattering series of encounters with grey-skinned humanoids. They invade his home, abduct him, examine him, probe him anally, torment him with dreams, plant apocalyptic visions in his head, and erode his sanity. Written in a riveting, fiction-like style, *Communion* became a phenomenal best seller, and more than any other event its publication is probably responsible for the proliferation of abduction reports in the late 1980s and 1990s and the emergence of a nationwide community of thousands of self-identified abductees.

It was in the context of a ufological community revitalized by the publication of *Communion* that I first began seriously examining the phenomenon of UFO belief. Although UFOs had long been a topic of interest in my Southern Californian upbringing, it was during the wave of interest following *Communion*—in some ways because of reading it—that I became more heavily involved in the UFO subculture, in Oregon in the late 1980s and early 1990s and continued that involvement after a move to Illinois. I attended interest group meetings and forums, met abductees, and interacted with those who were investigating sightings for MUFON and referring abductees to counselors and hypnotists. In fact, there was quite a lot of amateur hypnosis going on.

What I saw by 1989 was a complete shift in the social organization of UFO communities. Keel's account of the "flying saucer subculture" in 1975 is an instructive comparison: he describes a loose network of hobbyists focusing on material evidence for UFOs. Most belonged to scientifically oriented private research networks and were resolutely uninterested in the psychic, mystical, historical, or mythical dimensions of UFOs (Keel 1975: 885–87). In the post-*Communion* era of the late 1980s and early 1990s, by contrast, abductions were the main focus of ufology, and every UFO interest group contained self-described abductees.[2]

At a typical UFO group meeting since the late 1980s, a local investigator for MUFON, responsible for a cluster of counties, might give a rundown of developments that month—mostly reports of lights in the sky, followed up with interviews and the filing of reports. This contrasts strongly with the more lively forums that follow, with abductees moderating and providing the main viewpoints. All topics are admitted: alternative and mainstream religion, any paranormal topic, any alleged political conspiracy, and any new or old ideas in psychology or astronomy or physics or biology that might shed light on the UFO problem. The discourse relies heavily on the assumptions and jargons of popular and therapeutic psychology; abductees have come to be regarded as morally authorized victims whose voices must be heard and feelings respected.

Abductees and contactees are not just the stars of these new ufological communities; they are the experts. No educational background is necessary; in fact, the pronouncements of other so-called experts are sidelined when real people who have interacted with real aliens are in the room. Their memories, theories, and intuitions are treated as (not necessarily true) "information"—an important and all-encompassing category in ufological discourse—and the people at these meetings are hungry for it.

Epistemologically, the spirit of this discourse is agnostic. No idea is too absurd to be considered, but all ideas are provisional and subject to revision. Some see the abductors as good or bad extraterrestrials, angels or demons or fairies, manifestations of hidden domains of consciousness, or covert government operatives. Abductees with any of these viewpoints can share their experiences and commune with one another.

Amid this antinomian agnosticism, however, there are ideologically driven attempts to systematize the disparate data in contact reports. Much of this is in the form of channeled material, which tends to dominate the inevitable book tables at UFO meetings. But there are also informal local gurus. One, based in Seattle who used a generic-sounding name that may have been a pseudonym, offered counseling to abductees in the 1980s and 1990s and distributed his own cassette tapes detailing elaborate narratives and typologies. Such figures, including channelers who might technically be "contactees," are distinct from abductees or physical contactees themselves, who typically do not offer or accept tidy explanations for their narratives, while still greedily devouring any such information, whatever the source. If the alien abduction program can be seen as a kind of physical anthropology being performed on humanity, then in the same way the ufological community can be seen to be engaged in its own ethnological investigations of who the aliens are and how the different types can be categorized and why, or even whether, they are constituted as they appear to be.

Greys' Anatomy

Various alien types are reported in *Communion* and its sequels. Strieber early on distinguishes four types: "small robotlike" beings; "short, stocky ones in . . . dark-blue coveralls" with "wide faces, appearing either dark gray or dark blue in that light, with glittering deep-set eyes, pug noses, and broad, somewhat human mouths"; a type of five-foot-tall, "very slender and delicate" creature "with extremely prominent and mesmerizing black slanted eyes" and "an almost vestigial mouth and nose"; and, finally, "huddled figures . . . somewhat smaller, with similarly shaped heads but round, black eyes like large buttons" (1987: 29–30). One of the third type, delicate with hypnotic eyes, is pictured on the cover of *Communion*. The creature is more pale yellow than grey, the cranium is less bulbous than in most reports, and the Giaconda smirk typical of the cool detached manner that most abductees, including Strieber, report is missing, but it was this image, the classic Grey, that seized the ufological imagination. Untold numbers claimed to have affirmed their own alien abduction memories as a direct result of seeing this picture.

An exhaustive study published the same year as *Communion* by the folklorist Thomas Bullard cites a bewildering array of alien abductors, with the typical Grey only one species among a panoply that included mummies, trolls, sasquatches, and robots (1987: 239). The hairless, androgynous Greys and their cousins made up only 26 percent of Bullard's sample (238). Since then, they have overwhelmingly dominated the reports.

Even many of those who believe in the reality of abductions have suggested that the image of the Grey may have been constructed by the aliens —whose real appearance may be unknowable—because of its cultural resonances for us. This—whether one takes the perspective of believer, skeptic, or social scientist—leads to the question of why the Greys look as they do.

A skeptic within ufology, Martin Kottmeyer, sees the Hills' narrative as heavily influenced in detail by their culture and environment and adds,

"The fact that the Hills were a bi-racial couple may be relevant to why they stand at the creation of this tradition" (1994: 9). He tracked down popular-culture sources for the abduction and alien imagery, including H. G. Wells's emotionless, androgynous Martians (Kottmeyer 1990) and suggests that the Hills conjured up grey-skinned aliens, as opposed to black or white ones, as a way of preventing racial connotations from being imposed on their experience (Kottmeyer 1994).

This viewpoint is echoed by scholars who see the abduction narrative as redemptive for a society divided by race. Jonathan Z. Smith has called the abduction narrative a myth that transcends racial categories with the image of the blank, grey, alien Other (1994). The anthropologist Luise White claims that the abduction myth is "the opposite of essentialism; it argues passionately against racial exclusivity and depicts a universe in which races and even species must mingle and intermingle to survive. The men and women who [through being abducted] have seeded other galaxies argue against national and racial identities" (1994: 32).

Kottmeyer sees the aliens' grey skin as negotiating and transcending symbolic associations of white and black with life and death, good and evil, truth and falsehood, and so on. In almost every respect, he points out, the Greys are a middle ground. While not beautiful, "they can't be considered predatory or monstrous. . . . Their goodness and badness are equally denied (1994: 7; see also Matheson 1998: 299).

Grey is also the color of metal, science and technology, and coldness, and these are frequent associations with the Greys. Terry Matheson points out that aliens' large heads suggest "not so much . . . great intelligence as inordinate rationality, and their disproportionately large, black, pupilless (and thus expressionless) eyes could hint of sight without insight. . . . If ever a race of beings exemplified the negative consequences of rationality it is these eminently drab, boring, and virtually sexless creatures with their expressionless faces and emotionless ways" (1998: 298–99).

In these and other respects, aliens' bodies reflect an exaggeration of the rational and cerebral capacities and an atrophying of the affective, sensual, and erotic capacities. Reproduction for them has shifted entirely to the technological and utilitarian, away from the erotic and the genital, indeed, away from sexual dimorphism itself. These capacities and tendencies, however, are projections and are mapped on alien bodies that are isomorphic (two arms, two legs) with our own. Moreover, the relationship between abductees' and aliens' bodies betrays differences—in intelligence, morality, emotionality, vigor, and cultural level—that for centuries have been mapped onto racial differences in folk and academic thought. The aliens may come from outer space, but we can find the origins of alien body types in the structure of very terrestrial racial schemes.

Greys and the American Ethnoscape

As anthropologists, we want to read abduction narratives as emerging from rather than impinging on a human belief world. Even if we are being visited by immensely superior aliens, our visitors would be understandable and perceptible only after being fitted into a preexisting cultural scheme for categorizing beings, as has often been the case among human societies, with different peoples perceiving one another at first—and often thereafter as well—as ghosts, animals, angels, or devils. This should be equally true of imagined, posited, or otherwise invented visitors. For want of a better term, such a classification is *racial*—and we have no better term precisely because popular discourse has clung to concepts that anthropologists have had to abandon as scientifically untenable. Race is an appropriate template for viewing the abduction phenomenon because race has always been more mythology than biology.

In North American English, *black*, *white*, and *red* are longstanding terms for African Americans, Europeans, and American Indians, respectively, *yellow* and *brown* being more recent additions to represent East Asians and Hispanics. In an exploration of why American Indians are "red," Raymond Fogelson points first to an older black-white opposition in European folk ethnology that pivots on an "ancient Cold-Hot, North-South . . . axis" (1985: 10; see also Kossy 2001: 69–116). The Columbian encounter, and European oceanic expansion in general, supplemented this original dichotomy, Fogelson writes, by bisecting it with "a Wet-Dry, East-West axis encompassing a Yellow-Red polarity" (10). Here American Indians are associated with arid climates and Orientals with tropical ones. Temperaments and predispositions can be superimposed on this scheme, going back to Linnaeus. This East-West dichotomy converges to some extent with the Old World longitudinal divide between western European Aryans and darker, shorter, eastern Slavs, which nineteenth-century racist scholars such as Gobineau and Klemm described in terms of a divide between "active," western, light-skinned peoples and "passive," eastern, dark-skinned ones (Kossy 2001: 83).

The East-West cline, unlike the North-South (white-black) one, is a cline of indigenousness, too, and here it is important to look at the role of westward migration in Theosophical racial theory and its convergence with ideologies of manifest destiny. One of the more persistent racial themes in ufology has been an interest in tribal or "primitive" peoples, especially American Indians. Indians are in a sense to white Americans what humanity in general is to the aliens (or, what I will argue is analogous, what Anglo-Saxon Americans are to more recent immigrants).

For Europeans, the American Indian became associated in folk thought with a vainglorious vigor, strength, and individualism. Indians in this folk view were portrayed—and in popular culture continue to be portrayed—as destined for defeat and eradication, despite their physical strength. Vigor and a harmonious relationship with their natural environment are contrasted with technological and organizational deficiencies that doom them to defeat. One of the most enduring images of the American Indian in popular culture is the "last of his tribe," admirable, proud, defiant, and unbowed but doomed in the march of history. This Indian is seen as individualistic and, paradoxically, symbolic of the American ideal of liberty. In this view, his nobility is vicariously absorbed into the American sense of self even as the people themselves fade from history (Berkhofer 1978; Weatherford 1988: 117–31). But this nobility is also literally absorbed, as (again according to the national myth) scattered Native American genetic lines survive in an attenuated form in a new, mongrelized but coded-as-white majority.

This subtheme of the national myth has its blunter counterpart in New Age historiographic discourses. In addition to inventing what we recognize today as the alien conspiracy theory, George Hunt Williamson also innovated, in *Other Tongues—Other Flesh*, another trend that has become strongly associated with New Age and UFO lore: an interest in the role of the American Indian in human history and alien contact. *Other Tongues* sets out new terms for the occult approach to human history, focusing more sharply on Native Americans.

As Theosophy fragmented in the early twentieth century, meanwhile, Asiacentrism was being challenged in the domain of ethnology by Benjamin Lee Whorf, an anthropologist, linguist, and Theosophist who specialized in Mesoamerican and Pueblo peoples. Whorf, addressing the matter (like Müller) at the level of grammar, argued (unlike Müller) for the particular suitability of many Amerindian languages and their concomitant cosmologies for expressing revolutionary ideas in twentieth-century physics for which "standard average European" languages were poorly equipped (1941, 1950). For Whorf, this was a scientific revolution with spiritual implications. Whorf's romanticization of Native American languages in what was otherwise a Boasian, antievolutionist "linguistic relativity hypothesis," dovetails with Theosophical tenets such as the inevitable waning of Anglo-Saxon domination, anticipation of the new ascendant civilization (the Sixth Root-Race), and a call for the unity of science and religion. In more private pronouncements intended for Theosophist ears only, Whorf argued that America would be the home of the Coming Race, its destiny assured by the subtle infusion of Amerindian blood into a largely European-dominated gene pool. For him this Amerindian blood derived from a proto-Mongol stock older and purer than those that remained in eastern Asia (n.d.: 569). These mongrelized descendants of the Indians "will be the future and true lords of the Western Hemisphere, as indeed the colonization by the whites was also preparatory to this destiny. It has been, in point of fact, the function of the Indian to prepare the ground of a wild continent, which never before had known the tread of man, so that it could be entered and inhabited by civilized man" (568).

This shift in occult historiography was an American innovation. Like the *Book of Mormon* a century earlier (Wauchope 1962: 50–68) or the Mu (i.e., Lemurian) historiography of James Churchward (1931; Wauchope 1962: 28–49), Williamson's work draws the New World into a sacred Old World geography and history, while retaining a broadly Theosophical model. This recentering of world history toward the Americas was a necessary stage in the transplanting of occult racial concepts into the new American soil. This was later echoed in the resurgence of the ancient astronaut spurred by *Chariots of the Gods?* (Däniken 1969), arguably the most popular UFO book ever. An easy criticism of Däniken's view of history is that it sees Indians as effectively extinct and looks only to their ancient monuments, not their living cultures, for evidence of a civilization "high" enough to require hypothesizing alien intervention. But in this way Amerindian archaeology becomes "our" past, the heritage of all Americans, including European Americans. This privileged role of the American Indian, among the world's tribal peoples, as the seeding ground for a European-based New World civilization is, then, explicitly a genetic model—metaphoric in mainstream culture but real for Whorf and white New Age and secular liberal discourses that valorize any Native American ancestry, no matter how remote (see, e.g., Deloria 1970: 1–27; Churchill 1992: 215–22; Francis 1992: 109–43; and Kehoe 1990).

This New Age racial order is at the root of the racial schema whose branches are the alien and the "oriental." As we will see, this "occidentalism" of the noble savage complements the ignoble civilization of the aliens. But the aliens, as we will see, are an extension of an orientalism that was first extended to Eastern immigrants to the Americas.

Aliens and Immigrants

Mirroring in some ways the relationship between indigenous Indians and white settlers in American ideology is the relationship between white settlers and nonwhite or "less white" immigrants to America, including groups that had to "earn" their whiteness, such as southern Europeans, Irish, and East European Jews (Jacobson 1998). Again the relationships among ethnic groups ranged conceptually along this East-West cline have always been more shifting, more permeable, and more fraught with ambivalence (Said 1978) than has been the case with the harsh taboos against miscegenation that traditionally patrolled the black-white color line (which is essentially a North-South cline, whether Europe versus Africa or northern versus southern states). Much of this anxiety is rooted in the paradox of Anglo-Saxon anti-immigrant sentiment in a nation founded by Anglo-Saxon immigrants. These ambiguities are resolved only through a racial supremacism that transcends history and autochthony. In this, it has become expedient for Anglo-Saxon supremacism in the United States, overtly or covertly, to reproduce arguments and conceptual structures from traditional European racist anthropologies that defined Slavs, Jews, Orientals, and other structural easterners (including East Asians in the twentieth century and Arabs in the twenty-first) as simultaneously predatory and inferior Others.

A foundational narrative here is the Jewish blood libel, the belief, dating to the Middle Ages, that Jews require the blood of Christians, often babies, for nutritional or sacramental purposes (Trachtenberg 1943; Dundes 1991). This narrative unites two images: the predatory, conspiring Jew; and the physically weak Jew dependent on the essence of decent folk for his or her sustenance. This paradoxical combination of weakness and menace has structured anti-Semitism throughout history, up to and including the forged (but still widely circulated) nineteenth-century *Protocols of the Elders of Zion* and the Ariosophy of the Nazi era. The operative idea is that, individually and physiologically, Jews are weak, but they are a threat through their shrewdness and intelligence and their capacity for clandestine collective strategies. This idea, along with the vivid imagery of cannibalism or blood drinking, reverberates in other European folk beliefs as well and frequently converges with a class dimension. The emperor Constantine was rumored to require the blood of peasants for his nutritive therapeutic baths, it was no accident that the gaunt but nonetheless deadly Count Dracula was an eastern European aristocrat, and socialist rhetoric in the nineteenth and twentieth centuries drew heavily on the metaphor of the bloodsucking capitalist.[3]

These themes from anti-Semitism and its allied folk imagery have their echoes in official U.S. racial ideology. The intersection of anti-immigrant legislation and eugenics in the early twentieth century led, for example, to the identification of Jews as an oriental race whose physical deficiencies threatened to contaminate the Anglo-Saxon gene pool. Short stature, a compromised lung capacity, and other maladaptive effects of interbreeding or of breeding with other Asiatic groups were cited in defense of anti-immigrant policies and legislation. As one historian of this line of thinking points out, "Interestingly, this image of the Jews as small and physically weak, averse to labor and 'sensitive to pain,' was the opposite of the racial image of the American Negro, who was represented as oversized, frighteningly strong, given over only to physical activities, and immune to pain" (Hart 2002: 117). In this anti-immigrant rhetoric, the Jewish threat was thought to be inadvertent, unlike the plots for world conquest outlined in the *Protocols*, but physical weakness contrasts with the hardiness of "our pioneer breed" (and with the robust, individualistic Indians the pioneers succeeded).

Physically smaller than European Americans, East Asians, too, whether as immigrants or military adversaries, became associated with weakness, passivity, and a submergence of individuality in the service of a collective ideology that itself constituted the threat—a tendency associated with

Confucianism, with Japanese honor and the blindly loyal kamikaze pilot, and then with communism and a manufacturing sector based on fascist-style corporate loyalty. Popular imagery of inscrutability, unthinking devotion, and bloodlust dominated anti-Japanese propaganda in the 1940s. In the late twentieth century, the Oriental came also to be associated with technological wizardry, in this case as an economic threat. Arguably, East Asians for Americans fill the role Jews have traditionally had in Europe —economically successful Orientals suspected of being in league with shadowy, foreign, global agendas. In the twentieth century, fears of Japanese and then communist fifth columns in the United States led to popular stereotypes of short, foreign, emotionless Others as merciless, conspiratorial, and beholden to collectivism and authoritarianism—the very opposite of the free, individualistic American Indian and, by extension, of what European Americans see themselves as having become.

As in much anti-immigrant rhetoric, it is significant that the immigrant's homeland be seen as inhospitable, hence the reason for emigrating. This sets up a contrast between an overfarmed, overcrowded, used-up "old country"—often with a dysfunctional or stifling political life—on the one hand and, on the other, the unspoiled wide-open spaces and rich soil of America. One need only think of the Founding Fathers' sense of the decadent European aristocracy or the whole notion of the refugee, either economic or political. Here the East-West landscape itself maps a distinction between health and frailty that is also inscribed on racialized bodies.

Surely, Greys are not always metaphoric Orientals, either East Asian or Jewish, though it is hard to ignore the convergence in abduction reports with stereotypical East Asian physiognomic and characterological stereotypes. Betty Andreasson described one of her abductors as Chinese looking (Fowler 1990: 304), and the Hills, as we have seen, also compared their abductors to East Asians. Lyssa Royal, a channeler who works with abductees, is perhaps atypical in her (in its way Blavatskian) assertion that the extraterrestrials who originally seeded the Earth and manipulated human genetic history created "the Asian races on Earth" to give humans an evolutionary jump start. She writes, "If you look at the characteristics of the Asian races, you will find that there is a smaller amount of diversity. The concentration on individuality is not there. . . . [A] person . . . can be sacrificed for the good of the whole. . . . These [are] the key elements needed to bring about the probable reality on Earth that was desired" (Royal and

Priest 1992: 132–33). Nonetheless, such a view picks up not only on racist stereotypes at large in American popular culture but on currents of ufological thought as well. The abduction mythos, like Shaver's and Williamson's writings before it, extends the structure of this orientalist logic—of the physically weak, shrewd, elite outsider whose threat stems from a need to prey on his or her physical and moral superiors through conspiratorial behavior and technological advantage.

Science Fiction: Weak Bodies and Dying Planets

These themes can be found in *The War of the Worlds* as well as 1930s and 1940s comics. Flash Gordon, the original comic-strip space-adventure hero, was in constant conflict with Ming the Merciless, an explicitly Chinese Genghis Khan figure who ruled the planet Mongo (as in Mongol). The sprawling Flash Gordon narrative openly invokes anti-immigrant feeling, beginning with Flash crash-landing on Mongo after an attempt to use his ship to divert it from a collision course with Earth. As one scholar of "yellow peril" imagery writes, the evil races on Mongo "were but mere ripples, chain reactions from a cancerous core, which was inhabited solely by Chinese, or rather, constructs allegedly Chinese" (Ma 2000: 7; see also Wu 1982; and Marchetti 1993). Ming anticipates many attributes of the abducting Greys: cold, lithe, feline, implacable, inscrutable, and in control of vast technologies, in contrast to the blond, good-humored Flash Gordon, who operated mostly as a resourceful swashbuckler (Ma 2000: 9–10). If we try to trace other sources of the spindly Greys in popular imagery, we can look to film footage from the Nazi death camps of masses of emotionally numb, impossibly thin, large-headed, hollow-eyed, balding figures whose physical helplessness contrasts sharply with claims that these poor wretches had been bent on world domination. For 1940s America, such objects of pity were also an immigrant tide. Like the aliens, they come from a doomed world to ours and are threatening precisely through their weakness and need.

Kottmeyer (1990) has marshaled significant evidence against Budd Hopkins's claim (1987: 192), shared by many who believe in the reality of alien abductions, that abduction reports are convincing because they are unlike anything in mainstream science fiction and therefore cannot be attributed to its influence. Kottmeyer writes, in fact, "I ask, is there anything about

UFO aliens that does not resemble science fiction?" (1990). He argues in particular for the likely influence on Betty and Barney Hill not only of Keyhoe's *Flying Saucer Conspiracy* (1955), which Betty read before the emergence of the full details of the abduction, but of abduction-type scenes in the 1953 film *Invaders from Mars*. Also, a bald, noseless, earless, large-headed extraterrestrial with wraparound eyes was featured in an episode of the science-fiction television series *The Outer Limits* that aired twelve days before the February 22, 1964, hypnosis session in which Barney described and sketched his now famous alien image (Kottmeyer 1990). In turn, as has often been pointed out, the abduction of Travis Walton was reported in 1975 just two weeks after the airing of an NBC television movie based on *The Interrupted Journey* starring Estelle Parsons and James Earl Jones as Betty and Barney (Klass 1989: 25–26).

But Kottmeyer (1990) joins other historians of science fiction in gravitating toward *The War of the Worlds* ([1898] 1983) as a foundational text for how our culture thinks about the possibility of extraterrestrial life, in a way that has permeated all popular-culture representations of the alien. Of all Wells's imaginative works, most of them steeped in Victorian assumptions, only this one has left a lasting impression on American popular culture; indeed, it launched the entire alien invasion motif in mass culture and was popular in the United States long before Orson Welles's 1938 "panic broadcast." Those who—like Hopkins, apparently—have not reread it recently might misremember it as being more of the "monster that ate Cleveland" variety than anything reported by modern abductees. But a close reading of *The War of the Worlds* reveals shared themes.

The novel recounts the landing and devastating attacks of Martian invaders in England until they are halted by a susceptibility to bacteria to which humans have developed immunity. Like the vampire or the imagined medieval Jew, the Martians' doomed plans are motivated entirely by a need for human flesh.

> Strange as it may seem to a human being, all the complex apparatus of digestion, which makes up the bulk of our bodies, did not exist in the Martians. They were heads—merely heads. Entrails they had none. They did not eat, much less digest. Instead, they took the fresh, living blood of other creatures, and injected it into their own veins. . . . Blood obtained from a still living animal, in most cases from a human being, was run directly by means of a little pipette into the recipient canal. (Wells [1898] 1983: 132–33)

The Martians, then, are in search of alternative nutrients, apparently responding to a food crisis on their home planet. The narrator describes what can be ascertained about the Martian food chain.

> Their undeniable preference for men as their source of nourishment is partly explained by the nature of the remains of the victims they had brought with them as provisions from Mars. These creatures, to judge from the shrivelled remains that have fallen into human hands, were bipeds with flimsy, silicious skeletons (almost like those of the silicious sponges) and feeble musculature, standing about six feet high. (Wells [1898] 1983: 134)

In fact, this spongy livestock resembles the Greys of late-twentieth-century abduction reports more closely than the Martian invaders themselves do. But in the invaders we can also see the origins of some themes in descriptions of the Greys. Physiologically, there is the enlarged head and eyes and vestigial nose, ears, hair, and trunk, and the invaders, too, are emotionless and androgynous (134).

Although the Martian invaders are hardly aristocratic in their bearing, Wells portrays them as possessing a technologically and intellectually superior civilization. For a scientifically minded writer such as Wells, who studied under the Victorian evolutionist Thomas Henry Huxley, this is also expressed biologically. The narrator of *The War of the Worlds* remarks, in the midst of his description of the Martian anatomy, that

> a certain speculative writer of quasi-scientific repute, writing long before the Martian invasion, did forecast for man a final structure not unlike the actual Martian condition. His prophecy, I remember, appeared in November or December, 1893, in a long-defunct publication, the *Pall Mall Budget*, and I recall a caricature of it in a pre-Martian periodical called *Punch*. He pointed out—writing in a foolish, facetious tone—that the perfection of mechanical appliances must ultimately supersede limbs; the perfection of chemical devices, digestion; that such organs as hair, external nose, teeth, ears, and chin were no longer essential parts of the human being, and that the tendency of natural selection would lie in the direction of their steady diminution through the coming ages. The brain alone remained a cardinal necessity. Only one other part of the body had a strong case for survival, and that was the hand, the "teacher and agent of the brain." While the rest of the body dwindled, the hands would grow larger. (Wells [1898] 1983: 135)

The narrator's memory for publication dates is so precise because this is in fact Wells's tongue-in-cheek reference to his own anonymous composition, "The Man of the Year Million" (Anonymous 1893; see also *Punch* 1893). There Wells describes a future human strikingly like a Grey:

> Eyes large, lustrous, beautiful, soulful; above them, no longer separated by rugged brow ridges, is the top of the head, a glistening, hairless dome, terete and beautiful; no craggy nose rises to disturb by its unmeaning shadows the symmetry of that calm face, no vestigial ears project; the mouth is a small, perfectly round aperture, toothless and gumless, jawless, unanimal, no futile emotions disturbing its roundness as it lies, like the harvest moon or the evening star in the wide firmament of the face. (Anonymous 1893: 1797)

As for character, "emotion" will "fall within the scheme of reason" (1797) in this far future.

The notion that aliens might be some future version of ourselves has persisted in American science fiction and ufology. Betty Hill herself, although she rejects most of what is now being presented as the standard abduction scenario, has in recent years taken to the *Homo futuris* theme in describing her abductors.[4] In a memoir, she writes about returning to school to study archaeology and physical anthropology, relating how she asked the instructor to "evaluate" a bust that had been made from her and Barney's descriptions of her abductors, whom she now calls "the astronauts," "for I thought it might be 'future man'" (Hill 1995: 96). The instructor

> asked if he could keep it for a few more days, as he wanted other physical anthropologists to study it. When he returned it, he said they agreed this was "future man." We would look like this in about 25,000 years if we continue along the paths of evolution as we have been in the past. He was puzzled. This was my first semester in physical anthropology, so he wondered how I was able to do this. I told him it was not knowledge, for I had met him—future man." (96)

Hill is here picking up a line of thinking on evolution and extraterrestrials that can be traced to Wells's Huxleyan prophecy. The physiognomic aspects of Wells's view of future human evolution—bald, scrawny, with large heads and vestigial lower facial features and depleted lust and emotion—have been strikingly stable in popular-scientific writings in the intervening century (see, e.g., Wolstenholme 1963). The notion that Greys' bodies mark the future path of human evolution is echoed by numerous UFO writers, including Strieber, who suggests, among countless other hypotheses he agnostically pitches his readers, that aliens might be evolved beings visiting from Earth's future as time travelers (1987: 223–24). The French ufologist Aimé Michel, writing in 1969 before the explosion of reports of Grey abductors, notes that some of the early "little man" sightings

> usually fit in with the idea of an interpolation, in the future, of the past evolution of mankind (intensified cephalization, i.e. growth of the size of the head; regression of the vegetative organs, i.e. jaw, mouth, nose, and so on). In other words, just as though a biological and genetic technique had "done a job" on human nature in the very simplest manner, contenting itself with "stepping up the performance" in those features peculiar to it (which are linked to the use of the brain), and artificially accelerating the natural rate of evolution of mankind." (251)

Berlitz and Moore, writing about the Roswell aliens, concur: "the features of head enlargement, hairlessness, muscle deterioration, elongation of arms, loss of height, etc., might be said to be a perceptive guess of how we will look in the far future, the point from which the 'aliens' may conceivably have come" (1980: 114; see also Davenport 1994).

Wells's narrative, like his earlier novel, *The Time Machine*, prompts a resolution of a British class struggle, in this case with clean, healthy, scientifically minded working-class people set to triumph over a spoiled, soft, decadent upper class in an imminent struggle for survival under Martian domination (Wells [1898] 1983: 163–67). Analogous themes in American science fiction and ufology have, not surprisingly, a more racialized cast. Wells's contrast between two types of bodily vigor—the fattened, "beautiful" food herd that the upper classes will become and the lean, strong, "clean" working classes capable of decisive action—have an analogy closer to our purposes in the relation between humanity in general and the Martian invaders or between indigenous savages and European colonists. The Martians at first seem to be in some sense like the ideal survivor of their invasion: proactive, technologically proficient, unwilling to be cowed. But in the end the Martians turn out to be fatally weak: pampered by the sterile Martian atmosphere, they eventually succumb to microscopic germs to which warmer and more earthy indigenous humans are immune; they are "slain by the putrefactive and disease bacteria" (Wells [1898] 1983:177), in particular those thriving on the very corpses of their human victims. But despite the failure of the Martian conquest, we are left with the impression that a newly invigorated humanity can somehow emerge from the rubble, just as, as Whorf would say, a "new American" is felt to have emerged from the bloodiness of the Indian wars, combining the best elements of both.

Hybrid Vigor

We now turn to the theme of the emergence of a new humanity from the effects of an encounter with an invader. Just as racial concepts are often revealed in the question of interbreeding, and racial tensions and anxieties are sharpened, in the same way the question of the supposed alien hybridization program brings into focus many of the nascent anthropological themes in the abduction scenario. The effect of alien contact on the future of humanity has been an undercurrent in ufology from the beginning, but it reached its clearest articulation in the closing years of the twentieth century. The idea, from Blavatsky, that Venusians jump-started human evolution echoes throughout the ancient astronaut literature and has served as a kind of eugenic charter, both for the explicitly ideological contactee reports and, more subtly and indirectly, for the less ideologically explicit sighting and abductee reports. But abductee reports began to acquire a political flavor by necessity as the alien breeding program that emerged in the writings of abduction researchers began to emerge as a detailed scenario with implications for human destiny. Many abductees have told me that they cannot explain or defend the racial or political implications of the breeding program, and in some cases the eugenic and racialist implications troubled their more or less politically liberal consciences; they tell me they can only describe what they have seen.

Budd Hopkins, an abstract painter from New York City, began to track patterns in different abduction accounts in the 1970s (Hopkins 1981) and in 1987 published *Intruders*, which describes an Indiana family's repeated alien abductions through the generations. His primary abductee and witness, "Kathie Davis"—who later published her own account under her real name, Debbie Jordan (Jordan and Mitchell 1994)—brought the possibilities raised by Hill's pregnancy test to their logical conclusion: Jordan had been impregnated by alien abductors, followed by the removal of a hybrid fetus. This rapidly became a standard element of the abduction scenario and dominated the sequels (e.g., Fowler 1990) to *The Andreasson Affair*, which dwelled more and more on outer-space nurseries full of languishing hybrid babies and fetuses floating in liquid.

Although females' narratives, and themes of nurturing and loss, dominate abductee discourse, human men, too, are involved in the breeding program. One abductee, Bruce Smith, had a series of dreamlike coerced sexual encounters with Grey-type aliens—experiences that made sense to him only after attending a lecture by Hopkins. What followed for him was the mixture of anger at the aliens and parental pride and affection that many abductees report. Smith also began to be abducted into nurseries on board spaceships, where he was urged to interact with his hybrid brood in "dance/movement therapy sessions" as a way of providing bonding experiences of which the full-blooded aliens are incapable. The aliens indicated to Smith that millions of such children were being bred, adding, "The hybrid kids are going to populate . . . the earth directly sometime between the year 2020 and 2030. By then the earth will be a much different place. These hybrid kids are being prepared to live in that new environment and with the new spiritual frequency that the earth will vibrate in." "You," the aliens told Smith, "will be an elder to the new ones of ours on earth. . . . You will be the bridge from the old to the new; from the old planet to the new; old *Homo sapiens* to the new gene pool. You know so well the ocean of emotions your people have. . . . You can help them adjust, understand, accept and integrate; help them make the transition" (Smith 1990: 15; cf. Commander x 1994: 38–45). To hear Smith, like others, describe it, the Greys prey on his human, emotive capacities and his "seed" in much the same way that Wells's Martians ingested human flesh. For Smith, who gradually became impotent with everyone except his Grey paramours, "this idea of losing my sexual energy really weighed on my mind. Were the greys storing it up for the kids? Was passion needed besides sperm to make a baby? Maybe the greys drank my passion like an elixir. Maybe I was just a tasty bit of 'soul food'?" (16).

Researchers and abductees are divided over how to view the breeding program. Hopkins, for one, openly struggles to interpret the experiences positively: abductees, for him, "are, in every sense of the word, victims. And yet, unasked, they are also pioneers" (1987: 202). David Jacobs, a Temple University historian who followed Hopkins to become a leading figure in the abduction investigation field, sees the alien agenda as more menacing. The hybrids and aliens, he fears, will "integrate into human society and assume control" of the earth (1998: 251).

John Mack, a Harvard psychologist who in the 1990s rapidly ascended to the pinnacle of the degree-revering ufological community, even as his credibility was attacked within Harvard's halls, takes a more holistic and metaphysical approach. He notes the striking convergence of details in abductees' reports of how the breeding program operates but balances this with an acknowledgment (rare in ufology) of the complete lack of corroborating physical evidence. For him, this demonstrates that the phenomenon of abduction reports is operating on a nonphysical plane, one not subject to positivist materialist epistemology. Ultimately, for Mack the breeding program and the birth of a new species are metaphors for an ongoing and necessary expansion in human consciousness—which may or may not involve literal extraterrestrial visitors (1994, 1999). This minority viewpoint within ufology is shared at times by the shifting views of the agnostic Strieber. It is certainly supported by what biologists tell us, that interbreeding between species from different planets—even between related species adapted to different planets—is an absurdity (see Swords 1991). So, too, is the idea that a civilization capable of interstellar travel would rely on in vivo fertilization and gestation instead of genetic engineering. But abductees themselves know only what they have seen and usually find antipositivist perspectives such as Mack's unsatisfying. Even Mack acknowledges that the breeding program is as "literal and concrete" (1994: 395) for his own abductee clients as it is for Hopkins's, Jacobs's, or anyone's.

Most abductees are closer to Jacobs, seeing the hybrid program as part of a series of coming changes on the planet that involve evolution, environmental collapse, and some reordering of the global social order. Mack's abductee clients (1994: 414–17) provide us with some of the most orderly interpretations of the data. Like Wells's Martians, Greys tend in this view to come from a doomed world. Mack's client "Scott" reports that the aliens were from a planet that "was yellow, mostly desert, and lacking water. Once there had been trees and water, but something . . . 'went wrong' and [the aliens] 'went underground.' " They now live in an "artificial environment" on their home planet. Analogous changes are in store for Earth: "The aliens will only come 'when it's safer,' " Scott tells Mack. "But that will not occur until there are 'less and less' of us as we die off from disease, especially more communicable forms of AIDS that will reach plague proportions" (104).

"Joe," an abductee and himself a psychotherapist, tells Mack that the alien hybrid program and genetic engineering are " 'necessary' so that 'humans aren't lost in their race and their seed and their knowledge,' for 'human beings are in trouble. . . . A storm is brewing,' an 'electromagnetic' catastrophe resulting from the 'negative' technology human beings have created." He tells Mack that the purpose of the interbreeding is "evolutionary, to perpetuate the human seed and 'crossbreed' with other species on the ships and elsewhere in the cosmos" (186).

Andreasson, who tells us less about the aliens' world and regards them more as angelic helpers, nonetheless tells a similar story. She says it is not just a human genetic program; like Noah's, it involves all species, so that they can survive some form of mass destruction (Fowler 1990: 119, 201–3), as well as escalating infertility (213). The human-alien hybrid species, she suggests, will have a better balance of intellect, which humans tragically misuse, and emotion, which aliens mostly lack (19). Andreasson sees herself as part of a cohort the aliens chose for this program in the early 1940s: "Those who were contacted would be used in some way in the future to help people understand that the aliens were doing something beneficial for mankind and to help people not to be afraid of the coming of the aliens" (329).

Fowler, in interpreting Andreasson's experiences, builds directly on the Wellsian theories of Michael Swords, a university biologist with an interest in ufology. Swords suggests that the aliens represent a future course of evolution, including bodily features suggesting mechanization of reproduction and an artificial environment (1985: 8). These features, Fowler (1990: 224–26) and Swords both point out, are in fact neotenic. Fowler goes so far as to say that the aliens look specifically and significantly like fetuses (xxii, 213, 220, 223). In particular, the aliens look like larger versions of the hybrid fetuses in the incubators seen on board their spaceships, just as Andreasson described a vivid encounter, in a spaceship's "vivarium," with baby hybrids who were essentially greatly downsized Greys (104–6). For one thing, pedomorphism and neoteny reinforce the image of the alien as lustless but physically needy in other ways, as weak and dependent, selfish, and coming from a controlled environment (the womb) that spoiled and softened them. Mack writes, pointedly, that, although the purpose of the hybridization program seems to be hybrid vigor, " 'Vigor' seems a strange word in this context when one thinks of the listless hybrid children that have been described by so many abductees aboard the ships" (1994: 199).

Hybrid Programs and Contemporary Races

Fowler uses these thoughts as a jumping-off point for ruminations that, intentionally or not, sound straight out of Blavatsky. He writes that the aliens claim to "have coexisted with Man from his very beginning" and may share with us a common genetic ancestor, who

> may be traced to a highly advanced race of extraterrestrial beings who discovered our solar system millions of years ago. In the course of their scientific activities on this planet, they may have genetically altered one of earth's primates to make it in their own image. This would explain the amazing similarities between fetal apes and fetal man. . . . Have we any clues as to who these ancestors might be? Yes. Evidence indicates that mankind's heredity may be related to the tall, blue-eyed, blond, robed entities seen by Betty and others. It is apparent that whoever they are, the small fetus-looking Watchers are subservient to them. (1990: 227–28)

In sum, the progression of logic runs roughly as follows. Aliens are currently abducting humans and interbreeding with them, as evidenced by abduction reports. This interbreeding program seems to be multigenerational, and it is unclear when it began. Therefore, one can guess that it might be a permanent part of human genetic history and that humans themselves might originally have been the product of this interbreeding. (Once this conclusion is reached, a whole literature from Blavatsky to Zechariah Sitchin is immediately made comprehensible and relevant.) Human physical variation, then, like all facts about human physiology, must be the product of this alien interbreeding. Finally, it can then be assumed that some human ethnic groups are more purely alien in their ancestry than others and that different groups might be traceable to different alien groups. Once one has accepted the American cultural concept of race, the racial order becomes, for a UFO believer following this logic, a reflection of a cosmic hierarchy. The millennial themes so common in the abduction scenario, involving environmental and other cataclysms that the aliens can foresee and that justify the hybridization program, inevitably begin to take on racial themes. Who will be saved? And, if it is the hybridized human families that will be saved—the abductee families—who, exactly, are they?

Despite common claims by abduction researchers hankering for legitimacy to the effect that abductees come from "all walks of life," it is abundantly clear both anecdotally and in the opinions of many abduction researchers I have interviewed that, although there have been, for example, a few prominent African American contactees, the abductee population is overwhelmingly white. Barney Hill stands almost alone. Investigators tend to try to account for this as a problem of reporting, which can be attributed to cultural and social factors. Whatever the reason, the fact remains.

Although it is a topic most researchers avoid, several abductees have told me that they were told or feel that the dearth of nonwhite abductees is no accident. One told me that, although she has encountered African American abductees on board ships during abductions, she has gleaned from her interactions with aliens that the coming winnowing of humanity will deplete the nonwhite populations of the earth most heavily. Another abductee, one with a leftist, countercultural orientation, told me that he has come to feel that the reason blacks are abducted less frequently is because the aliens are less able to "deal with" the bodily, physical—as opposed to cerebral or spiritual—predisposition of black people. Donna Bassett, the journalist who infiltrated John Mack's abductee support group for *Time* magazine (Willwerth 1994) and subsequently led an investigation of Mack, told me in 1994 that Mack's circle of abductees was also foretelling the decimation of nonwhite races. Abductees have expressed to me sadness and anger over this scenario, but, once they have interpreted their own experiences in a certain way, the conclusions seem for them inevitable.

Here, of course, there are strong parallels with scenarios for the emergence of the Sixth Root-Race in early-twentieth-century Theosophist writings (Besant 1910; Besant and Leadbeater 1947), which also suggest that natural disasters will wipe out portions of humanity, followed by the emergence of a future race from the remaining, largely white, mostly American population. With the Theosophists, too, divinely ordained racial extinctions sit awkwardly alongside sincerely held egalitarian and antiracist views. The submersion and disappearance of races whose time has passed are simply part of the natural order of things.

In ufological discourse, however, these racial themes, which most abductees and researchers struggle to repress, sometimes do erupt in fully formed racist ideologies, as is the case with Robert Girard, whose self-published book *Futureman: A Synthesis of Missing Links, the Human Infestation of Earth, and the Alien Abduction Epidemic* (1993) does not flinch from racist conclusions. He follows the ancient astronaut view of human evolution, including his own theory that the black, red, and yellow races represent earlier, imperfect attempts by aliens at genetic engineering, while the white race ("Self-Aware" man) represents a spiritually superior product of the alien-bred Cro-Magnon lineage destined to rule the other races. Alien abductions, he claims, are recent and part of a fresh attempt to preserve these superior genetic strains when the great mass of overbreeding brown-skinned humanity is exterminated in the near future (1993; Kossy 2001: 38–40). Girard, who is also a prominent UFO bookseller, veered from his usual titles by offering the controversial racist, pseudo-scientific best-seller *The Bell Curve* (Herrnstein and Murray 1994) in his Christmas 1994 catalogue, adding in a capsule review that the book

> will provide information to anyone reading or contemplating the ideas expressed in . . . *Futureman*. Whether you want it, like it or believe in it or not . . . the only (and last) workable solution to catastrophic overpopulation will be the outright extermination of vast numbers of humans who are incapable of making any meaningful contribution to that civilization. These number well into the billions among us now: humans who have absolutely no purpose or justification for being here. . . . Given the enormity of the crisis facing our species, and by extension, all of earth's living species, there must someday come the deliberate elimination of (hopefully) the vast majority of humans now living. (Arcturus Books 1994: 3)

Most UFO believers have no sympathy with such a view, but Girard's genocidal rage is in one sense only a logical progression from the millennial visions many abductees are reporting and the fact that those who claim they are part of the breeding project are almost all white Americans.

Hybrids as an Ethnic Group

Another logical evolution from the abduction scenario has emerged only within the past decade. Although Williamson and Adamski discussed the presence of aliens among us, it is only since the early 1990s that there has been a strong movement of people from abductee families claiming alien or hybrid identity for themselves. This emerged slowly at first, with Hopkins and Jacobs reporting that some of their clients were wondering if some of their own, Earth-dwelling, human-looking children might not be alien hybrids, just as their half siblings in orbiting hatcheries were (Hopkins 1987: 283; Jacobs 1992: 153–86; Jacobs 1998: 70). The prolific New Age pulp writer Brad Steiger coauthored a series of books beginning in the 1980s (B. Steiger and F. Steiger 1981; B. Steiger and S. Steiger 1992; see also Mandelker 1995) alerting humanity to the emerging presence of these "star people" or "star children," all with heavy religious overtones. One chapter, "Rearing the Star Child," gives advice to parents such as "I have found that star-shaped, luminous decals are excellent for decorating a child's ceiling" (B. Steiger and S. Steiger 1992: 163). Steiger also presents a "Starbirth Questionnaire" as an aid to determining if the reader is a star child. The long list of telltale symptoms includes sinusitis, imaginary childhood friends, seeing "a bright light even when your eyes are closed," painful joints, "a more than normal attraction . . . to the name Leah or Lia," and a feeling that "your father and mother were not your true parents" (B. Steiger and F. Steiger 1981: 46–47). Dual human and alien identity is also a strong theme among Mack's clients (Mack 1994, 1999), many of whom are self-identified aliens or hybrids, and Mack, like the Steigers, painstakingly refuses to distinguish between reincarnation and interbreeding, physical and spiritual reality, and the metaphoric and the real.

The social function of alien self-identification is structured similarly to the phenomenon of reincarnation beliefs in mainstream U.S. society: in contrast to societies with long-standing reincarnation traditions such as, for example, some indigenous North American groups, middle-class American reincarnation beliefs usually serve to set the believer apart from his or her community and kinship network rather than weaving him or her into it more firmly (Harkin 1994: 194–95). Middle-class reincarnation is almost never within the family and tends to be expressed in past-life memories focusing on romanticized ancient civilizations such as pharaonic Egypt or classical Greece, out of all proportion to the statistical representation of those societies in the accumulated human population. Mack's clients who report past-life memories fall into this pattern as well (Mack 1994). In a sense, being the reincarnation of an alien is a further extension of this radical-individualist trend.

But inevitably alien self-identification adopted the modern American discourses of identity politics and minority rights. The first issue of *Other Wise*, an Olympia, Washington, zine devoted to alien-identified families, describes the childhood of its editor, who was "mostly a normal kid—except for one thing. Tucker had a Secret that she was hiding behind her pigtails and skinned knees. . . . Lots of nights Tucker went to bed scared and had nightmares about people learning her Secret and not liking her anymore because of it."

We can see in this growing movement a co-optation of most of the themes in minority politics discourses, such as negative media imagery that encourages prejudice against "real aliens, not the tentacled monstrosities from movie studios" (Estron 1996: 5). There is even an organization called ETADO, the Extra-Terrestrial Anti-Defamation Organization (Alexander 1997). A book called *E.T. 101* (Jho 1990) counsels those coming to terms with their alien identity. Other publications use the jargons of abuse survivors, parents of special needs children, and homosexual outing. Just as the abductee Leah Haley's children's book *Ceto's New Friends* (1994) introduces children to alien visitation (much as *Adoption Is Forever* and *Heather Has Two Mommies* counter for children the stigma of other unconventional families), in the same way a page from *Other Wise* no. 3 urges parents of hybrid children to "be honest with them about their heritage" and tells us, "Hybrid kids are fun, but challenging. Some of the challenges can be: strange sleep-wake cycles (corresponding to day length on another planet), weird taste in foods, and something called 'hybrid vigor,' which translates to 'very busy, into-everything kid.'" (As with Steiger's questionnaire, one is reminded here of quizzes designed to alert parents to their teenagers' drug use, which merely list symptoms of adolescence.)

Inevitably, if unintentionally of course, this is partly an acquisition by "unmarked," nonethnic, mainstream Americans of the moral authority of an oppressed minority. I have been told repeatedly that abductees are likely to have Native American or "Celtic" ancestry—that is, whites with these ancestries. *Celtic*, of course, is not an ethnonym used in Irish American communities, while abductees of Native American ancestry almost never have enough of it to be involved with Native American communities or to experience racism as a visible minority. Being an abductee or hybrid is one of the few ways an American WASP can be ethnic.

Conclusion

Since the UFO movement can be expected to continue to shift and innovate as rapidly as it has done in the past, one cannot predict the future course of the alien self-identification movement. Certainly, it bears this resemblance to earlier phases in the history of ufology as anthropology: like Blavatsky's theory of evolutionary meddling from Venus, like the Aryan space brothers of the 1950s, and like the complex image of the Greys, the belief in new aliens among us is an attempt to weave contemporary ethnoscapes into a divine plan that is explicitly hierarchical.

An occasional hope expressed by UFO enthusiasts is that encounters with extraterrestrial intelligence will somehow act as a catalyst that will lead to world peace or the bridging of differences among human groups. (The dark side of this is the common conspiracy theory that, for example, a faked alien invasion by global elites will be used as the excuse to impose a monolithic New World Order on humanity; see, e.g., Hayakawa 1993.) But, as we have seen, differences, the very idea of ethnicity and race, are part of American cultural conceptions of what it is to be human. Insofar as aliens are incorporated into preconceived notions of humanity, they will be accommodated as a part of—not a transcendence of—existing evolutionary, racial, and ethnic dimensions on which our conceptions of human diversity are already arranged. This is what gives us George Hunt Williamson projecting anti-Semitic fears onto an alien infiltration of our social institutions; Betty and Barney Hill abducted and probed by "men" who morph from Irishmen to Chinese to specimens from an ethnological slide show; thousands of white middle-class Americans reporting that they have been kidnapped and raped by high evolutionaries trying to save their race and ours simultaneously; nightmare fantasies of genocide, for which we can blame the aliens, not whites; and a growing number of abductees and their children believing that they themselves are downtrodden immigrants, adding grey or green to the palette of white, brown, red, black, and yellow Americans.

I have tried to leave aside here the question of what, if anything, abductees and contactees are really experiencing, which may or may not be a phenomenon better categorized as neurological, spiritual, or something else. But the narratives and imagery they employ are immediately woven into an existing coherent and evolving folk anthropology that is already structuring most thinking about race and difference, a folk anthropology that dips into and out of academic anthropology at surprising junctures. Academic anthropologists, after all, have (for good scientific and political reasons) stopped making pronouncements on racial difference, but, since most Americans "know" that race is real and must mean something, someone has to be providing some answers.

Notes

I wish to thank Lyell Henry, Donna Kossy, James Moseley, and Angela Sorby for reading and commenting on drafts of this essay. Myrdene Anderson, Tom Benson, Adi Hastings, Rupert Stasch, and Michael Swords assisted me in finding sources. Additional insights have been developed through discussions with Debbora Battaglia, Jodi Dean, Susan Lepselter, John Brent Musgrave, and the late Valerio Valeri. I am also privileged to build on the work of Donna Kossy and George Stocking; they were there first. Chris Holmes and Corky DeVault joined me in some of the interviews I conducted. Most of all, I wish to thank the many UFO experiencers, investigators, and others who have shared with me their insights and stories, including Martin Cannon, Edward Carlos, Forest Crawford, Marc Davenport, John Foster, Raymond Fowler, Leah Haley, Ronald Hoag, Budd Hopkins, David Huggins, David Jacobs, the late Annie Livingston, Mark Perk, Elizabeth Clare Prophet, Mark Rodeghier, Derrel Sims, Corey Slavin, Bruce Smith, Frank Stranges, Debbie Tomey, the late Karla Turner, and Katarina Wilson, as well as many whose identities I will protect. I only hope that my attempt here to provide terrestrial cultural and historical contexts for the UFO experience as it is articulated and understood will not be interpreted as an aspersion on anyone's sincerity or sanity.

1. There is a strong strain of anti-Semitic conspiracy theorizing that makes ufological connections, including especially the work of Milton William Cooper (1991) and David Icke (e.g., 1997). Both are controversial but still well known in both right-wing conspiracist and ufological subcultures. These themes also converge in the literature of the Nation of Islam, which one could characterize as an anti-Semitic sect headed by a UFO contactee (Kossy 2001: 101–15).

2. At no point, however, have any significant number of UFO enthusiasts, investigators, believers, or even abductees had anything to do with UFO "cults" such as the Laugheads (Festinger et al. 1956), Bo and Peep (A.K.A.. Total Overcomers, A.K.A.. Heaven's Gate), or the Raëlians, despite such groups' high media profile and their attraction to sociologists and scholars of religion (see, e.g., Lewis 1995).

3. My thanks go to the late Valerio Valeri for pointing out some of these connections.

4. She has gone so far as to say that abductions have nothing to do with reproduction, that the vast majority of reports are psychological in origin, and that "no one has been abducted more than once" (Hill 1993).

Alien Tongues

DAVID SAMUELS

> "Yes. So that's that much, REM41. And then comes a number from 1 to 6, that classifies the language for one of the possible orderings of the verb and subject and object. This one is a 3—that means its order is verb followed by subject followed by object. Very roughly speaking, of course."
>
> "We wouldn't need that one, for all we know," said Anna, "if we ever acquired a non-humanoid language."
>
> "Why? Would they all have the same order?"
>
> "No, dear. There's no particular reason to expect that nonhumanoid languages would *have* verbs, subjects, or objects, you see."
>
> "But then how could it *be* a language?"
>
> "That," they told her, "is precisely the point."
>
> —Hagen [1984] 2000: 209–10

Would they even have them? Tongues, that is? Tongues capable of the fine motor control to form *tɛɪk mi tu jɔɹ lirɚ* in another planet's language? Or would they perhaps communicate via voluntary control of pheromones? Other odiferous emissions? Through—let's all say it (or think it) together—telepathy? Would humans be able to communicate with visitors from another planet at all? How would we recognize their communications as communicative? And in the absence of that recognition, how would we recognize any possibility of common humanity in these strangers?

Space, time, communication: braided obsessions the twentieth century. If it can be legitimately claimed that "The twentieth century began in 1905" (Bate 1998: 311) with the revelations of Einstein, that ground had been prepared by a number of other events in the preceding generation. The Michelson-Morley experiments in 1887 led to the conclusion that the Earth did not travel through an ether in its orbit around the sun and also produced the anomaly of the constant speed of light that resulted in Einstein's equations. Freud's work on dreams and the unconscious quietly reached the public in 1900. Experiments in telegraphy and telephony had given rise to early "sender-receiver" models of communication (Harris 1996), whereby communication was conceptualized as the clear transportation of "messages" from "sources" through "transmitters" across a "channel" to a "destination" via a "receiver" (Shannon 1948). And in the last quarter of the nineteenth century Giovanni Schiaparelli had discovered the "canals" of Mars, which fired imaginings of a great Martian civilization.

What are we? Where are we? Are there other beings anything like us somewhere else? If these questions received new kindling at the cusp of the twentieth century, they reached a kind of culmination in mid-century. Radio astronomy had its beginnings in the 1930s—although Nikola Tesla, in his Colorado Springs laboratory, had detected radio signals from space in 1899—when Karl Jansky at Bell Labs and Grote Reber in his Wheaton, Illinois, backyard constructed radio antennas to monitor the skies (Reber 1940). The search for extraterrestrial intelligence (SETI) had its origins in 1959 with the publication of Cocconi and Morrison's conjecture that extraterrestrial intelligences, if they wanted to be found, might likely communicate at 1420 MHz, which corresponds to the time period of the hyperfine transition of neutral atomic hydrogen. At Cambridge in 1967, Jocelyn Bell's discovery of the first pulsar was at least jokingly referred to as the LGM signal—LGM standing for "little green men." A few years later, in the 1970s, four National Aeronautics and Space Administration (NASA) spacecraft—Pioneers 10 and 11 and Voyagers 1 and 2—were each outfitted with a "message in a bottle," an attempt to reach out and communicate with whatever kinds of spacefaring beings might stumble across these vessels in three hundred thousand years or so.

In this essay, I want to explore how assumptions about language and communication have informed the imagining of interactions with alien intelligence—including the assumption about what "intelligence" might be. In these scientific musings about intelligence one often finds the sense that it is manifested in performances of universal "problem solving"—that any spacefaring beings would have grappled with and solved certain universal problems of mathematics and science. Various imaginings contain assumptions about the elements that would warrant the possibility of communication as well, especially the mid-century variety of communication that was linked to information theory. What must exist in order for communication to take place? Shared codes? A shared universe of semantic concepts? (And do these concepts exist prior to the codes?) A means of making utterances publicly accessible? (And are these publicly accessible utterances encodings of "thought"?) These imaginings of language and communication have often led to the production or description of alien tongues that are simultaneously opaque and transparent: *opaque* because they are alien, *transparent* because they are languages. As Connie Isele states (quoted in Debbora Battaglia's introduction to this volume), "ET communication often comes through to my consciousness in the form of my own thoughts." Roy Willis's revelation of alien(ated) voices is similarly doubled, as Battaglia notes. The voice is simultaneously "immensely far away and from deep inside me." The voice speaks in "flowing, powerful . . . English," and yet Willis is at the same time perfectly aware that this speech is being translated. This combination of clarity and obscurity is further paired with the idea that *intentionality* must lie behind any interpretable communicative act, an intention that often is assumed to find its expression in the purported universality of mathematics. In the course of my discussion, I will wend my way between science and fiction, for the imagining of alien languages has thematic resonance with both.

Dreaming of Mars

The nineteenth century ended with new fantasies of life on Mars. The evidence of a great Martian civilization was obvious from Earth. Not with the naked eye, of course, but once telescopes of sufficient power were developed the canals germinated a fantasy of Mars as the seat of a wondrous civilization of canal-builders—beings who had tamed the hostile environment of the red planet by lacing it with irrigation conduits that traced their spiny fingers to the source of water at the polar icecaps. Or perhaps it is clearer to say "telescopes of *in*sufficient power," for part of the waking from the dream of Mars lay in lenses powerful enough to render surface features of the planet with sufficient clarity.[1] But perhaps it is better to say "*apparently* lay in lenses powerful enough," for the idea of Martian life was hardly resolved by sharper vision. Deep imaginings of Mars have been with us from Schiaparelli's original 1877 observations to the recent findings of the two Mars exploration rovers Spirit and Opportunity.[2]

Were the canals created by intelligent beings or by the English-speaking misinterpretation of Schiaparelli's *canale*? No matter. The dream of life on Mars preoccupied French speakers in Paris and Geneva as well. We cannot lay the responsibility at the feet of English. But the American astronomer Percival Lowell was perhaps the greatest scientific proponent of Martian civilization at the dawn of the twentieth century. The express purpose of his eponymously named Lowell Observatory in Flagstaff, Arizona, was "an investigation into the condition of life on other worlds, including last but not least their habitability by beings like [or] unlike man. This is not the chimerical search some may suppose. On the contrary, there is strong reason to believe that we are on the eve of pretty definite discovery in the matter" (quoted in Sheehan 1996: 105). Lowell concluded that the canals on Mars were undoubtedly the result of intelligent beings faced with global drought, who had solved the problem though massive irrigation systems: "the most self-evident explanation from the markings themselves is probably the true one; namely, that in them we are looking upon the result of the work of some sort of intelligent beings" (106). At the closing of the American frontier and before the horrors of the world war, Lowell wrote three books—*Mars* (1895), *Mars and Its Canals* (1906), and *Mars as the Abode of Life* (1909)—that presented turn of the century readers with a mirror and yardstick for their civilization's own accomplishments.

On the nature of that Martian intelligence, Lowell was unwilling to speculate. "As to details of explanation, any we may adopt will undoubtedly be found, on closer acquaintance, to vary from the actual Martian state of things; for any Martian life must differ markedly from our own" (1895: 278). Yet the question was inevitable. What might they be like, these Martians? In appearance? In intelligence? They must be rational beings in order to have constructed something on the scale of the canals. Their minds must work with exemplary focus, and their society must be highly organized on a planetary scale, in order for them to have solved a massive problem such as global irrigation with such engineering might and aesthetic grace. They must also have overcome problems of communication of monstrous proportions. Would they be able to communicate with us? Or we with them?

Clarity and Opacity

In Edgar Rice Burroughs's notes for *The Gods of Mars*, we find (some typed on his manual typewriter, some worked out in his scribed hand):

1st zode 6 am (accurate sunrise)
2———8:24 am
3———10:48
4———1:12 Pm
5———3:36
6———6:00
7———8:24
8———10:48
9———1:12 am
10———3:36 am

Here Burroughs worked out the decimal segments of a Martian revolution on its axis in terms of the duodecimal Western clock system.[3] Below this, Burroughs continued with Western clock equivalents of Martian time units carried out in some cases to four decimal places.

TABLE of TIME (MARTIAN)
200 tals .8867 E secs—1 xat = 2 minutes 57.24 E sec
50 xats—1 zode
10 zodes—1 PADAN (DAY) 1 revolution of Mars upon its axis
67 PADANS = 1 TEEAN (month)
10 TEEANS = 1 ORD (YEAR)

---

10 zodes—88,620 Earth seconds
1,477 " minutes
24 hrs 37 min Earth time
1 zode = 2 hrs 27 min 42 sec or 2.461 2/3 hrs

---

1 xat = 2 min 57.3 sec

The obsession continued. One Martian year was equal to 670 Mars days, or 686.98 Earth days. Mars (or Barsoom, as it was called by its natives), according to Burroughs, had a reverse leap year: each year divisible by four had 669 days rather than 670. There were other additional refinements of calculation, but Burroughs's handwriting became cramped by dint of having reached the bottom of the page.[4]

This was all worked out in the lower-right quadrant of the notebook page. Down the left-hand margin, typed neatly, Burroughs made a more conventional glossary of Martian terms (*Sator Throg*—a Holy Thern of the Tenth Cycle) that included the following temporal equivalents:

tal—second)
zat—minute) see table
zode—hour)

The system was, on the one hand, opaque—almost deliberately so. Burroughs worked out its opacity in loving detail, with units of time equivalent to 2 minutes 57.24 seconds. On the other hand, the system was entirely transparent: a tal is a second, a zode is an hour. Speaking Martian isn't so different from speaking English.

Burroughs was an inveterate inventor of languages.[5] He took care in the logic of language, as in other domains. In *The Chessmen of Mars*, for example, he presented the Martian game of Jetan with rules complete and interesting enough to be included in John Gollon's *Chess Variations: Ancient, Regional, and Modern* (1968). The notes described above are in the service of demonstrating the logical rigor of Barsoomian symbolic systems. Indeed, for Burroughs, one might conclude, language was nothing more than a logical system of reference. Turn to his most famous fictional creation: the apes who reared Tarzan taught him a language whose morphology included rules for compound nouns—*den* means "tree"; *balu* means "baby"; *balu-den* (baby-tree) means "stick, branch, limb"; *ry* means "crooked"; *ry-balu-den* (crooked-baby-tree) means "bow."

Imagining that nonhuman species such as primates and Martians might possess the capacity for humanly recognizable language places Burroughs in the context of both fictional and scientific discourses about advancement and the capacity for language that trace back to the Renaissance (Lenain 1997). Burroughs's Martian work is of interest here, for it brings the question of communication into contact with the dream of Mars and the possibility of Martian civilization that was so fashionable at the beginning of the twentieth century.

One of the most prominent cases in this context was that of Mlle Hélène Smith, the pseudonym of Catherine Élise Müller, a medium in Geneva at the end of the nineteenth century. The pseudonym was given to her by Theodore Flournoy, whose six-year psychological study of Mlle Smith's séances contributed to the early development of the theory of the subconscious mind.[6] The question surrounding mediums appears to have been whether they actually contacted the spirits of the departed or instead contacted a portion of their own minds to which they lacked conscious access. As Todorov has written of this case, "deception is ruled out from the start" (1982: 258). Harry Houdini, in the 1920s, embarked on his crusade to expose spiritualist fraud (which included his membership on a five-member panel appointed by *Scientific American* in 1922), but in the late nineteenth century the veracity of spirit mediumship does not appear to have been at issue.[7]

Mlle Smith's utterances have attracted the attention of linguists interested in glossolalia (Yaguello 1991). But if the case of Mlle Smith is known among linguists and semioticians, it is probably because one of the spirits she channeled spoke "Hindoo," or a mixture of Sanskrit and glossolalia that Flournoy termed "Sanskritoid." Because of this, Flournoy enlisted the "eminent Orientalist" Ferdinand de Saussure to consult. The mystery of Mlle Smith's Sanskrit utterances seems to have occupied Saussure's imagination and energy, as his efforts to discover the organization of epic poetry in hidden anagrams would in later years.[8]

Saussure's involvement in Flournoy's study of Mlle Smith places the question of alien life in the context of the birth of modern linguistic and semiotic theories. While Saussure worked on Mlle Smith's Sanskritoid utterances, another of her "novels," as Flournoy called them, involved the channeling of spirits from Mars, who spoke Martian.

Flournoy credited the public popularity of the idea of life on Mars as the source of Mlle Smith's inspiration to focus on that distant locale. He cited evidence that the conversation of Mlle Smith's circle of friends "more than once turned in the direction of the habitability of Mars" ([1901] 1994: 88). He also appealed to the "echoes in the popular and everyday press" that followed on Schiaparelli's discoveries—popular articles by the astronomer Camille Flammarion ("Inondés de la Planète Mars") and the drawings of

Caran d'Ache ("Mars est-il habité?") that were appearing in *Figaro* at the time—to help his readers "understand at which point the idea of Martian humanity now had to be made a part of everyone's current notions" (294).

Flournoy turned to Flammarion's *La Planète Mars et ses conditions d'habitabilité* to reinforce the verity of his explanation.

> "We dare to hope," says M. Camille Flammarion, at the beginning of his excellent work on the planet Mars, "that the day will come when scientific methods yet unknown to us will give us direct evidences of the existence of the inhabitants of other worlds, and at the same time, also, will put us in communication with our brothers in space." And on the last page of his book he recurs to the same idea, and says: "What marvels does not the science of the future reserve for our successors, and who would dare to say that Martian humanity and terrestrial humanity will not some day enter into communication with each other?" ([1901] 1994: 87)

Flournoy is skeptical. If there are Martians, he does not believe that Mlle Smith is in contact with them. He places this imagined communication with our space brethren alongside such utopian notions as "wireless telegraphy" ([1901] 1994: 87).

In its structure—as a language—Mlle Smith's Martian performs the simultaneous transparency and opacity seen in Burroughs's notes. On the one hand, Flournoy credits Martian with the sense of the fullness of a language, concluding that "it is, indeed, a language and not a simple jargon or gibberish of vocal noises produced at the hazard of the moment without any stability" ([1901] 1994: 241–42). It is not simply vocability or glossolalia. Flournoy admits of Martian that it has phonemes and words. It has a definite aesthetic style and tunefulness, a musicality and rhythm that are distinct from those of French, although all of its sounds can be found in French. "Just as one distinguishes by ear foreign languages which one does not understand. . . . In this the Martian, indeed, bears the stamp of a natural language" (154–55). In this regard, Flournoy noted that high vowels occurred 73 percent of the time in the Martian, as opposed to 32 percent of the time in French utterances. Similarly, low vowels occurred only 8 percent of the time in Martian speech, whereas in French they occurred 48 percent of the time. Flournoy also noted that that there was a stability of sound-meaning relationships over the span of utterances. While arguing that it is clearly a construction (of Mlle Smith's subconscious mind),

Flournoy thereby placed Martian in the same category as other invented languages such as "Esperanto and Volapük" (242).

On the other hand, Martian is no more than "an infantile travesty of French" (Flournoy [1901] 1994: 154). Between February 2, 1896, and June 4, 1899, Mlle Smith produced forty spoken or written texts (Martian had its own unique orthography) that were eventually translated. For months, between February and November of 1896, attendees at Mlle Smith's séances badgered Astané, her Martian personage, for translations of the Martian utterances.[9] On examination of the translations, Flournoy discovered that syntactically and semantically Martian was completely transparent to French.

The standard French system of address included *monsieur*, *madame*, and *mademoiselle*. Martian mirrored this with *métiche*, *médache*, and *métaganische*. Flournoy found that he was able to construct exact word-for-word interlinear translations of the Martian utterances.

Cé Evé plêva ti di bénèz éssat riz tès midée durée
Je Suis chagrin de te retrouver vivant sur cette laide terre
"I am sorry to find you again living on this wretched earth."

Despite the paltry syntactic rules that could be derived from the corpus of forty texts, Flournoy concluded that "the rules of that [Martian] grammar, if it ever sees the light of day, will be only the counterpart of, or a parody upon, those of French" ([1901] 1994: 159). From the limited data, Flournoy was able to construct a table of "personal pronouns, articles, possessive adjectives, etc." in which the Martian form mapped transparently onto the French. That is, from the perspective of French, Martian had no exotic grammatical forms: no dual plural, no honorifics, no noun classification, no animacy distinctions. Everything was as it is in French.

The relexification is not necessarily complete. My study of Mlle Smith's utterances showed that there did appear to be an application of regular grammatical rules. For example, a systematic creation of the future indicative seems to be accomplished by adding an *-ir* postposition to the stem: *parler* is to *triné* as *parlera* is to *trinir*; *voir* is to *vétéche* as *verras* is to *véchir*. For other verbs, only the future indicative form is available: *furimir*, *andélir*, and *uzénir* stand in identical relationships to their French counterparts *aimerai*, *apparaîtra*, and *attendra*. This regular appending of *-ir* to denote futurity appears to be a grammatical rule and not merely a preference.

On the other hand, the system did not seem to maintain a consistent morphology with respect to French, and it may be that Mlle Smith's linguistic consciousness did not extend to the morphological level. The third-person singular equivalent of *trouver* in Martian was *bindié*, but the known Martian forms for *retrouver* were *bénèz* (first-person singular) and *bénézéé* (second-person singular) rather than, as one might expect, some form of *bindié* with a prefix. (It may be, of course, that vocalic alteration or the suffix *-ez* was meant to substitute for the *re-* prefix of French, but this would violate Flournoy's observation of utter transparency.) Similarly, there appeared to be no reflexive construction in Mlle Smith's Martian unless the reflexive pronoun could be parsed as a separate word: *s'approcher*, *s'elever*, and *s'envelopper* appear, in Martian, to be identical to *approcher*, *elever*, and *envelopper*. The corpus is too small, and the elicitation too unsystematic, to draw any conclusions. But it may tell us something of Mlle Smith's linguistic consciousness if her sense of "language" stopped at words and did not extend to the smaller meaningful units of morphemes.

These possible inconsistencies notwithstanding, Flournoy concluded that Mlle Smith's Martian was merely a complete relexification of French. He even noted the use of a Martian equivalent for the French phonetic *t* in inverted questions ([1901] 1994: 160): Kèvi beremir-m-hed, *quand reviendra-t-il?* ("when will he return?"). Flournoy concluded that there was no other explanation for Mlle Smith's Martian than relexification, as "the very possibility of [a] correspondence absolutely word for word would remain an extraordinary fact without a parallel, since there is not a single language that I know in which each term of the French phrase is always rendered by *one* term, neither more nor less, of the foreign phrase" (160). Still, the complete relexification of a language, maintaining stable referential content, is a phenomenon of great creativity—whether it was a circus act, a psychological illness, or an entrancement—and bears further investigation. It also raises, again, the question of transparency between human languages and their corresponding imagined alien analogues.

Transparency and Telepathy

At least Mlle Smith's Martians spoke to Earthlings in what they purported to be their native language. While issues of communication are an ever-present theme in science fiction (Meyers 1980), the issue is often addressed without actually performing an alien language for the reader. The problem of communication is also ever present in Robert Heinlein's *Stranger in a Strange Land* (1961). Heinlein's story of Valentine Michael Smith, the Earth infant who comes home after having been raised by Martians, reveals a great sensitivity to interactional pragmatics and the problem of polysemy in his American English encounters. At the same time, one gets the sense that Valentine Michael Smith is surprised by the very possibility of multiple meanings. Communication on Mars is more direct and clear, with less potential for ambiguity and misinterpretation. This is in part because Martians are more advanced than humans and in part because Martians are able to communicate telepathically. The two go hand in hand, of course. Communicative transparency is the clearest marker of technological or cultural superiority.[10] If Mlle Smith's Martian language was transparent to French, we cannot credit the superior logical construction of French thought for that transparency. But due to the directness of telepathic communication it is always a sure bet that the creatures are of an order of intelligence superior to our own.

This also relieves the author of the task of depicting the language as it is performed. At numerous points in *Stranger in a Strange Land*, Heinlein *describes* Valentine Michael's Smith's Martian speech: it sounds "like bullfrogs fighting cats" (1961: 34), "a strange, choking speech" (54), or "a croaking meaninglessness" (64). But with the exception of a single word, *grok*, which is explored with some interest throughout the novel, Martian language is never *enacted* for the reader. Even when Gillian Boardman learns some of the language, Heinlein simply describes it: "Jill startled him by addressing him with the correct honorific for a water brother, pronouncing it three octaves higher than any Martian would talk but with sore-throat purity of accent" (194). Eventually, as she becomes more fluent, that fluency is represented in italic type, which replaces the descriptions of croaking unfathomableness.

> Mike said in Martian, "*My brother, this is an Old One?*"
> "I don't know, Mike. They say he is."
> He answered, "*I do not grok an Old One.*"
> "I don't know, I tell you."
> "*I grok wrongness.*"
> "Mike! Remember!"
> "Yes, Jill." (245–46)

FIG. 1. An image of Martian life that was transmitted to Donald Menzel during one of "the large number and wide variety of committee meetings that I must attend." (From Donald H. Menzel, "An Earthling's View: Meet the Martians," *Graduate Journal* 7, no. 1 [1965]: 220–34.)

On the other hand, while sound images (signifiers) are never presented to the reader, the question of linguistic concepts (signifieds) is paramount to the interaction between the characters, whether they speak Martian, English, or (in the case of Dr. Mahmoud) Arabic. By the end of the novel, Mike is able to communicate telepathically, the dream of Mars meeting the dream of direct and transparent telementation (Harris 1981).

My Favorite Martian

The Mariner 4 flyby in July of 1965, which produced the closest photographs of the red planet up to that time, reopened questions of Martian life and inspired one of Texas's most prominent Indo-Europeanists. The *Graduate Journal* of the University of Texas at Austin dedicated an issue to "Planets and People." The issue featured a serious treatment of the surface of Mars by the astronomer Gerard de Vaucouleurs. Another astronomer, Donald Menzel, offered speculation about the possibility of life in the universe and a fanciful collection of his watercolor paintings of Martian beings (fig. 1). The noted science writer and editor Lyle Boyd teasingly speculated that Jonathan Swift knew that Mars had two moons (as he wrote in *Gulliver's Travels*) because (like Heinlein's Valentine Michael Smith) he had been kidnapped by Martians as a baby before returning to Earth.

As his contribution to this collection, Winfred P. Lehmann, of the university's linguistics and Germanic languages departments, wrote a science fiction story. In "Decoding the Martian Language," Lehmann toyed with

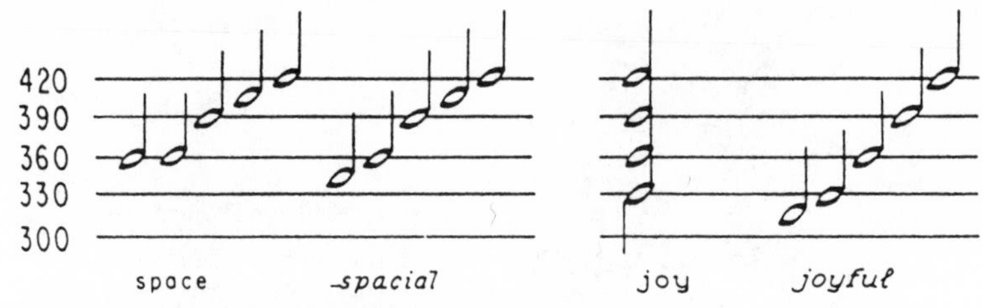

FIG. 2. W. P. Lehmann's Martian language sketch, showing (in HZ) the derivation of adjectives from nouns through shifts in the sequence and combination of tones. (From W. P. Lehmann, "Decoding of the Martian Language: Coordination of ILU and WGW," *Graduate Journal* 7, no. 1 [1965]: 269.)

the problem of how alien speech might be made sensible. The situation at the beginning of the story is depressing. Martian presents Earth's linguists with a system of musical communication in which phonemes apparently appear at random within a series of chords and arpeggios. As no one was able to translate even the simplest Martian utterances, Lehmann writes, "The prestigious Yeabean Prize in Non-terrestrial Study was withheld by the Purundi Parliament for the first time" (1965: 266).

The breakthrough in Martian linguistics—and the discovery that it had parts of speech identical to those of Earth languages—occurs when Dr. Sensai, director of the Language Reduction Center of the Interplanetary Leisure Unit (ILU), thoroughly dejected by his group's lack of progress, embarks on an extended leave of absence in southern Mexico. There he attends a conference at which he learns of Mazateco whistle speech, and the idea that the Mazatecs are able to communicate through the melodic patterns of whistling, without the necessity of distinctive vowels and consonants.[11] With this insight, Sensai is able to reanalyze the Martian utterances, paying attention to the musical tones and the relationships between them (fig. 2). This enables the ILU to determine that the arpeggios denote nouns and verbs, the former characterized by upward movement of the tones, the latter by the reverse. Nouns are further marked by a repetition of the first tone of its sequence. "Adjectives are derived from nouns by lowering the first tone by ten cycles per second" (Lehmann 1965: 269). Because pronouns involve repeating the first tone of a sequence thrice, "Martians were greatly delighted by Beethoven's Fifth Symphony, for it seemed to them a toying talk in praise of the ego" (269).

The repercussions on Earth are astounding. The Sounds replace The Letters as the central focus of education in the humanities. Earth's poets begin incorporating Martian tones into their work. Earth children are given elementary school training in Martian. Azorean whistle speech and West African drumming are proposed as keys to interplanetary communication and the music of the spheres. Lehmann ends his story with a wry dig at present day humans—one that still resonates in an age of language death. A joint congress passes a resolution "urging the governments of both planets to increase the grants for communication research on the grounds of the tremendous ignorance of varieties of language" (1965: 272).

"Come Visit Us If You Have Time"

Lehmann's fictional notion that Martians were particularly pleased by the tones of Beethoven's Fifth Symphony had its counterpart in the real world. Ironically, arguments about Beethoven occupied discussions by the committee compiling the musical examples to be included in a phonograph record that was to accompany the Voyager spacecraft on their journeys beyond the solar system.

Voyagers 1 and 2 were not the first spacecraft to be outfitted with a "message in a bottle." Pioneers 10 and 11 had both been launched with plaques announcing the presence of the capsule's senders. Each plaque bore depictions of a human adult male and female in relationship to the size of the satellite; a sketchy depiction of the solar system from which Pioneer originated; and a diagram of that system's location in relation to fourteen pulsars and the center of the galaxy, given in units of time equal to the transition of molecular hydrogen (the standard set by Cocconi and Morrison in 1959). The LAGEOS (LAser GEOdynamic Satellite) satellite was sent into high Earth orbit to measure continental drift in 1974. It is expected to reenter Earth's atmosphere in about eight million years. Because of this life expectancy of the satellite's orbit, NASA asked the astronomer Carl Sagan to design a plaque for the satellite so that whoever is around in eight million years will have some idea of what its purpose was (Sagan 1978: 9–10) (fig. 3).

The communications directed at beings hundreds or thousands of light-years away were similarly directed to the people of Earth. For both audiences, the communicative codes of science were privileged. Mathematics

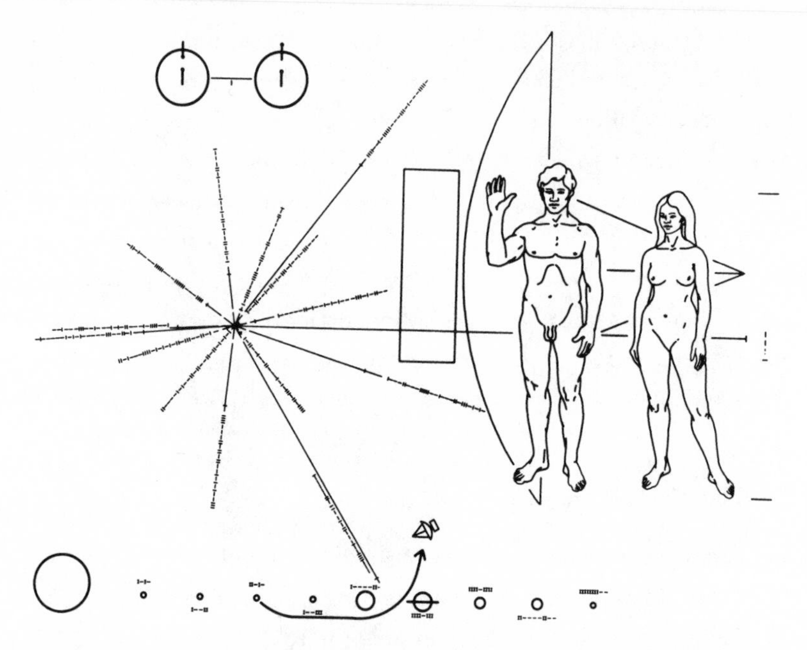

FIG. 3. "Hi, what's new?" The plaque designed by Carl Sagan for the Pioneer spacecraft. (From "Mission Descriptions: Pioneer 10 & 11 Spacecraft," http://spaceprojects.arc.nasa.gov/Space_Projects/pioneer/PN10&11.html.)

was the lingua franca: philosophical musings aside, it was assumed that 2 + 2 = 4 and hydrogen is hydrogen, on Rigel as well as Earth. If the Rigelians were technologically and scientifically advanced enough to be monitoring space, they had figured that out. The design of messages directed at space aliens took these notions of problem solving as the universal key to solving the problem of decoding the message.

Carl Sagan carried through this theme of science and mathematics as a common tongue both in his search for extraterrestrial intelligence and in his 1985 novel, *Contact*. But the idea was hardly new. As noted earlier, Nikola Tesla, working in his Colorado Springs laboratory in 1899, had received radio waves from space. He came to the conclusion that what he was hearing were radio signals broadcast from Mars. His conclusion was based in part on his sense of the universality of certain principles. Tesla's recollection of the event was that he heard repetitive signals grouped together as the integers 1, 2, 3, 4. In an interview in 1923, Tesla said:

> Twenty-two years ago, while experimenting in Colorado with a wireless power plant, I obtained extraordinary experimental evidence of the existence of life

on Mars. I had perfected a wireless receiver of extraordinary sensitiveness, far beyond anything known, and I caught signals which I interpreted as meaning 1–2–3–4. *I believe the Martians used numbers for communication because numbers are universal.* (*Albany Telegram*, February 25, 1923, emphasis added)

As this took place before the idea of radio astronomy became commonplace, Tesla's assertions were largely rejected by his peers. He continued to attempt to send signals to Mars, publishing pieces in newspapers and journals for decades after his initial encounter (1901, 1907, 1909, 1919). Gugliemo Marconi also saw radio as a means of communicating with the inhabitants of other planets, and he subscribed to the idea that the language of numbers would provide a lingua franca for this communication.[12]

While the emphasis on scientific and mathematical universals as a basis of interspecies communication has a long history, the group that would create the Voyager message combined notions of science, logic, language, expressiveness, communication, and mathematics in a way that created a special place for music in its thoughts about interstellar messages. This growing interlacing of science and aesthetics could be seen—or heard—in the events that occurred when the Arecibo radio telescope in Puerto Rico was reopened in 1974. There the dedication audience of two hundred was witness to the broadcast of a binary signal to the stars using the facility's 500,000-watt transmitter. The message is decodable as a picture composed of 1,679 light or dark cells on a 73 x 23 grid (1,679 is the product of the prime numbers 73 and 23). The message includes the first ten integers; the atomic numbers of hydrogen, carbon, nitrogen, oxygen, and phosphorus; the chemical formula of DNA; a rough depiction of the double helix; an even rougher depiction of a human being; a sketch of the solar system, with the third planet offset; and a sketch of the radio telescope from which the message originated (Drake 1978: 62–63).[13] For all the cold logic behind the form of the message, it also had an aesthetic dimension—one that was aimed at the Earthbound audience for the binary performance.

We wished to send about ten characters a second, both because this would cause the signal to be detectable to very large distances and because such a signal would sound pleasing to the dedication audience. We thought that about three minutes of such a transmission would be enough—more might be boring. . . . The message was successfully sent on November 16, 1974. . . . It took 169 seconds to send, and as the warbling of the message changed to the steady tone that marked the end of the message, the emotional impact on many of the audience was evident—there were tears in many eyes and sighs to be heard. (62–65)

While earlier messages had been largely concerned with communicating scientific information—biology, astronomy, chemistry—the design of the Voyager message took a decided turn from science to the humanities. The case in which the Voyager phonograph record and its stylus are held repeats the information on the Pioneer plaques about the location of the solar system in relation to various pulsars and continues to use the stable transition of hydrogen as the benchmark for all temporal units, including the instructions on what speed the record should be played (16 2/3 rpm). But whereas earlier messages were "visual greeting cards" (Sagan 1978: 23), the Voyager record contains multiple media and much more than science: 118 diagrammatic and photographic images, greetings from President Jimmy Carter and United Nations Secretary General Kurt Waldheim, spoken greetings in fifty-five human languages and one whale language, a soundscape suite evoking the evolution of life on Earth, and ninety minutes of music from around the world.

The inclusion of the whale greeting offers an important insight into the mind-set of the members of the committee working on this project and an important caveat to the group's dedication to the centrality of mathematics as the basis of communicative intent.[14] The first group of scientists working on SETI issues, inspired by the work of John Cunningham Lilly in the area of interspecies communication between humans and cetaceans (1967), dubbed themselves the Order of the Dolphin (Drake 1978: 47). The idea of nonhuman intelligence, and the potential diversity of intelligent life in the cosmos that whales and dolphins implied, fired the imaginations of these astronomical dreamers. When the time came to include audio greetings from the Earth's intelligent creatures, in a performance of open-mindedness the scientists included a sample of humpback whale songs that zoologist Roger Payne (1970, 1983) was convinced were indeed greeting formulas (Sagan 1978: 26–27).[15]

The choice of the fifty-five human languages for inclusion was somewhat haphazard. Space and time constraints on the disc precluded the idea of including a phonemic or grammatical key to any single language. Sagan's initial idea had been to record the twenty-five most commonly spoken languages of the planet. The group's initial appeal to the United

Nations Committee on Outer Space was accepted, but it yielded only a dozen languages. (Ralph Harry, the Australian delegate, delivered his greeting in Esperanto, the invented international language that Flournoy had compared to Mlle Smith's Martian.) The remainder of the speakers were recruited from among a network of Sagan's colleagues, friends, and friends of colleagues at Cornell University. This perhaps explains why the final list of languages spoken on the recording includes Sumerian, Akkadian, and Hittite, which were spoken in ancient Sumer, Mesopotamia, and Anatolia, respectively, but are heard only in ancient language classrooms today. There was no Mazateco whistle speech, which may have disappointed Lehmann's scholars of The Sounds. The group's desire to have representation of the world's most commonly spoken languages, its assumption that national rather than linguistic representation was important for the completeness of the document, and the constraints of time, space, and logistics meant that thousands of minority languages were not included. A map included in the book that reports the activities of creating the record (Sagan et al. 1978) demonstrates the way in which huge geographic areas could be "represented" by colonial languages (English, French, Spanish), especially if one ignores the problems of dialects and creoles (Haiti is represented by French) in addition to those of minority languages and vernaculars.

The question of inclusiveness also haunted the choice of music for the recording. The importance of music as a form of communication can be sensed in the fact that the Voyager disc itself, and the book that chronicles the making of it, is dedicated "To the makers of music—all worlds, all times." The greetings section of the record didn't include any musically based speech surrogates, but musical expression was an important part of what the committee wanted to present to any Aliens who might eventually intercept the craft. Sagan had been intrigued by the idea of including music for a number of reasons. For one, he wrote, "Our previous messages had contained information about what we perceive and how we think. But there is much more to human beings than perceiving and thinking. We are feeling creatures" (1978: 13). While conceiving of music as a language of the emotions, at the same time Sagan also trusted in music's purported relationship to mathematics for its communicative power across the galaxy. Music could reveal something of human emotional life, but at the same time "Harmony has a distinct mathematical character" (13). Here again we encounter math as the common tongue of all problem-solving species,

FIG. 4. *Close Encounters*: human and alien communicate in a musical duet. (From *Close Encounters of the Third Kind*. 1977. Directed by Steven Spielberg.)

and thus of interstellar communication, interlaced with ideas of aesthetics and expression in communicative action. This layering of mathematics and aesthetics also played a crucial role of the communication of the aliens in the film *Close Encounters of the Third Kind*, which was released just a few months after the launch of the two Voyager spacecraft. The breakthrough event occurs in Dharamsala, India, where a large group of worshipers sings the five-note sequence that marks the duetting and learning of "a basic tonal vocabulary" at the climax of the film (fig. 4).

The selection of music for the recording was a complicated process and one that was made frenetic by the late decision to change the speed of the record from 33 1/3 to 16 2/3 rpm, thus effectively tripling the amount of time that was available for musical performances. Timothy Ferris coordinated much of the production of this portion of the project. Ethnomusicologists Robert Brown and Alan Lomax were contacted and made helpful suggestions, as did Murry Sidlin, the music director of the National Symphony, and Martin Williams, curator of the jazz collection at the Smithsonian Institution. The final selection of the twenty-seven pieces on the recording included Javanese gamelan; Senegalese percussion; Pygmy, New Guinean, and Australian Aboriginal singing; Mariachi music; Chuck Berry; Japanese shakuhachi; Louis Armstrong; Peruvian and Solomon Islands panpipes; a Navajo Nightway chant; Blind Willie Johnson; as well as Chinese, North Indian, and Georgian performances.[16] These works muscled out a number of Western art pieces.[17] Arguments in favor of Haydn, Wagner, Debussy, Vivaldi, Tchaikovsky, Copland, Handel, and others eventually gave way in favor of a selection of classical pieces by Bach and Beethoven. (The recording does include brief selections by Mozart, Stravinsky, and Holborne.) The most decisive criterion, according to Ferris, was that a number of works by a single composer would aid in "facilitating 'decoding' by extraterrestrial listeners" (1978: 163). Another, according to Sagan, was that he was "very sensitive to the feeling that Bach and Beethoven represent the best of the musical tradition of the west, the culture that launched the spacecraft" (1978: 18). In this, as in many decisions regarding the musical selections, competing questions of globalism, nationalism, humanism, science, and culture were solved in part by an appeal to authenticity: Miles Davis's version of "Summertime," or Louis Armstrong's "Melancholy Blues"? (Armstrong.) A Russian folk song sung by Nicolai Gedda, the Russian pop song "Moscow Nights," or the Georgian folk song "Tchakrulo," suggested by Lomax? (the latter, in part because Gedda was Scandinavian and the group became convinced of the Georgian song's age and traditionality). Beethoven and Bach were argued to represent, in some sense, the most authentic version of the Western classical music tradition and the culture from which it had sprung.

Voyagers 1 and 2 passed Pluto's orbit in 1989. Voyager 1 is currently the most distant man-made object in space, approximately 8.1 billion miles from the sun. As of this writing, the spacecraft is expected to soon enter the area of termination shock. This is the region where the solar wind begins to wane, thus marking the place where the sun's gravitational influence on bodies in space begins to diminish and the area of interstellar travel begins to unfold.

Lost in Translation

The scientists who grappled with the issues of alien communication for the Voyager recording (not a linguist or anthropologist among them, mind you) faced recurring questions of interpretation and translation. These issues also plague science fiction writers. And so it is perhaps no accident that Carl Sagan, in addition to consulting physicists, astronomers, and biologists when creating the Voyager record, also contacted the science fiction writers Isaac Asimov, Arthur C. Clarke, and Robert Heinlein.

The idea that a simultaneous translating device of some sort could enable communication between speakers of even radically different languages has some moments in the history of science fiction writing. In

Murray Leinster's classic short story "First Contact" ([1945] 1998), two ships—one, the Llanvabon, from Earth, the other not—stumble across each other while making scientific studies of the Crab Nebula.

The two species communicate in some strikingly different ways. Unlike the Earthlings, who use "sound waves in air for communication" (Leinster [1945] 1998: 95), the crew of the other ship communicates via frequency modulations of the shortwave band (a form of telepathy). At the same time, the crew of the second ship uses this frequency modulation and "variations in wave forms" to create a phonemic system that corresponds to the vowels and consonants of spoken Earth languages.

This knowledge makes it possible for the crew of the Llanvabon to create a "mechanical translator" that will convert sound patterns into microwaves and back again. Still, translation as such is not possible—only the transposition of one phonemic system into another. In order to communicate, the two crews must work out an agreed-upon code, including "arbitrary symbols for objects . . . relationships and verbs and so on" (95).

The possibility of a successful outcome of the communications in "First Contact," however, does not hinge on the possibility of reference only but also on the possibility of tropes. Tommy Dort, the Earth scientist in charge of communicating with the other ship, senses that they might be likable creatures because he detects an all too "human" irony and humor in their response to the situation. "They were not humans, but they had a very human sense of the ridiculous" (98). The possibility of sharing rests on a sense of the psychic unity of all creatures who achieve the capability of light-speed space travel. Dort theorizes that there must be analogous evolutionary processes at work across the galaxy: "But their brains worked alike. . . . He would hate the idea of killing even non-human creatures who understood a human joke" (105). This unity of mental processes, then, ignoring the cultural specificity of humor, extends beyond rationality to encompass dry irony and gallows humor as well. The commonality of the two species also extends to their intelligence as seen in problem solving: both ships' captains come to identical solutions to the mutual dilemma they face.

Kim Stanley Robinson stakes out a more ambiguous perspective in his story "The Translator" (1994). Here, Owen Rumford, the chief of Rannoch Station, a trading outpost in deep space, must negotiate and avert a ritual war between the Ba'arni and the Iggglas that every 144 Rannoch years scorches to destruction the surface of the planet on which the station stands. Rumford's problem is that the translation box he relies on to transact his trades is somewhat ill-equipped for the delicate job of diplomacy. "It was an old bulky thing, in many ways obsolete; you had to type in the English half of things, and it would only translate between English and the alien languages in its program—no chance of any alien-to-alien direct contact" (291). The two languages, as presented by Robinson, are quite different in their phonology, morphology, syntax, and semantics. Ba'arni consists of clicks and tones and has a great deal of polysemy that the translator can only partially solve by context; Iggglas has neither tenses nor verbs. For Robinson's Rumford, unlike Leinster's Dort, these linguistic differences are not surmountable in the image of the common mind; rather, they are "another indication of a different reality" for the two species.

In the course of his mediation,[18] the Ba'arani say something to Rumford that the box translates as "Tell them we are ready to (x-click B-flat to C-sharp click sequence; see dictionary) and the hateful poison birds will die in traditional manner." On entering the unknown term into the dictionary, Rumford learns: "X-click B-flat to C-sharp click sequence: 1. Fish market. 2. Fish harvest. 3. Sunspots visible from a depth of 10 meters below the surface of the ocean on a calm day. 4. Traditional festival. 5. Astrological configuration in galactic core" (293). Here, Rumford comes face-to-face with the logician's problem that Sagan's and Tesla's concentration on numbers and the periodic table were trying to overcome: natural languages are not structured for truth value the way algebraic formulas are. Somehow Rumford is able to complete the negotiations to his satisfaction, saving the trading outpost for another 144 years. Let someone else worry about it when the time comes. In both Leinster's and Robinson's versions of mechanical translation, the process is difficult. It necessitates interpretation and creativity on the part of the beings making use of the device.

In the popular series of *Star Trek* television programs, on the other hand, a device known as the Universal Translator acts rather magically so that all creatures on the program speak in comprehensible English. Clearly this device is mostly a sop to the show's writers, actors, and viewers, making it possible for everything to be presented in the language most commonly spoken by both the show's creators and its audience. This being the case, however, it is interesting that the device sometimes becomes a focal point of a plotline and that its functioning is sometimes explained within the fictive universe of the script. The workings of the Universal Translator were first introduced in an episode entitled "Metamorphosis." In it, Kirk and Spock, brought against their will to a planet by an unknown energy cloud, modify the translator in order to communicate with their abductor. In the process, another character (as it turns out, Zefram Cochrane, who had discovered warp drive but mysteriously disappeared from Earth years earlier; well, Star Trek continuity is too difficult to explain in this essay) inquires about how such a thing might be done.

COCHRANE: What's the theory behind this device?

KIRK: There are certain universal ideas and concepts common to all intelligent life. This device instantaneously compares the frequency of brain wave patterns, selects those ideas and concepts it recognizes, and then provides the necessary grammar.

SPOCK: Then it simply translates its findings into English.

COCHRANE: You mean it speaks?

KIRK: With a voice or the approximation of whatever the creature is on the sending end. Not 100 percent efficient, of course, but nothing ever is. Ready, Mr. Spock?

Perhaps the only way to make sense of this explanation is to read Mr. Spock's line with as much irony as one can muster. More recently, the Universal Translator has been theorized to contain massive dictionaries and grammars of every known language in the *Star Trek* universe. But it must somehow be able to translate entirely new languages as well, based only on the phonetics of utterances, without any context in which to distinguish, for instance, the utterer's meaning from that of the utterance.[19]

Speaking Klingon

One of the more interesting practices to emerge out of the global *Star Trek* phenomenon (Greenwald 1998) has been the dissemination and circulation of the Klingon language. An Associated Press story of May 10, 2003, reported on the need for workers at a mental hospital in Portland, Oregon, to find a Klingon-English translator. Because Multnomah County human services is obligated to provide information in all languages spoken by its mental services clients, the county included Klingon among the languages it might possibly want in order to serve those of its patients who would speak nothing else. This, the report concluded, put "the language of starship Enterprise officer Worf and other Klingon characters on a par with common languages such as Russian and Vietnamese, and less common tongues including Dari and Tongan."[20]

The association with mental hospitals reinforces the association of alien languages, as in the case of Mlle Smith, with the glossolalia of the mental patient. But a number of speakers of Klingon claim that it is the fastest-growing language in the world—no, the galaxy. This is undoubtedly a matter of percentage growth rather than the number of speakers. And it appears that a good deal of Klingon use is as a literary practice, especially on the Internet. Still, one hears impossibly apocryphal stories: of the English-speaking tourist lost in Japan who got directions to his hotel in Klingon or of the parents who were reported to social services because they were raising their infant as a native speaker of Klingon. Will the real global lingua franca please stand up?

Klingon, of course, is the language invented for the belligerent aliens on *Star Trek*. It is "the official language of the Klingon Empire" (Okrand 1992: 9). The original Klingon utterances were created for *Star Trek: The Motion Picture* by the film's associate producer, Jim Povill, and a dialect actor, James Doohan, who portrayed the engineer Mr. Scott on the television series and in various films. Beginning with the third *Star Trek* film, *The Search for Spock*, however, the creation of a language for the Klingons fell to Marc Okrand, a Berkeley-trained linguist who studied with Mary Haas and wrote his dissertation on the grammar of Mutsun, a Native American language of California (Okrand 1977).

Constructed languages have an interesting history. Suzette Haden Elgin—a linguist with a doctorate from the University of California-Davis (1973), the author of the feminist *Native Tongue* science fiction trilogy (Elgin 1984, 1987, 1994), and the creator of Láadan, the language at the center of that novel—refers to them as "conlangs." J. R. R. Tolkien, drawing on his background in philology, constructed Elvish for *The Lord of the Rings*. Today computer software has made language generation easier. As of this writing, Richard Kenneway's Constructed Language website lists more than three hundred (http://www2.cmp.uea.ac.uk/~jrk/conlang.html, accessed May 8, 2005); Dean Easton's site lists over a thousand (http://www.geocities.com/Athens/Acropolis/9219/conlib.html, accessed May 8, 2005). But, as Elgin points out, constructing a language that is *interesting* is still a challenge.

The first thing to be said about Okrand's *tlhIngan Hol*, then, is that, as conlangs go, it is interesting—and not only because of its increasing number of users. Having been brought into the process midway, Okrand made the decision to create the language so that all of the existing elicitations of Klingon would be syntactically well formed and semantically meaningful utterances. He then went through every episode of the *Star Trek* franchise and translated every line spoken by a Klingon character into the native tongue of the character's home world, deriving vocabulary and syntactic forms as needed. Because Klingons are warriors—or at least the Klingons that viewers get to see represent a warrior class—Doohan and Povill had loaded the soundscape of the language with every acoustic form that English speakers might interpret as harsh, guttural, or violent. There are lots of unvoiced fricatives and affricates. The sounds of the language do not make use of minimal distinctive features of place and manner. For example, in English there is a regular series of stops and fricatives that distinguish voiced and unvoiced forms in the same place within the mouth: *b/p, d/t, g/k; z/s, zh/sh*. Klingon consonants appear to be distributed around the mouth so as to take greatest advantage of the dramatic possibilities of voiceless stops and fricatives. Like Apache and Navajo, for instance, Klingon has a voiceless lateral affricate *tł* (written *T* in Okrand's orthography) but not the voiced counterpart also found in those languages, *dl*.

Okrand constructed Klingon as an alien language that is not transparent to English, and at the level of morphology and syntax he certainly succeeded. In something of a linguist's inside joke, the unmarked declarative word order for a Klingon sentence is the object of the sentence followed by the verb and then the subject (OVS), the inverse of English, which is SVO. In Klingon, to say "dog bites man," you would say "man bites dog" (though Klingon does not have a word for dog).

So, the first thing to say about the Klingon language is that it *is* a language. It has nouns and verbs, the nouns distributed syntactically as subjects and objects. Its particular distribution of constituents is extremely rare but not unheard of on Earth. While there appears to be a global preference for subject preceding object in human languages (Tomlin 1986; Hawkins 1994), OVS languages, while extremely uncommon—only 4 of Tomlin's sample of 402 languages—can be found, for example, in the Amazon (Hixkaryana and Apalai in Brazil and Barasano in Colombia).

Klingon has intensely regular ordering of five types of noun suffixation: (1) augmentative/diminutive, (2) number, (3) qualification, (4) possession/specification, and (5) syntactic markers. The example Okrand offers in his grammatical sketch is:

QaghHommeyHeylIjmo'

Qagh	*-Hom*	*-mey*	*-Hey*	*-lIj*	*-mo'*
Error (N)	Diminutive	plural	Evidential	Possessive	Resultative
			(apparent)	(2nd person sing.)	(because of N)

"Due to your apparent minor errors" (1992: 29)

Each of Klingon's syntactic features can be found in languages on Earth, though not in the collection found in Klingon. Like Native American languages such as Koasati and Washo, Klingon makes use of an animacy hierarchy, so that beings capable of language are marked for plurality with a distinctive suffix (*-pu'*). (In Washo, this includes "personified animal protagonists in stories" as well as human beings [Mithun 1999: 558].) Like the Kiowa-Tanoan languages, Klingon body parts are also classified with a distinctive plural marker (*-Du'*). (Ancient Greek, as well, had a dual plural that denoted plural objects that naturally come in pairs, such as body parts.) Like Yana, Klingon has a distributive plural that can be interpreted as "scattered pieces"—a useful concept for beings that so relish hand-to-hand blade combat. Like Turkish or Chukchi, Klingon is agglutinative. It has grammatical rules for locating an action, though not much of a system for marking direction of movement. It has grammatical markers for topic. Nouns take no gender, and third-person singular pronouns are similarly neuter, as in Navajo and Apache. Klingon has no tense, but it has an aspectual system similar to Hopi, which includes the distinctions between perfective and incompletive aspect and between punctual and durative.

Unlike Mlle Smith's Francophile Martian, then, Klingon is clearly alien, in the sense that its syntax cannot be transparently mapped onto English. In the play of opacity and transparency, however, it is still recognizable as a human language. For one thing, the physical apparatus of production is identical. Obviously, this is in part because Klingon is designed so that actors can pronounce it using the vocal tracts they use to speak their own languages. But it is interesting that Mlle Smith's Martians also apparently spoke with a human apparatus. Valentine Michael Smith, as well, was able to enunciate Martian using his human tongue, lips, teeth, and vocal folds, strange though it may have sounded. Vocal sound remains an important aspect of how aliens are judged.

Given the phonology of Klingon, an alien species that wants to conquer the Earth might do well to speak a language that has many voiced consonants and continuants—a language such as Láadan, for instance. Proposed in Elgin's *Native Tongue* trilogy as a distinctly women's language, a way of representing women's experience, Láadan also features a range of sounds that are, compared to Klingon's warrior phonemes, almost stereotypically feminine. Láadan contains no unvoiced stops at all—no *p*, *t*, or *k*. Its range of consonants includes voiced stops, nasal continuants, voiced and unvoiced fricatives, liquids, and semivowels. Láadan is a tone language, as well, giving it a musical "lilt" compared to the harsh, emphatic delivery of Klingon.

As a constructed language, Láadan also has a unique grammar. The unmarked declarative sentence structure is VSO (verb-subject-object), with clause-initial speech-act particles and clause-final evidential particles. But Láadan is intended as a human language to be spoken by the women of Earth. Klingon is imagined as an alien language. Yet, as we have seen, Klingon has an analyzable syntax that shares its features with a range of human languages, though in a number of seemingly unsystematic and somewhat randomly selected ways (rather than ornate or exquisitely developed systems such as the classificatory counting system of Yurok).

At the level of semantics of nouns and verbs, however, as Mlle Smith's Martian was to French, Okrand's Klingon is little more than relexified English. This may be an after effect of Okrand having developed the lexicon from the English lines delivered by the Klingon characters. His more recent publications (e.g., Okrand 1997) acknowledge such features as dialectal variation, metaphorical extension, and idiomatic phrases. Still, when you look something up in the Klingon dictionary you generally see one English gloss for the term—and a single-word gloss at that. *QoS* is a verb that means "be sorry." Do you want to accuse someone of being boring in Klingon? The word you want is *Dal*, a verb that means "boring, be boring." The one exception I found—a notable exception given all the linguistic and anthropological work that has been done on color terminology and Whorfianism—is that Klingon has a single term, *SuD*, a verb, which glosses as "be green, blue, yellow" (Okrand 1992: 108).

One long-standing aspect of thinking about the differences between languages has been the idea that different languages cut up the world differently. Saussure, for example, demonstrated that the distinction between *rivière* and *fleuve* in French is not equivalent to the distinction between *river* and *stream* in English. One does not necessarily discover this structural difference when comparing the lexicons of English and Klingon. It is, however, the central project of encodings of Láadan in Elgin's *Native Tongue* trilogy. The Láadan project was to find lexicalizations for semantic concepts that would make women's experiences easy to talk about, to find ways of cutting up the world of experience in ways that had never been done before. And it certainly succeeds at the level of discovering a new semantics, offering lexical items with glosses such as "nonholiday, a time allegedly a holiday but actually so much a burden because of work and preparations that it's a dreaded occasion; especially when there are too many guests and none of them help" (*radíidin*); and "the act of relinquishing a cherished/comforting familiar illusion or frame of perception" (*zhaláad*). Klingon does not seem to do this work. This may be one reason (the cultural force of the franchise of which it is a part obviously being another) why Klingon has gained in popularity while Láadan languishes in comparative obscurity.

Of course, the Klingon dictionary does not contain every lexical item found in English; for the most part the lexicon includes only those concepts that have been expressed by a Klingon character in *Star Trek*, a comparatively small corpus of utterances. The Klingon locative and directional adverbials, in relationship to either a speaker or cardinal points, are comparatively limited. As the Seattle playwright Marcy Rodenborn discovered, Klingon has no word for *south*. In her short play *Antietam Redux* (1997) one of the characters needs to end his work at a Civil War reenactment in order to get to a *Star Trek* convention.

YOUNG WOMAN: Do you want some Yankee prisoners?

YOUNG MAN (looking up): Wha?

VINCENT: Well, I don't see—

YOUNG WOMAN: Take us prisoner—you might get promoted even higher and get to sit with Lee.

YOUNG MAN (urgently): We have to be at Trek Con in three hours!

YOUNG WOMAN: We'll make it.

YOUNG MAN (really freaking out): Yeah, but I get to be Klingon High Commander this time. I've never been a High Commander. I have to prepare for the ceremony of KaoPa. It's Kao Pa—

YOUNG WOMAN (pacifying): There'll be time.

(She turns to LETTY and VINCENT.)

Think about marching up to Magnolia house with two Union soldiers in tow. Whaddaya say?

VINCENT: You were just dead.

YOUNG WOMAN: No, we only nicked ourselves. Come on!

(VINCENT and LETTY look at each other and smile.)

VINCENT: Get along now.

(VINCENT gestures to have them march before him.)

LETTY: And yell loudly, "The South will rise again!"

YOUNG WOMAN: The South will rise again!

YOUNG MAN: WoQ mojqa' boq'a'!

(They all look at him.)

It's Klingon. WoQ mojqa' boq'a'! That actually means "The great alliance will become a political power again." There's no word for South in Klingon. You could also say, "tugh malotlhqa'bej" which means "soon we will definitely rebel again!" In fact, that might be the better—

LETTY and VINCENT: Quiet, Yankee!

(They exit.)

Klingon's semantic transparency to English may be changing. As people work on translations of Shakespeare and the Bible, metaphorical extension and other expansive forces may push Klingon to become more opaque in its semantics, as it is in its syntax.

Conclusion: Alien Languages, Alien Realities

The questions raised by constructed languages such as Klingon and Láadan are at the heart of the imagining of alien tongues. How are languages and realities connected? Does the possibility of communication depend on the possibility of similar life experiences? These questions are played out in the dance of opacity and transparency that I have explored in this essay.

In the film *The Day the Earth Stood Still* (1951), Klaatu enters his flying saucer after his meeting with Dr. Barnhardt in order to plan his demonstration of power for the next day's lunch hour. To the strains of the theremins used in Bernard Hermann's musical score, Klaatu calls (one assumes) his superiors and speaks the lines: "Imre Klaatu naroant. Makro pruvow beratu lukdentso imoplit. Yabu teri akso b'getyo berengi degus" (fig. 5).

FIG. 5. "Imre Klaatu narroant": Klaatu discusses his plans with the home world. (From *The Day the Earth Stood Still*. 1951. Directed by Robert Wise.)

Part of Klaatu's alienness lies in his use of alien language, part of his superiority in his willingness and ability to so perfectly deign to speak ours. He must teach Mrs. Benson a phrase of his native language (Klaatu borada nikto) in order to assure his survival. In that language, and the understanding that only through command of alien forms of communication can we hope to curtail the destructiveness of the robot Gort, the audience encounters (as Battaglia writes in the introduction to this volume) the dissociative E.T. effect of modernity: Who are we? Who are they? Are they anything like us?

As it turns out, however, Klaatu's language is not wholly made up at all. It is not gibberish—not a random sequence of syllables meant to sound like a language. Rather, it is a constructed language. But who produced it? The screenplay contains only the instructions "Klaatu starts speaking into a built-in microphone in his own strange language. He speaks in rapid-fire explanation, continuing to talk," until the screen dissolves to the next shot. Was it devised by the screenwriter Edmund H. North? It is not found in the original 1940 Harry Bates short story ("Farewell to the Master") from which the film was adapted.

In the April 1978 issue of *Fantastic Films*, Tauna La Marbe provided readers with an analysis of Klaatu's language.[21] According to La Marbe's dissection, the language is a mixture of "Latin, French, English, Greek, Cipher, and transposition code." (*Cipher* refers to a rearrangement of the letters of a word and *transposition code* to the regular substitution of each letter in a word with another letter. The name Klaatu appears to be a coded form of Harry B, which would refer to Harry Bates, the author of the short story on which the film was based.) Klaatu's first sentence, then,

"Imre Klaatu naroant," was produced by La Marbe as "Emoere Klaatu Narroante." The first word is thus ciphered *me*, a phonetic transposition of *are*, followed by the character's name and then a Latin-derived verb *narroante*, "narrate-previous." She interprets this as meaning "This is Klaatu, reporting as previously agreed." La Marbe argues that each of Klaatu's alien utterances is decipherable by similar means. "Because there are so many Earth root languages involved," the editors mused, "the speculation may be raised that Klaatu's race once 'seeded' our world with much of its present population. Or, that in the far distant past we may have had the same ancestors, from beyond the reaches of even Klaatu's spaceship, who seeded both worlds. It would account for his totally human characteristics in any event" (see the essays by Battaglia and Lepselter in this volume).

Again we see the dance of clarity and opacity, the desire to be human and alien simultaneously. That dance is similar to another, which is the dance around universality and particularism, in the internal structures of languages and in the relationship between languages and the minds, cultures, and experiences of their speakers. The bandleaders for this dance could be called Chomskyanism and Whorfianism.

Neal Stephenson's *Snow Crash* (1992) is a Chomskyan novel. In it, Hiro Protagonist is faced with a debilitating computer virus called Snow Crash, which reduces anyone exposed to it to uttering nothing but blithering babble. The blood of those infected with the virus can be used to create a drug that has the identical effect. Hiro consults a virtual librarian, and learns that the virus is, in a sense, reaching deep into people's minds to release the ur-language within. Playing on the biblical story of the tower of Babel, Stephenson's novel dramatizes the idea that there once was a single language spoken by all humans—and makes strong gestures toward the notion that this language was Sumerian. At one point, Hiro says to the librarian, "You mentioned before that at one point, everyone spoke Sumerian. Then, nobody did. It just vanished, like the dinosaurs" (203).

The Snow Crash virus causes something that sounds like glossolalia. The librarian tells Hiro that "glossolalia comes from structures buried deep within the brain, common to all people" (Stephenson 1992: 192). In this, he is in agreement with Victor Henry, a colleague of Saussure's who reexamined Mlle Smith's Martian language to determine whether her glossolalia might reveal anything about the origins of human language itself ([1901] 1987). Snow Crash causes people to revert to the state they were in before languages began diverging. The novel asserts that the historical diversity of languages is itself the result of an infection. Before that infection, the fate of languages was to be unified and whole. The sense of merging diversity is metaphorically played out in the images of code switching, linguistic imperialism, and globalization in the character of the Japanese rap star Sushi K.

> He learn English total immersion
> English/Japanese be mergin'
> Into super combination
> So he can have fans in every nation

The idea that all human brains are hardwired with a single language is clearly in the Chomskyan realm, but in the end the novel takes a turn toward the Whorfian. Hiro must keep the virus from spreading because language diversity is mankind's only protection against fascism.

By contrast, Samuel Delany's 1966 *Babel-17*, winner of the Nebula Award, is a wildly, almost carelessly Whorfian novel.[22] In it, language is also a virus—one that changes the thought processes of the person immersed in the language. An intergalactic war is the centerpiece of the novel. The protagonist of the story is a renowned poet, Rydra Wong, who is asked to decode some enemy transmissions that the military has intercepted. As it turns out, the transmissions themselves are the weapon. As you learn to think in Babel-17, you are compelled to behave in certain ways.

The theme draws on the so-called "strong" version of the so-called "Sapir-Whorf hypothesis"—the idea that languages determine the thought of their speakers, that if a language doesn't have a lexical item the mind can't have the concept. Rydra Wong explains: "Imagine, in Spanish *having to* assign a sex to every object: dog, table, tree, can-opener. Imagine, in Hungarian, *not being able to* assign sex to anything: he, she, it all the same word" (Delany 1966: 81, emphasis added). The linguistic theory of the novel is contained in those modals. Languages force their speakers into boxes. We experience and operate in the world because of what our languages make possible. Rydra eloquently ruminates on the problem.

> Nominative, genitive, elative, accusative one, accusative two, ablative, partitive, illative, instructive, abessive, adessive, inessive, essive, allative, translative, comitative. Sixteen cases to the Finnish noun. Odd, some languages get by with only

singular and plural. . . . No way to say *warm* in French. There was only *hot* and *tepid*. If there's no word for it, how do you think about it? (112)

Babel-17 is a very useful language, cognitively speaking. Thinking in Babel-17, Rydra is able to escape from a web that entrapped her in English because "Switching to another language creates another reality" (Delany 1966: 177). But it has no first-person singular pronoun and thus gives the individual *I* no way of asserting any thought outside the linguistic framework. And the word for the Alliance (the good guys) in Babel-17 translates literally into English as "one who has invaded." "While thinking in Babel-17 it becomes perfectly logical to try and destroy your own ship and then blot out the fact with self-hypnosis so you won't discover what you're doing and try to stop yourself," Rydra explains (215).

The irony of the novel is that the enemies are not "aliens" in the sense I have been discussing throughout this essay. Rather, they are people from Earth who have relocated to new colonies in deep space. Rydra Wong is troubled that the people thought of as the enemy read and cherish her poetry just as much as do members of the Alliance.

But perhaps it is best to stop with the misused image of Whorf's linguistic relativity principle. For Whorf based his principle in part on his interpretation of Einsteinian physics, with which we began. The Whorfian and Chomskyan views of language can be considered within the context of twentieth-century science, which also gave us science fiction and the imaginative dreams of communication with aliens. And so I note, as one final piece of the puzzle, that in 1924, seven years before he began graduate study in linguistics at Yale with Edward Sapir, Benjamin Lee Whorf tried to work out his concerns about the conflicts of science and religion by writing a science fiction novel. According to Walter Meyers (1980), *The Ruler of the Universe* may have been the first science fiction novel to use the theme so prominently displayed at the conclusion of Klaatu's visit: man's destruction by means of his own nuclear hubris. Unfortunately, or fortunately, the novel was never published.

Notes

1. Sagan and Fox (1975) provided a map that laid Percival Lowell's canal network over maps generated from the photographs taken by the Mariner spacecraft, dem-

onstrating "virtually no matches between Lowell's canals and real surface features" (Dick 1998: 42).

2. The visual and technological attention to Mars has revealed evidence of changing seasons (Schiaparelli), canals (Lowell), and vegetation (Trumpler, Sinton). These observations fueled both a sense of Mars as a site of life, if not civilization (see McKay et al. 1996 for an analysis of the organic life attributed to the "Mars rock"), and a sense of Mars as a possible home for civilizations to come (note, e.g., Robert Zubrin's 1996 argument for terraforming and colonizing Mars). Dick 1998, especially pages 25–69, is an excellent resource for the history of imagining Mars as a home to life.

3. The reckoning of Barsoomian time makes its appearance in chapter 16 of *The Gods of Mars*, "Under Arrest": "Late in the afternoon a messenger arrived from Zat Arras to inform us that we would be tried by an impartial body of nobles in the great hall of the temple at the 1st zode* on the following day, or about 8:40 A.M. Earth time." The asterisk after *zode* guides the reader to an editorial footnote that explains:

> Wherever Captain Carter has used Martian measurements of time, distance, weight, and the like I have translated them into as nearly their equivalent in earthly values as is possible. His notes contain many Martian tables, and a great volume of scientific data, but since the International Astronomic Society is at present engaged in classifying, investigating, and verifying this vast fund of remarkable and valuable information, I have felt that it will add nothing to the interest of Captain Carter's story or to the sum total of human knowledge to maintain a strict adherence to the original manuscript in these matters, while it might readily confuse the reader and detract from the interest of the history. For those who may be interested, however, I will explain that the Martian day is a trifle over 24 hours 37 minutes duration (Earth time). This the Martians divide into ten equal parts, commencing the day at about 6 A.M. Earth time. The zodes are divided into fifty shorter periods, each of which in turn is composed of 200 brief periods of time, about equivalent to the earthly second. The Barsoomian Table of Time as here given is but a part of the full table appearing in Captain Carter's notes.
>
> TABLE
>
> 200 tals . . . . 1 xat
>
> 50 xats . . . . 1 zode
>
> 10 zodes . . . . 1 revolution of Mars upon its axis.

4. In Porges 1975: 148. The accuracy of Burroughs's reckoning of time on Mars for the purposes of making a calendar is open to question. For a digest and assessment of various authors' attempts to devise a Martian calendar, see Thomas

Gangale's "Mare Chronium: A Brief History of Martian Time, 1880–1999," at http://pweb.jps.net/~gangale4/chronium/chronfrm.htm. Accessed May 4, 2005.

5. As an army cadet, Burroughs was posted to Camp Grant, Arizona, just south of the San Carlos Apache reservation. It is pure conjecture to suppose that he was exposed to questions of language and translation in this polyglot region of the country, but John Carter, Warlord of Mars, begins his adventure in Arizona.

6. In his introduction to the German edition of Flournoy's study of Mlle Smith, Carl Jung credits Flournoy with having assisted with some mediation between Jung and Freud after their falling out.

7. For more on Houdini's work against mediums, see Kasson 2001.

8. For more on the work of Saussure outside the *Course in General Linguistics*, see de Certeau 1996; Gadet 1989; Harpham 2002; Lecercle 1985; Starobinski 1979; and Todorov 1982.

9. In fact, Cifali (1994) argues that Mlle Smith's "Martian" only became what it was because of this insistence—that the development of Martian as a language was as much a creation of the insistent questioning of her interlocutors as it was of her utterances.

10. But see William Golding's *The Inheritors* (1964), in which telepathic Neanderthals are replaced by *Homo sapiens*, who must overcome their lack of telepathy by developing language and technology. From Poe's early proto-science-fiction stories on, telepathy has been a strongly recurrent theme in science-fiction writing. Stone 1969 is a collection of a dozen or so classic short stories.

11. Writing in 1965, Lehmann cites Cowan 1948. See also Sebeok and Umiker 1976.

12. Marconi's pronouncements appeared on the front page of the *New York Times* on January 20, 1919 ("Radio to Stars, Marconi's Hope"). A great deal of information on Tesla and his involvement with interplanetary communication is available on the Web. See, for example, the encyclopedia entry for Tesla at http://en.wikipedia.org, accessed September 3, 2004; and the Tesla Memorial website at http://www.teslasociety.com, accessed October 7, 2004.

13. Although the sketch of the human lacks genitalia, it is "rather masculine-appearing" (Drake 1978: 63). F. D. Drake, who designed the message, wrote that he settled on this picture because a more unisex version "looked as much like a gorilla as a human" (63). It is notable that these visual messages were all created by astronomers and physicists, not artists.

14. The committee members were Carl Sagan, F. D. Drake, Ann Druyan, Timothy Ferris, Jon Lomberg, and Linda Salzman Sagan.

15. The idea that cetaceans hold a key to understanding extraterrestrial languages also appears in Elgin's *Native Tongue* trilogy, in which one program for communi-

cating with aliens involves the use of dolphins; in the film *Star Trek IV: The Voyage Home*, a spaceship threatens Earth when its attempts to communicate with whales go unheeded because of the extinction of the species.

16. A comprehensive website about the Voyager mission and the "Golden Record" is maintained by NASA's Jet Propulsion Laboratory. A complete playlist of the music that was included can be found at http://voyager.jpl.nasa.gov/spacecraft/music.html, accessed May 8, 2005.

17. There is no Elvis Presley on the record nor any Beatles recordings, it seems because of complicated copyright issues. The committee had to secure releases and pay mechanical fees for all the recordings. Nor is there any country western music on the recording, despite some arguments that this style of music would reflect the tastes of the people who actually put the Voyager spacecraft together.

18. One might wonder why two groups that have conducted ritual warfare against each other every twelve-score years for as long as anyone can remember would never have learned each other's languages.

19. How, for example, would even a very powerful dictionary distinguish between metaphorical and literal meanings or idiomatic and more standard utterances, let alone between languages that distinguish gender in the noun phrase or use the same kinship term for "mother" and "mother's sister"?

20. The cynical and joking response to the inclusion of Klingon prompted the county to withdraw the language from its list.

21. The article is available on the Web, at http://www.dreamerwww.com/fanfilm/fanfilm2.htm, accessed May 2, 2004. This is perhaps the best website dedicated to *The Day the Earth Stood Still*, but it was down—hopefully, temporarily—during the completion of the present essay.

22. The inspiration to compare *Snow Crash* and *Babel-17* came from my encounter with an essay by Tracy Seneca that has circulated on the Web since 1994. Although I reach very different conclusions about the two novels, I would not have considered comparing them otherwise. Seneca's essay is available at http://besser.tsoa.nyu.edu/impact/f93/students/tracy/ tracy_midterm.html, accessed April 19, 2004.

The License: Poetics, Power, and the Uncanny

SUSAN LEPSELTER

This is an essay about class and conspiracy, desire and limitation in America. It's also about UFOs and the invisible human structures that can be glimpsed, sometimes, by the glow of their weird lights.

One thing they shed light on is the poetic interplay between the ordinary and the fantastic in stories about power and its fallout. How are these stories shaped by the inarticulate disappointments of everyday life? And how do people make sense of power's twin effects, restriction and possibility, forces that coarticulate with uncanny simultaneity?

Uncanny stories are always haunted by questions. In the stories I want to tell here, the most central question (and the most maddeningly elusive) hovers over the constant, porous interplay between seemingly binary oppositions, the real and the imaginary, and their more material correlates, limitation and potential. How is the interplay between these oppositions lived, embodied, and saturated with social meaning? In this essay, I want to think about such issues through two complementary perspectives on the uncanny, "ethnography" and "theory," approaching parallel problems in two sections through distinct genres of critique.

Although I keep these large questions in mind, and they are haunted by the uncanny specter of UFOs, the stories I want to tell in this section revolve around the mundane, ordinary figure of *the license*—a lived trope that performs the simultaneous forces of restriction and possibility emanating from modern experiences of power.

The word *license* can suggest lawless freedom—a licentious abandon. And there's also the sense of *license* as a degree of freedom that is ultimately shaped by its own containment. In this sense, freedom is meted out by the authority of the state in its markers: tags and documents, concrete indices to an abstract idea of a social contract with power. The physical license you hold in your wallet always implies freedom to act but maintains awareness of the law circumscribing the action. It reminds the actor that freedom has been granted and can be taken away—by what Taussig (1997) calls "the magic of the state" and others call the *powers that be* (see Dean 1998).

When it works, the agreement to move without anxiety inside a licensed realm seems natural for those whose imagined community includes the "we" of the representative-based state. Yet for those who don't feel part of the franchise this ordinary zone of sanctioned freedom feels strange. Bureaucratic signs and procedures grow fabulous, charged with overdetermined meaning, and the conflict between law and freedom, which is supposed to remain unmarked, can grow uncanny in its emergent visibility. The *source* of power is felt to be simultaneously hyperpresent and hidden. And its conflicts are expressed in a struggle for something like *poetic* license, which takes *the real* itself as the site of struggle.

One site of struggle over the real is Area 51, which is part of the vast complex of the Nevada nuclear test site and Nellis Air Force Base, birthplace of the Stealth Bomber and the U-2. Area 51 is a heavily guarded place in the middle of nowhere in the Nevada desert that was supposed to remain a federal secret. This is where, some say, the powers that be hid the UFO that crashed in Roswell, New Mexico, in 1947. Some say government scientists dismantled the UFO to figure out how it worked. Some say those scientists took apart the extraterrestrial bodies, examining their exotic organs and strange blood. And some say the government and the aliens conspired together. They let the aliens abduct us, steal our sperm and eggs, and make hybrids of aliens and humans to survive what's coming.[1]

The stories I tell here arise at the interface between the fantastic, terrible shadow cast by Area 51 and the everyday life that goes on in the small local settlement closest to it: Rachel, Nevada, with a population that fluctuates at more or less ninety. Rachel was a community dwindling to nothing after the closing of a local tungsten mine in the 1980s, but it has since become famous for its proximity to Area 51. In 1990, the Little A'Le'Inn sprang up there—a cafe in a doublewide trailer whose elaborate UFO theme made it stand out from other small rural cafes (including one that had failed several times over the years in the same location). I worked there as a waitress for a couple of months in 1997 and 1998, to write about the stories I heard. There were paintings of aliens on the bar and photographic evidence of UFOs on the wall, stacks of libertarian newspapers, gift shop shelves in a corner filled with alien mugs and Area 51 T-shirts, a gun behind the bar, and antigovernment signs and cartoons everywhere: *Bill and Hillary: Twin Air Bags*. The cafe and inn (there were five trailers out back where travelers could stay) brought lone UFO pilgrims and busloads of tourists into the remote desert of central Nevada.

Passionately argued conspiracy theory mingled here with the cadences of everyday talk and the long, quiet spells of any out-of-the-way cafe. Into suddenly cool indoor space from the glaring sun or vast pressing darkness that lay behind its metal doors came retired RV travelers and hired hands from the nearby farm, cowboys and down-and-out drinkers, lone drifters and families with kids, military personnel from the base, and solitary guys who everyone knew had a job "up there" in some working-class capacity at Area 51 but couldn't talk about it—they'd go to prison if they mentioned where they were employed. Maybe they spent their days up there fixing the plumbing or driving a van, who knew? Much as you could talk about what the government and the aliens were doing up there, everyone just knew not to ask too much about what anyone sitting in the cafe really did for a paycheck in the same place.

And, of course, there were people who worked at the cafe and inn itself. They washed the dishes. They did the laundry, carrying piles of rough white towels in their arms. They mopped the floors and scraped the grills and served the Alien Burgers. Some of the cafe workers were locals, but many had just drifted to this strange place in the middle of nowhere and later drifted off again. A topic of conversation that came up now and then was that several of these drifters had driven for years without driver's licenses.

Alongside the die-hard rural Western discourse against the licensing of guns, alongside the endless rumination about UFOs and what the government was hiding up there at Area 51, people talked, sometimes, about the anxieties raised by the Department of Motor Vehicles.

One afternoon, a dishwasher named Ken—who was stretched out in the back of my car, with his wife Linda riding in front—told me that everything about you lies in the opaque black coding bar on the back of your driver's license. I'd heard suspicious talk about driver's licenses before from antigovernment conspiracy theorists and fundamentalist Christians. In Austin, Texas, where I'd done previous fieldwork with UFO experiencers and where I stopped on my way to Rachel, Carla, the former leader of the UFO Experiencers' Support Group, had shown me a videotape made by Alex Jones, a local radio show host with a conspiratorial vision. Carla sent it along with me to give to the people at the Little A'Le'Inn, whom she felt would identify with it as she did. Carla and I watched the tape together in her Airstream trailer near the outskirts of town. She dragged intensely on her cigarettes as she took in Jones's message for the umpteenth time. In one segment, Alex Jones could be seen protesting the new procedure of *thumb printing* at the Austin Department of Motor Vehicles (DMV). *They* want to register you through the body now—not just to leave their mark on you, as is promised in the Book of Revelation, but to capture the mark of your physical individuation, to track you with your own embodied trace. Links from Alex Jones's website, it turned out, led to a whole slew of antilicensing outrage. A Christian family in Alabama was suing the state for demanding that the licensing of drivers be accompanied by social security numbers (SSNs). The biblical mark of the beast was recast in the ordinary procedures of state bureaucracy; in its tracking and surveillance the state was becoming profanely omnipotent, displacing the awesome power of God with the power of computers.

The encroaching pervasiveness of social security numbers, long felt to be part of Satan's plan by some apocalyptic Christians, intensifies as it appears to be mandated in more and more venues. A sample letter to the government in the movement to "Resist Enumeration" argues:

> More and more people are beginning to ask why–why does the government need all this personal information linked to my SSN? And why am I being pressured into getting a social security number for my children?

> The Bible provides answers to these questions, along with instruction on how we should respond to the ever-increasing demands for citizens to be numbered. God's People are admonished, by clearly stated example, to resist being numbered by government.
>
> We're told that King David wanted to "know the number of the People" under his authority (2 Samuel 24:2). And, Satan caused David to number all Israel (1 Chronicles 21:1). God's Word further states that David's command to number Israel "was evil in the sight of God" (1 Chronicles 21:7). Because of the People's acquiescence to the king's enumeration plan, God sent a plague UPON THE PEOPLE (1 Chronicles 21:14). The "People" are now, once again facing new demands from the modern day "kings" to be numbered and registered. And again it is the responsibility and duty of the PEOPLE to resist; regardless of how powerful or godly the particular ruling authority claims (or appears) to be, and regardless of the sincerity of their justifications. For, it is the PEOPLE that will be held accountable if they do not resist. (http://www.networkusa.org, accessed June 2004)

Here the emphasis on the word *people* foregrounds iconicities between two fundamentalist texts, the Bible and the Constitution. Just as the power of the state tries to usurp the power of God, the power of a monarchlike, computerized system usurps the power of democracy: *the "people" are now again facing new demands from the modern day "kings."* Carla, who grew up in a strict Christian home, no longer went to church (and no longer ran the UFO abductee support group), but she religiously attended a Constitutional Study Group to track the encroachments of these powers that be.

This resemblance between biblical and constitutional narratives against the surveillance of kings is not interpreted historically (that is, it does not discuss the biblical background of the writers of the Constitution.) Rather, the paradigmatic, or simultaneous, axis is foregrounded. And so the resemblance becomes not historical but poetic. A structure is felt to lurk below the surface of such resemblances, and, just barely visible, its glimmer becomes uncanny. The parallelism between signs becomes yet another sign, pointing to a referent too large and pervasive to fully grasp.

But you don't need a Christian paradigm (or any explicit ideology) to identify with such feelings. Rather, you need a specific orientation toward power, an inchoate sense of your own distance from its invisible source, and a feeling of things slipping away into vast computerized networks (see also

Dean 1998). The prophecy nods to a felt sense of our world being changed into another world, transformed by rushing technological advances in surveillance. This feeling acquires apocalyptic weight and biblical grounding.

Now, as we sped along the empty desert highway, Ken took my license again and examined it. The thin magnetic strip, I noticed, actually resembled the redacted, blacked-out segments of documents released grudgingly by the government in UFO-related documents secured through the Freedom of Information Act. The horizontal shape of the strip suggested a line of writing "inside" or "beneath" it.

Ken said: "*They got everything in there*—when you were *born*, what you did in the *military*, where you *lived*, what *crimes* you done . . . just . . . everything!" Such items, even if they are on file (and who knows?), can never add up to "everything" about the phenomenological self, but the flat list was deepened for Ken by the immense single metafact that *they know*.

For the second time in less than a month, I was taking a middle-aged cafe worker—Ken's wife Linda this time—to get a driver's license in Tonopah, the next town to the west, 110 miles away. Our car was the only one making its way through the desert, through federally owned ranchland and the invisible borders of military property. We craned our necks to watch F-16s swoop in formation in the sky just south of the road, then stopped the car to blow the horn at meandering cows.

Two weeks before I'd taken a fifty-four-year-old woman named Lee on this same trip. Lee was a drifter and had come to Rachel after reading in the *Weekly World News* that aliens frequented the cafe. She herself was part alien—a hybrid, she said. She'd known since she was a little girl that something wasn't right. Her parents seemed foreign to her, and the world was not her own. Then one day she was abducted. *Take me, take me, I want to go*, she'd said, lifting her arms to the sky. When they returned her to earth, she knew that her real father was an alien kept hostage at Area 51 by the powers that be.

One day Lee had asked me to take her to get her driver's license at the DMV. For decades, she'd drifted through the country without one, but now she wanted to get right. And so I took her on out to Tonopah and sat with her while she pored over the test. I watched the intensity of her concentration while she labored over questions of the law. She flunked the test so badly that the girls behind the desk looked at her with wide eyes and asked if she had the right booklet. On the drive home, she announced a decision to take her camper and move on out to Tonopah, to park somewhere in the desert near the DMV and go back every day to the clean, cold office until she passed the test. It would be a symbol of entry into some indescribable realm of legitimacy, with her picture on it. "Why not," she said, "it's free. The test is free." And the next day she was gone, off to begin a quest.

Linda, Ken, and I looked futilely for Lee now as we drove along the route she'd come before. We knew she was parked illegally somewhere out here in the scrubby desert, living without running water or any way to get more, vulnerable to anyone who came along. Her ramshackle camper was filled with photos of some past life and dozens of water bottles for the battles at the end of the world. She'd told me once that she came from a planet that had no birth certificates, money, or temperature. *It's not like your earth where I come from*. Bureaucratic tokens such as money and birth certificates—and licenses—were as naturalized on earth as temperature, and deep down she *remembered* a home without them. Now she was going to stay in this barren place for easy access to the DMV. For her, the driver's license was an ambivalent passport into the world of power and law.

Linda, my current passenger, had been licensed at one time, unlike Lee. But Linda had gotten into some bureaucratic tangles when she moved between states. In her forties, she had a gaunt face that seemed much older. There was a look of pain in her eyes and in the square set of her jaw, and nearly every morning she was in fact painfully ill, often doubled over in pain from a stomach-stapling operation that had taken off two hundred pounds but never set right inside her. The stomach-stapling operation was an ordinary, material sign indexing an alternate imagined self and its potential life story. I hoped it really was the only thing making her so sick, for she'd come to Rachel from a life of small-time prostitution and drug addiction in Las Vegas.

In their final weeks in Vegas, Linda and Ken had been desperate. When Pat, the owner of the Little A'Le'Inn, came to the Salvation Army there to look for new workers, it was a stroke of fortune, though not the kind people hope for in Vegas. But Linda said without it she'd be dead. She couldn't have survived Vegas much longer.

Once things had been different. She had built a decent working-class life, modest but respectable, based on hard work and skill. She'd been a waitress for a decade in one of the hyperclean and regular chains that thread across the United States. At the little desert cafe in Rachel, waitressing with quick movements and forearm-stacked dishes, Linda spoke of her years at the Tucson Pie Hut as a marker of professionalism and, more, of a different orientation toward the world before things had slipped out of control.

She said: *We went to Vegas on a dream.* Like many who flood into that city, they wanted not just to get rich but to start over. When they got there, though, nothing worked out the way they had planned. They gambled and partied, giddy with the carnival of possibility after years of the military and solid, decent work that never quite goes anywhere. Their drug use went out of control, and the foundation of working-class life seemed to slide out from beneath them before they realized what was happening. In their final weeks in Vegas, Linda and Ken, along with Ken's brother Alex, had given up hope and were homeless, sleeping under a bridge.

Ken was half a generation younger than his wife, a handsome African American man with a distant smile. Often I wondered what Ken thought when the bar at the cafe was full of the local white rural men, the cowboys and farmworkers and drinkers who sometimes made racist jokes as if he weren't there. Ken's brother Alex, a Desert Storm vet who worked as a cook in the cafe, sometimes sat on the steps of my trailer and reminisced about life back home. He sang an old hymn he'd learned from their grandmother, one I'd heard from UFO abductees in Texas: *The earth is not my home, I'm just a-passin' through.* But it was Ken who seemed to be just passing through. In Rachel, he affected a mood so impenetrably affable that it seemed sometimes he *wasn't* really there, as if he were reserving his real opinions for a less unreal place. And then he would burst into sudden rages that evaporated again as if they hadn't occurred.

But today in my car, musing about the magnetic strip on the driver's license, Ken seemed not to mind about anything. It was good to get away even for a half-day's trip to the Tonopah DMV. A month earlier, his brother Alex had been wrongly charged with driving a stolen car—it wasn't stolen, but the person who sold it to him hadn't bothered to change the tags. Now the three of them had no legal car, no way to go anywhere unless someone else would drive them the two hundred miles to Vegas on their day off. And it was clear, though they never said so, that a black man driving an illegally tagged car would certainly be stopped in rural Nevada. Last time they had a day off and bummed a ride to Vegas, Ken and Linda had come back depressed; without a car, they didn't know what to do and sat the whole time staring at the cinderblock walls of their cheap motel room.

But life in rural Nevada was a new frontier, and they were again starting over. The three of them were anxious to fix things up, to become legal. They were all living in a trailer a few steps from the cafe, had fixed it up *real nice* with plants and decorations, and had adopted a puppy from the Travises' latest litter. Unlike the intoxicating possibility of Vegas, starting over in Rachel was overlaid with the historical narrative of a stark and sober pioneer story. Ken and Linda were *clean*—"don't even *want* the drugs here," said Linda—the desert itself was "like a rehab center." Here, she said, you take responsibility for yourself. You work all day, and you're too tired to party afterward, and you have to be at the cafe at 8 A.M. Yes, the cafe workers would drink after shift and maybe drive on out to the black mailbox where UFOs were spotted, hopping into a car with some young tourists . . . and sometimes one guy was late to work with a hangover, but he kept trying to get back on track. For all the workers trying to start over after an abject turn in Vegas, a "rehab" discourse mingled with an imagined pioneer discourse. Their conflation created the promise of a new frontier for the self.

The "up from Vegas" workers saw themselves differently here, and shyly, on this road trip to get licensed, Ken and Linda told me of their new dream. They had drifted long enough; they would settle and live here. They would save up their wages and tips. With hard work and time, they would buy land across the Extraterrestrial Highway from the Little Ale'Le'Inn, and on their land they would build a UFO-themed putt-putt golf course. They had planned it all—*the tourists drive up and have nothing to do after eating an Alien Burger, well now they can come play* UFO *putt-putt golf*. Ken and Linda would be their own bosses; they would own their land.

This didn't happen. There were struggles between Pat and the Salvation Army workers, and after a while the lot of them left Rachel. A year later no one at the cafe knew where they were anymore.

But that day Linda entered the frosty, gleaming office of the DMV. Although there was never a line, never more than one or two people in the place, you had to make an appointment a week in advance—an empty gesture of bureaucratic rationalization that made the Rachel people smirk. And that day Linda passed her driver's test. Afterward we went to Burger

King to celebrate Linda's new license. They insisted on buying me lunch. She had passed back into the franchise of the state.

Then, driving through the hard-bitten military base town of Tonopah, with its dusty hills and severe-looking casinos, something happened to dampen Linda's accomplishment. Our car was pulled over by a police officer. He had, I think, done a double take at a black man driving in the deeply rural West with two white women. The cop vaguely hinted at a driving infraction but didn't even bother to issue a false ticket. He just wanted to know why we were driving in his town. He manipulated a heavy silence, creating a thick sense of trepidation. And when he saw that my driver's license and plates were from different states he looked baffled. I'd never bothered to get a new license after I'd moved to New York City from Texas, and I had never worried about it. As he stared ominously at my license, I could feel us bluffing and dueling, him flashing the power of the state and me flaunting the disregard for minutiae that indexed my own middle-class ease, two small expressions of the powers that be. But in his eyes I saw us all as a motley bunch at his mercy. It was tense until he decided to just let us go.

I was relieved to get away. But an uneasy feeling subdued us. I was angry; it was so clearly a racist harassment. Ken and Linda dreamed out the windows as we sped past the Tonopah Test Range, with its 1950s-style rocket at the fence. The setting sun turned the desert copper colors. Ken slept, and Linda told me about her life, repeated her waitressing resume, her history of moving around the country with a military dad. *You know I come from a good family*, she said.

Two hours after we'd been stopped by the police officer, Linda, Ken, and I descended the last hill to see Rachel, ten more miles down the road in the valley below, a tiny encampment that from here looked both staunch and vulnerable in the nothingness of the desert. That's when Linda spotted the UFO. It was hovering on the coppery mountain to the north, a blinking and unnatural glitter, like a mirror tilted to signal us. *Wake up Ken, she said, That's a UFO, there it is.* Ken and Linda watched it with attentive acceptance. *Yeah—that's something.* As we neared, the thing seemed to grow, becoming more metallic and gleaming more brightly with each mile.

There's nothing up there usually, Linda said. *I've come this way before, there's nothing. It's just the mountain. That is a UFO.* I couldn't argue—I, too, had come this way many times and had never seen anything like this on the mountain. A few miles later the bright, growing gleam disappeared as if a switch had been thrown. An unsettled feeling of the uncanny was palpable, specific as scent.

We had sped out of the world of ordinary power, away from the downward pull of racist cops and frosty DMV offices. Now power was emanating instead from Area 51, the awesome center of inscrutable omnipotence, the place where the magic of the state gets infused with the supernatural. The cop's small, homely injury of the hour before evaporated in this shift to imagination. Yet this unidentified shining object was not wholly shocking. The mystery of its power was still inside the experienced fabric of things.

Did Ken and Linda think this UFO was an alien spaceship or a top-secret military experiment? As usual, it did not seem to matter. What resonated was the very *fact of power*—its vastness, its hidden sources, and its just visible clues. What mattered was its potential for transformation and the strange pleasure of tearing holes in the real. In the cafe, Linda and Ken told everyone about the UFO, how it had glittered and then *just like that* disappeared. They didn't mention the cop.

Later I talked to an old rancher who laughed at the UFO idea, teased me about it with his dead serious, western style of teasing, and finally said we'd seen the sunset reflection of some metallic piece from the old ghost mine up on Tempiute Mountain. But that, I thought, was uncanny, too. The old mine was the trace of dreams that had existed long before Lee's or Ken and Linda's, where other pioneers had come to dig for prospects, to wreck their bodies, to die or move on. A few old miners still lived in Rachel, struggling with state and corporate agencies for a few dollars, requesting their due compensation for busted up backs and lungs and sick and tired of all *the forms*.

Theorizing the Uncanny

While there is a long history of ethnographic writing on religion, what of the uncanny eruptions into ordinary postmodern life—eruptions that are, in discourse and experience, often located "outside" traditional social-spiritual structures? And how does the indeterminate nature of what the ethnographer is trying to represent infect the way he or she chooses to portray it in writing?

This question of representation is more than a matter of simple style; it bleeds into all the others. Thinking through the uncanny heightens my sense of the "something more" (Stewart 1995: 5–6) in story, and my own ethnographic voice in this essay tries to mimic its poetic process. Uncanny narrative reminds us of how even ordinary language strains to exceed its literal, referential domain through its metaphoric and indeterminate capacities. Through its emphasis on poetic structure, its allegorical levels of unconscious political struggle, and the layered history of its voices, uncanny stories foreground and amplify the ambiguities inherent in all narrative—my own ethnographic one included.

One thing is clear: the uncanny in America is ambivalent about power, ricocheting between centrifugal and centripetal desires (cf. Bakhtin 1981). It sometimes seeks to unify story fragments into master narratives and then fractures them again. On the one hand, it strains toward rupture; on the other, it works through an obsessive attention to structure.

This tension between structure and its breakdown informs both the uncanny and the poetic capacity of language. I suggest that the uncanny is strongly linked to what Roman Jakobson (1960) called the poetic function of language, from which there arise inseparable aesthetic and social implications. Below I want to briefly discuss some elements in the work of Tsvetan Todorov and Sigmund Freud, two major theorists of the uncanny, and connect them to Jakobson's understanding of the poetic function of language.

In Todorov's (1975) structural sense of literary genre, the fantastic, the uncanny, and the marvelous exist in direct relation to each other. What Todorov calls the "fantastic," not the uncanny, however, is most like Freud's ([1919] 1963) description of the *unheimlich* (the uncanny).[2] In Todorov's generic scheme, the uncanny means that a strange, troubling effect is resolved by the end of the story through its final attribution to natural causes. In what he calls the "marvelous," the strange effect belongs to another world in which magic events are part of the order of things. But the fantastic, he says, is never resolved one way or the other. Is it natural or supernatural? The fantastic "occupies the duration of this uncertainty" (1975: 25).[3] A hesitation develops between structures of expectation. Todorov's fantastic creates a liminal space between the real and the imaginary and makes manifest the tension between them.

Although Todorov's definition of the "fantastic" (rather than the "uncanny") more closely correlates with my own understanding of American UFO discourse, he mentions briefly that the uncanny depends on a sense of encroaching "taboo," a disturbing return of some secret impulse. As he acknowledges, this is his one point of agreement with Freud: for Freud, similarly, the uncanny signifies a dreadful return of the repressed.

Freud writes that the unheimlich is revealed but was supposed to remain hidden (especially surrounding death or object loss, e.g., castration).[4] It would seem, he writes, that the unheimlich would be simply the opposite of the ordinary German word *heimlich* or *heimisch*, (familiar, native, or belonging to the home); it would seem that the unheimlich would be frightening simply in opposition, because it is *un*familiar. But the truth is more complex. Tracing the history of the two words, Freud finds that among its shades of meaning, *heimlich* (familiar) sometimes means its opposite, *unheimlich*.

> What is *heimlich* thus comes to be *unheimlich* . . . *heimlich* is not unambiguous . . . on the one hand it means that which is familiar and congenial and on the other, that which is concealed and kept out of sight. . . . Thus *heimlich* is a word the meaning of which develops towards an ambivalence until it finally coincides with its opposite, *unheimlich*." (Freud 1963: 375–77)

This foray into what he considers "the aesthetic . . . [domain] of feeling" suggests that the uncanny presents a problem of poetics. It reveals a glimmer of the chaos always hinted at in the ordering principles of opposition. On one level, here is an opposition (heimlich/unheimlich) that merges and becomes disturbing through the loss of its *difference*. It is a merging both longed for as a kind of ultimate union and abjectly feared because, "coinciding with its opposite," the wiping out of difference means the loss of meaning, a chaotic absence of distinction.

This play between difference and unification in language recalls the poetic function and the effects of repetition. Freud says that the uncanny disrupts the ordinary flow of time when an otherwise unremarkable event inexplicably recurs, seemingly pointing to an invisible agency or design through what he calls "involuntary repetition" (Freud 1963: 390).

> We of course attach no importance to the event when we give up a coat and get a cloakroom ticket with the number, say, 62; or when we find that our cabin on board ship is numbered 62. But the impression is altered if two such events . . .

happen close together, if we come across the number 62 several times in a single day. . . . We do feel this to be uncanny and unless a man is utterly hardened and proof against the lure of superstition he will be tempted to ascribe a secret meaning to this obstinate recurrence of a number." (390–91)

In this passage, the feeling of the *unheimlich* begins to match up with a feeling about form. The events or images themselves are meaningless. It is when they are suddenly revealed as related to each other that their connection grows charged with the intimation of hidden significance, a "secret meaning," or an intuition of relations that seem to be—somehow—purposefully constructed.

As Roman Jakobson (1960) famously wrote, the poetic function of language foregrounds the "palpability" of signs with attention oriented to the message itself. It "deepens the fundamental dichotomy of signs and objects" (358), turning the major emphasis of the signifier from reference to poesis. Through "the reiterative figure of sound" (359), the flow of speech is "experienced as it is with musical time" (358; see also Feld 1994: 190). Jakobson's insight was that these effects occur through the poetic use of repetition with variation. For Jakobson, too, these features give an intimation of the structural relations in language that, on the level of everyday talk, are usually unconscious. Repetition with variation "projects the principle of equivalence from the axis of selection into the axis of combination. . . . Equivalence, normally the device of selection, is promoted to the constitutive device of sequence" (358).

This is virtually a cubist insight, or like the ineffable sensation of seeing your own bones in an x-ray, the structure beneath the skin of things. One of its effects in poetry is a feeling of heightened significance that transcends the referential meanings of the words themselves into a gesture toward their underlying linguistic relationships. In the uncanny, a similar experience of just-glimpsed parallels and heightened significance moves urgently toward its "something more," the just-glimpsed "secret meaning." There is a *feeling* of a hidden "deep structure," which if seen in its entirety would finally "make sense" of the immanently open-ended fantastic.

Within the charged social spaces that give rise to an "escape into the subversive power of strangeness" (Steedley 1993: 76), then, repetition with variation produces not just a sense of formal aesthetic pleasure but even more seductively and urgently the intense feeling of meaningfulness that is the engine of uncanny discourse's social life. And a sense of irreducible openness combines with a sense of underlying, always-incomplete structure, one that is still imagined as potentially—often apocalyptically—unified.

The Fantastic, Uncanny Real

Uncanny and fantastic narrative dismantles conventions of realism and replaces them with irreducible uncertainty. But at the same time, when told outside the bounds of fiction, it usually demands to be read as *real*, as true, that is, to some ambiguous but felt and embodied experience. When the uncanny is encountered as part of an ethnographic relationship, therefore, the emotional force of its stories compels the listener to attend to the teller with the same openness demanded by the genres of ordinary personal narrative. But in fantastic stories what is the referent? Where do you locate the real?[5]

Perhaps the places to look are in the trails of resemblance these stories produce—the repetition with variation that becomes a sign in itself. Then you might hear the distorted echoes of histories whose wounds have never healed. In narratives of aliens conquering the borders of vast worlds and intimate bodies, you might point to innumerable, unspoken narratives of class, race, and gender and to multiple, still bitter histories of colonization, destruction, and loss. You could look to the piled-up moments of class-, race-, and gender-inflected fantasy and humiliation that are swallowed as soon as they occur, leaving their traces in the everyday texture of life. For the hidden "it" of the uncanny is not necessarily a single, unified object but rather the *too-muchness* of an entire social field of interconnected memories and experiences striving to create a story that makes sense.

Through the uncanny, in other words, we can sometimes see other ways of entering into the lived terrains of class and race and gender—categories that, if spoken as abstractions in many social worlds, sound too flat, too distant and formal to encompass the overlappings and partialities of their embodied and felt effects. You might think, first, of the workings of everyday life. In a passionate critique of British sociological objectifications of class and gender, Carolyn Steedman writes of working-class "longing" in her own mother's desire—not for revolution or even class solidarity but rather for redemption through the material things that lay out of her reach, clothes and houses, which grew charged and powerful. Instead of projecting an "articulated politics" of either class or gender, Steedman asks, "what becomes of the notion of class-consciousness when it is seen as a structure of feeling? . . . Class and gender, and their articulations, are the bits and pieces from which psychological selfhood is made"(1986: 7). Then coveted things become signs in an alternate life story, one that rides the back of everyday life and its random disenchantments.

Here, as in the uncanny, stories can circle around their missing objects, infusing the boundaries of categories such as class and gender with their disturbances and desires. Sometimes to enter inside those structures of feeling we call class, race, and gender is to notice the ways in which they don't stay put on their own foundations. The spaces of *departure* from the rooted signs of class position are often the most intricately imagined, as well as the most despised. There is the disgrace and voluptuousness of giving up while falling from one class position to another. There is the parallel shame of desire exposed amid the pervasive narrative culture of class mobility, the visible straining after a still unnaturalized habitus. These liminal spaces themselves become fertile ground for uncanny elaboration, for stories of unwanted dislocations and sublime flights from the ordinary. Then tropes of a watchful, panoptic, cosmic-political government or aliens resonate with submerged understandings of (and ambivalence toward) hegemonic power as pervasive and structuring to the core—a core that still protests but in the language it is given.

This is not to say, of course, that abductees or UFO witnesses come only from a specific class, race, or gendered position (although it is true that specific uncanny narratives take hold with particular force in specific social worlds). Rather, I am trying to tease out oblique understandings of power, social imaginaries that are co-constructed from multiple points of view. Here I try to write against those high-popular models of intellectual history that numbingly trace changes in public consciousness through a sort of rationalized canon of American Events; in this model, for example, "we" lost faith in the government because of the Kennedy assassination, the Vietnam War, and Watergate. You could argue whether Vietnam or Watergate was the turning point that led to the groundswell of antigovernment sentiment and thus the turn to "conspiracy theories." Or, objecting to the naturalized "we," you could reinvigorate the argument by pointing out that many oppressed groups, such as Native Americans and African

Americans, had mistrusted the government long before the 1960s. But for uncanny discourse such an interruption is still not a productive enough difference. For instead of the monolithic master narrative of American consciousness, you are now faced with an equally familiar image of parallel but uncontaminated social memories, each "belonging" to the heirs of its own group only. In contrast, social memories viewed through uncanny perspectives lead to a different historical narrative model. Their signs do not stay put inside the track of identity. They force you to notice the play of many social memories, from many different times and places, arranged in hybrid forms that intensify their points of connection. Dense with partly recognizable tropes, half-articulated memories, and condensed, intensified, and rearranged particles of other social narratives, they complicate theories of cultural replication and discursive circulation (Urban 1996) and remind us of the complex mediation of all semiosis.

Through the uncanny, perhaps, *the naturalized* may grow contingent with the latent critique in its stories of alternate possibilities. Things as they are, things that appear to be as they must be, threaten to fall apart. In the light of an uncanny space, these naturalized rules *almost* appear to be what they are, constructions. As Turner (1981) wrote of the liminal, this space breaks down code into its parts, which loom grotesquely out of order. They acquire the horror of taboo in Mary Douglas's (1966) classic sense of the term, of things out of place that threaten a naturalized order. Douglas recognized that such ambiguity has its seductions as well as dread; "the richness of poetry depends on [it] . . . aesthetic pleasure arises from the perceiving of inarticulate forms" (37).

Like poetry, they are glimpsed in their constitutive parts. But if they were to appear *fully* as conventions, they would no longer be uncanny. In the latter case, their repetition and parallelism would create fully crafted, politically rich, aesthetic critiques. In the poetic decomposition of the uncanny, however, such critical denaturalization isn't ever fully complete. It remains half articulated, emerging not in conscious protest to oppression but in more oblique reactions to power. An alternate order starts to form in the imagination, rising from the partially visible hegemonic one—an order in which elements from various imaginings blend, intensifying all their effects. You could say that too much ideological light and air stunt the growth of the uncanny's distortions.

There are myriad differences in specific uncanny discourses, of course.

Still there is something to notice, even if it keeps slipping away. Perhaps this thing I am after does occur tactically, or just as a side effect in situations of overt oppression, when options for resistance fold into despair—where options for resistance seem to be shutting down, during genocide or intense fast occupation—places where there seems to be no way out except finally through apocalyptic destruction, rising desperately from the message itself. In effect then, a social perspective on the uncanny twists the ongoing anthropological question of agentive "resistance," in this case with a sense of the ambivalence and ambiguity in the encounter among power, imagination, loss, and desire.[6]

In a social understanding of the uncanny, then, a few essential themes emerge. One is a sense of vague but pressing danger that is uncannily expressed not so much by direct reference to specific social conditions as by attention to the poetics of the secret message. Another is a sense of contingent experience inextricable from its telling in narrative—a slippery experience that can't be finalized by official truths or totalizing hegemonies. With one foot inside the dominant, the uncanny plays on the liminality of partially articulated ideology—a semiemergent "political unconscious" (cf. Jameson 1981). The uncanny story denaturalizes dominant histories, imagining ghostly pasts and potential futures in elaborated discourses of nostalgia and apocalypse. But the story's endings are not predetermined. Out of such longings emerge restriction and possibility, containment and freedom, and license to imagine.

Notes

I would like to thank the people of Rachel, Nevada, for their friendship and hospitality during my stays there. I also thank Debbora Battaglia, Erica David, Jodi Dean, Aaron Fox, Kathleen Stewart, and my dissertation writing group for comments on earlier drafts. All errors are, of course, my own. This essay is dedicated to the memories of Joe Travis and La Rae Fletcher of Rachel, Nevada—vibrantly warm and spirited people who are sorely missed in Rachel and beyond.

1. For much more about Area 51 that is beyond the scope of this article, see Darlington 1997 and especially the illuminating ethnographic journalism of Patton 1998. More on life around Area 51 is also detailed in Lepselter, 2005.

2. For instance, Todorov uses the example of Hoffman's tales to analyze the "fantastic" genre, but these same tales are used by Freud to interpret the *unheimlich*.

3. "In a world which is indeed our world . . . there occurs an event which cannot

be explained by the laws of this same familiar world. The person who experiences the event must opt for one of two possible solutions: either he is the victim of an illusion . . . and laws of the world then remain what they are; or else the event has indeed taken place . . . [in which case] reality is controlled by laws unknown to us. *The fantastic occupies the duration of this uncertainty*. Once we choose one answer or the other, we leave the fantastic for a neighboring genre. . . . The concept of the fantastic is therefore to be defined in relation to those of the real and the imaginary" (Todorov 1977: 25, emphasis mine).

4. This connection between the uncanny and repression has been productively understood ethnographically to interpret fabulous experiences under conditions of social repression, especially surrounding the idea of the vanishing "homeland" or "native" in modernity (see, e.g., Steedley 1993; Tsing 1994; and Pemberton 1994). For instance, as Ivy (1995) points out, the yearned for, nostalgic rural homeland became a marker of the uncanny in Japan as it was repressed by the forces of modernity. The world of origins and nature becomes densely imagined as both safe and terrifying, natural and strange, and filled with the returning spirits of a repressed realm of the natural. This idea of ambivalence toward the vanishing real occurs also in the uncanny poetics of the hometown in the United States (Lepselter 1997).

5. For an illuminating discussion of the problem of the real in UFO discourses, see Dean 1998. The "real" as a discourse in UFO worlds is elaborated in Lepselter 1997. In terms of my further observations here, also see Dean 1998 and Roth 1995 for elaboration on images of race and colonization in UFO discourse.

6. As Mary Steedley puts it, writing of Karo uncanny narratives at the border of totalizing, modernist forces in Indonesia:

> These stories are not simply products of individual imagination; nor are they transparent reports of what happened to a certain time and place. They exist within socially constituted patterns of domination and subordination, and within culturally defined patterns of meaning. They are structured by Karo narrative conventions as well as by the social context of their telling. Directly or indirectly they refer to other stories, other experiences, other moments in the teller's life. . . . But these stories are not told as illustrations of some officially established generic truth. They are told because of their strangeness: because they are partial misfits within an official order of things. (Steedley 1993: 239)

"For Those Who Are Not Afraid of the Future": Raëlian Clonehood in the Public Sphere

DEBBORA BATTAGLIA

This essay is a call for ethnographic work and broader anthropological research along three lines.

The first is to critically engage the social phenomenon of *technoscience spirituality*—by which I mean "hard faith" in science and technology, future. The second is to expand our understanding of the relation of this phenomenon to mass media production, circulation, and reception. The third is to approach the work of producing ethnography as a complexifying "supplement" (Battaglia 1999) to existing disciplinary knowledge of the faith-science-media articulation. From this approach, ethnography can, on the one hand, destabilize prior knowledge and on the other hand open conventional programs of representation to the possibility of exceeding themselves through interdisciplinary and also intermethodological engagement.

Taken in these concrete yet indeterminate terms, new pathways open to "studying out" from our disciplinary comfort zones (as all the essays in this book in some sense do) while acknowledging that the gravitational pull of disciplinary methods and histories is not altogether a bad thing. Bearing in mind this creative tension, I offer some moments from "the fields" of the Raëlian movement as a case in point.

> I saw the Elohim insert a cell taken from my forehead into a huge aquarium-like machine . . . and then watched a perfect copy of myself grow in just a few seconds.—Raël, *Yes to Human Cloning*

> "Let us embrace Science and the new technologies unfettered, for it is these which will liberate mankind from the myth of god, and free us from our age-old fears, from disease, death, and the sweat of labor."—Raël (rael-science-select-owner@yahoogroups.com, accessed December 26, 2002)

The Raëlians are a creationist-science religious movement that claims between 2,800 and 55,000 members worldwide—depending on your source—who are drawn to the idea that "extraterrestrial scientists created life on Earth" (a signature of official e-mail messages). These "Designers" human beings, created "in their own image" using advanced cloning technology.[1] Thus, for Raëlians the God function was performed by scientists—a point that distinguishes them from most intelligent design creationists (Pennock 2001), who conscript science into a (mainly) Christian politics and belief system (Harding 2000). One effect of this unequivocal atheism is to open up social space for defectors from the world religions who wish to remain, in the words of one devout subject (a former Muslim and neurobiologist then doing research at Harvard), "deeply religious" but also "advocates of science." The Raëlian emphasis on creativity, and on human beings as their creators' supreme "*artworks in progress*," further encourages a social eugenics and expressive culture in which the physical person becomes the focus of technologies of "genius," as Raël terms mankind's inherent capacity for higher consciousness.[2] The movement's signature "sensual meditation" and instructions in psychosocial discipline and interpersonal refinement, alternative health, and so forth are offered for the slender price of admission to annual seminars in East Asia, Africa, Australia, Europe, and the Americas. And the reward for realizing one's genius is nothing less than immortality. Friendly surveillance spacecraft observe individuals' progress, and scan and archive the DNA of the "awakened" for use in cloning them offworld should humankind violently destroy Planet Earth. The bombing of Hiroshima—Year One of the Raëlian calendar—and more recently the World Trade Center, as well as Middle East terrorist attacks and the war in Iraq, are given as evidence that all this is a matter of urgent anthropology. If I were to seek a succinct image of the Raëlian religion, I would describe it as a make-love-not-war peace movement, gone to science and technology. Thus, Raëlian "philosophy" reconciles the presumed "secular turn" in modernity (De Vries 2001) with a view of the physical person as a sacred scientific site. Offering community to "those who are not afraid of the future," the movement extends itself through "dissemination" events that deliver its messages and through tabloid-friendly publicity.

However, the creative center of the movement is the charismatic figure of His Holiness Raël—the French-born singer-songwriter, Formula I race car driver, and prophet formerly known as Claude Vorilhon (who calls himself the "fastest prophet on Earth").[3] Raël's messages to the faithful and others stream through the Internet and e-mail ether, and engage talk radio and television hosts, and world and local leaders, sometimes with the bestowal of honorary titles as Raëlian priests—for instance, on Senator John Kerry (for opposing George Bush), on the rap singer Eminem (for his protest video "Mosh"), on the mayor of San Francisco (for supporting gay marriage), and on others who make progressive news. Raëlians are less interested in UFOs than in "who's inside them," as I often heard it put, although their spiritual language and faith sites are often shared by other so-called UFO religions. But no other movement or religion has a Baby Eve (fig. 1).

Baby Eve

> Can you believe it? I went to speak at a private high school in Connecticut about human cloning, and the kids hadn't even heard of the Raëlians!—Gina Kolata, science correspondent, *New York Times* (personal communication, April 2003)

As was indicated to me by every one of the journalists I interviewed on the topic, the Raëlians' celebrity status among new religious movements, and consequently their media draw, is entirely a result of its human cloning agenda. Media interest peaked on December 26, 2002, when Brigitte Boisselier, director of Clonaid.com and a bishop in the Raëlian movement, announced in Florida that she had cloned a baby girl, who was to be called Eve. In no small part due to the phenomenally mediagenic Boisselier, the

FIG. 1. Baby Eve, a clone is born. (From the *New York Daily News*, December 28, 2002.)

announcement sent a seismic shock across the global mediascape, rekindling public and professional bioethical debate over human reproductive cloning and by extension therapeutic cloning, human genetic engineering, and assisted reproduction more generally.[4] Clonaid's website, which offers designer babies and pets cloned to order for a sizeable fee, did nothing to stem the tide of public response. To be sure, debate among secular ethicists was more formally than substantively rational and did not exclude established figures such as Leon Kass, who urged that the visceral negative response to the idea of Eve be taken as a sign of collective public wisdom; it was "thin" also in broader arenas. For example, on Court TV, an attorney in the state of Florida filed a preemptive lawsuit to place the alleged Baby Eve in the custody of court-appointed guardians on the grounds that she was the object of a criminal action before her life (by any legal definition) had even begun.

On the one hand, there is no better evidence than this that "something is going on in media all its own that reflects less on the particular events being reported than it does on the nature of our cultural pre-occupations and the way in which we process them" (Rushkoff 1996: 20).[5] And Raël and his publicists would embrace the argument that this "something" relates to how "the web of new media nodes can serve to foster new cultural growth" (21) but also new cross-cultural connections on a planetary scale. Thus, a colleague of mine could return from fieldwork in India, bearing the gift from Assam of *The Sentinel*'s December 28 front-page story of "The World's First Human Clone," with numerous follow-up stories on "Virtual Faith" and "The Man Who Met E.T.,"—subtitled "Is There a Faith Boom Out in Space?"—and "If Genes Were Wishes" in *The Telegraph Guwahati*, January 5, 2003.[6]

Yet the operations of media engagement are more contingent and complexly configured than any straightforward media optimism can justify. Simply on the level of my own research with Raëlians (intermittently in Canada, in the United States, and on the Internet since the summer of 2001) the birth announcement was immediately destabilizing. By day's end on December 26, I found myself—utterly surprised by the announcement and lacking the faintest notion of what was going on (alongside most of the Raëlian administrative "structure")—dodging science correspondents from the *Wall Street Journal* and other major newspapers, nonplussed. Frankly, my lack of information was a relief, given that I was unsympathetic to the tactics of the Raëlian publicity machine, which would render the scientific business and moral issues of human cloning a public spectacle on a global scale. Too, the media fallout was creating a living nightmare for Raëlians I knew personally. One couple's subsistence gardens near Raël's residence in Canada were trampled and their privacy wantonly invaded by paparazzi for weeks after the announcement. Other Raëlians tucked their star-logo pendants under their clothing and in effect sent their religious identities underground for months afterward. Blessedly, the story all but vanished from even talk radio and the tabloids by late January (it would resurface on anniversaries) near the time that an inside journalist who had offered to organize a scientific team of experts to confirm the cloning experiment abruptly broke off relations with Clonaid, suspecting a hoax. However, the phenomenon of "publicity," and as well the category of the "hoax," had, as I would learn, very different values for those on the peripheries than for the Raëlian structure. This fact presented no small challenge for ethnographic writing which would "converge with the real" (I take the phrase from Walter Benjamin), as diversely positioned subjects and media were busily co-constructing this.

Awakening

I began doing fieldwork with Raëlians in 55 A.H. (After Hiroshima), when I attended an "awakening" seminar for the faithful and anyone curious about the religion in the farming and industrial outskirts of Valcourt, Quebec Province, on the bucolic residential grounds of the Jardins du Prophete. This was the headquarters of the Raëlian movement in North America. At the time, its most prominent buildings were the hangar-sized UFOland museum and adjacent condominiums, a conference hall, and a four-hundred-seat performing arts theater and auditorium, all designed and built by Raëlian volunteers. There was a small reed-lined lake and spacious lawn on the grounds and a wooded campground with cabins, space for tents and trailers, and a few office buildings and facilities. From Valcourt, Raël and the guides of the structure, including the bishop-guides Daniel Chabot, a clinical psychologist and Raël's then likely successor, and Brigitte Boisselier, the bishop-chemist and director of Clonaid who announced the arrival of Baby Eve, coordinated their travels to annual seminars and quarterly ritual celebrations, each one a culturally distinct event. The annual seminars typically drew upward of six hundred persons in each location and together with the monthly and quarterly gatherings were almost the only occasions when Raëlians could "show themselves to themselves" (Myerhoff 1986: 261) as a sizable offline community, though, again, culturally themed. For example, one young woman described the Raëlian seminar in her Japanese homeland as "Asia-land"; a Swiss citizen explained that in Europe Raëlians were "more ceremonial" and saw Raël "like the Pope"; and in Canada a Toronto resident explained that it was "very Quebec" to stomp and clap in unison when Raël appeared onstage, "like in an ice hockey arena." Las Vegas was "very New Age," and Australia was "like a beach party." Note that I had asked the question "Are the seminars where you come from like this one?" Perhaps knowing that I was an anthropologist, the response took the form of highly reduced cultural images—as if produced for an album-sized "family of man." Yet beyond the seminar fields a very real online network was promoted and maintained; indeed,

Raël describes the Internet as a "religious experience" and the space of "electronic democracy" (cf. Turkle 1984) for "diffusing" the faith.

Anyone attending an annual seminar should have read Raël's foundational text, *The Messages Given by Extraterrestrials*—often simply called The Messages or The Book.[7] This is an account by Raël of his conversations with extraterrestrials in the French countryside in the early 1970s aboard a saucer-shaped spaceship. Here, so the story goes (and we could read it in The Messages, on printed exhibition labels in UFOland, on the Rael.org website, and in print media or hear it told on television or radio talk shows), Raël was invited to learn the truth that the first human beings were decidedly not "relatives of monkeys" but clones of the Elohim: "Those Who Came from Above."[8] In his more recent book, *Yes To Human Cloning* (2001), Raël and his coauthors elaborate a vision of a future world of "biological robots," "cyborgs" and "transhuman" entities where geniuses liberated from physical and psychological pain and brute labor can pursue their scientific and artistic interests and sensual pleasures. When Raëlians state their goal of "living The Messages" or "living The Book," they are voicing a faith in science as elemental to a spiritual ethics of self with the potential to generate a social blueprint for rationally enhanced personhood.

This utopian vision of rationality, which valorizes empirical facts and logic—not excluding what Raymond Williams terms the "structure of feelings"—is contrasted with the "mysticism" and pitiful ignorance of prescientific "primitive" (though still alien-created) peoples. A prime example is taken to be the "cargo cult" phenomenon in Melanesia. And, of course, friends urging me to visit UFOland's exhibition wonderland were certain I would be interested in this, must know about this, as an anthropologist: how people in their ignorance used imitative magic, not science, to influence alien aircraft to disgorge their "cargo" wealth not to colonizers and missionaries but to the local people, who should rightfully possess such powerful things.

Meanwhile, Raël himself played fast and free with "the facts" of Clonaid's actual location, resources, and project history—even boasting of the "hundreds of thousands of dollars worth of free publicity" he had garnered from previous disinformation campaigns (e.g., a former Clonaid laboratory in the Bahamas turned out to be a post office box). This gave no Raëlian that I knew of cause to doubt the movement. Global knowledge of the Elohim's existence is a sacred mission for the Raëlians, and "publicity" is a means through which to accomplish it. Only when The Messages are heard by all will the alien creators return to Earth to reunite in a productive relationship with humanity—not as Other but as Ancestor—and save it from its own violent impulses. Whatever the reality status, human cloning was in 2001 a rhetorical vehicle par excellence for reproducing more and more Raëlians, more and more "buzz." Thus, while it hardly takes a Raëlian genius to discern the logic of the cargo cult in this late capitalist representational economy—manufacture a body, actual or virtual, and They, the artistic offworld scientist-creators, will come and by a sympathetic logic so too will their human consumer offspring—to decontextualize publicity from its redemptive function would be to misrepresent the Raëlian worldview. And a Raëlian reader of a former version of this essay firmly reminded me of this problematic of faith-based "publicity," which sacrificed the Movement's peace and security to the necessary evil of demon journalists.[9]

Too, acts of publicity are embedded in the movement's commitment to public "diffusion" of knowledge in other, more open forums. In their dialogic mode, diffusion events include street-corner pamphleteering, lunchtime meetings, and art exhibitions in libraries and other public spaces, as well as performances linked to the apostasy campaign against the Roman Catholic Church (e.g., cross-burning actions across the street from public schools) and the circulation of petitions against the wars in Afghanistan and Iraq, gay and lesbian rights parades, and disrobing-for-peace demonstrations on the steps of the U.S. Capitol Building and at the Federal Bureau of Investigation (FBI) headquarters in Los Angeles—the latter citing a model of feminist protest from late-nineteenth-century Ghana, where women dressed skimpily as men mocked the hubris of tribal warfare (Delafosse 1913). Overall, then, the poetics and politics of the Raëlian religion locate a psychosocial "cyborg personhood" (Haraway 1991) at the armature of future life worlds, with the effect for me of raising larger questions about what counts as evidence and truth, and for whom, at the faith sites of postmodernity. It is on this note that I would invite you to enter the portals of some Raëlian cultural spaces and encounter some of the forms imagination takes where science is sacred, with a view to asking whether we should be going there.

Oxygenation

It is the first day of the Valcourt Summer Seminar. The theme this year is "the playful mind." "When the Elohim created life," Raël tells us in his opening address, "it was a *game*." This idea of "the game" of creation and the theme of the "ludic spirit" will run throughout the exercises and events of the next five days. But one exercise will always be taken seriously. This is the collective practice of "sensual meditation" that marks the start of the program of every seminar day. Sensual meditation is the unifying event of the local monthly gatherings wherever Raëlians live and of the larger regional quarterly gatherings that celebrate turning points in Raël's spiritual history of "awakening."[10]

At 9 A.M. sharp, then, I join the four-hundred-plus participants, most of us wearing our poly-cotton white robes called *djalabas*: our sartorial passports to the meditation exercises, purchasable at the time of registration. We settle into the plush theater seats, setting our Walkman radios to channels where the French spoken by Raël and the Quebecois of the other speakers will be translated simultaneously into English, Japanese, Spanish, and Portuguese. Newcomers are informed that these exercises are "nothing dangerous" and totally voluntary: this is not a "cult." We are told that the exercises will aid us in opening the machine of our body, opening the machine of our brain, and not to worry if we don't get quick results—we are seeking an efficient result. Now close our eyes, like the cameras to the world, so there is a black screen. We are going to go inside the machine of our body. Air is entering our body and leaving it again. Deeply, deeply. Oxygenating ourselves consciously. We shouldn't be afraid of oxygenating ourselves. As we breathe deeply in, deeply out, our internal computer will increase its efficiency. The oxygen—"compliments of the Raëlian Religion"—allows us to cleanse our body of toxins. "While you oxygenate yourself, listen to yourself breathing, your own rhythm is the rhythm of your genetic code . . . we open ourselves like a flower, let ourselves be penetrated by infinity." "Our cardiac rhythm slows down" and "we feel the large black eyes in the sky that look down at us with so much love." And now our voyage of harmony is about to begin. A wave of heat is rising from our toes slowly upward to our brains, to the luminous spot, like a laser dot, between our eyes and above, like a spiral. We follow the spiral inward; we are at the brain, the very heart of ourselves. Now we will begin to leave the room, like a balloon (I think of the pastel balloons of the stage design, suddenly understanding). We travel through the roof; we have a global vision of ourselves. And when we are ready we will begin to move back again down toward the planet Earth, toward the blue ball, as if we are in a space shuttle. We see Africa, all the continents, as we go back through the clouds, gently. We try to spot the little lake, the lawn, the cabins. And now we reenter the atmosphere of this great hall, all these people in white, in harmony.

In the last day's most intense meditation, we are led in imagining our own deaths, leaving our bodies behind. As Raël did, we travel to another planet, are reborn there, and afterward reenter the Earth, given our bearings as we hear that George W. Bush is unfortunately still the President of the United States. A photojournalist from the *Sunday Times of London* approaches me as I drift out of the auditorium with everyone else after the meditation. "That was fucking sinister, don't you think? I mean, Raël will revive you after you've died." I look at him as if he'd come from another planet. And as I return to objectivity I realize how pleasurable has been my abduction by technoscience spirituality. We reenter the auditorium after the break to the orchestral signature of Strauss's *Also Sprach Zarathustra*—which people here recognize as the theme from the film *2001: A Space Odyssey*.[11]

Dancing with a Martyr

> Hey Joe, where you goin' with that Book in your hand?
> Hey Joe, where you goin' with that Book in your hand?
> I'm goin' out to tell the people,
> That the Elohim are about to land . . .
> I heard it on CNN,
> Clonaid's gonna' clone the first human being.
> —A Raëlian band (to the tune of "Hey Joe" in the style of Jimi Hendrix)

Open another window, it is another day, and for some an entirely dissonant environment to the contemplative space of meditation—a "bordello" environment: the midweek open-air disco. On the large lawn beside the lake, which is hung with little floating UFO-shaped lanterns, huge speakers on black metal stands create a ring, the prosthetics of a sophisticated sound system. Soon they are pounding out popular Quebecois, American, and world music. Eventually someone motions for me to join in the dance, and I do. As many do, I dance with all and sundry. Then I notice that Raël has arrived in his gleaming white Jeep Cherokee with his young wife Sophie. Brigitte Boisselier, the chemist and director of Clonaid, arrives at the same time. Raël is dressed as usual in casual whites. Boisselier wears a little black party dress. This is the woman one anticloning spokesperson for the religious right has referred to as "The Devil." Boisselier and I have talked before, have had critical exchanges on her project of human reproductive cloning, but most especially the commodification of human babies—price, twenty thousand dollars—and the "designer baby" eugenic marketing that Clonaid brashly employs on the Internet (she will tell the CBS *Evening News* on June 3, 2003 that Clonaid is "not a company" but a "brand name" as she defends herself in a federal Internet fraud case). But at the moment we both want to dance. She waves and smiles, and we end up dancing with each other until someone from the sidelines calls her away. Still dancing, I watch them talking. He leaves. She returns and tells me, leaning in to speak in my ear above the loud music, that the Food and Drug Administration (FDA) has just sealed her laboratory.

Recall: It is summer 2001. Public, religious, and bioethical interest in human cloning is front-page news. Recently, Boisselier has spoken by invitation to a U.S. congressional committee, articulating her commitment to human cloning as a matter of faith-based, pro-choice reproductive rights, her commitment to helping couples and others who wish to produce a baby, for example, gay and lesbian couples, or the terminally ill man who will tell her, "I want to be reborn like a blank tape with the possibility to live only what I enjoyed." She cites parents such as the ones who are sponsoring her laboratory research at the moment: their ten-month-old child died accidentally in a minor surgical operation. The parents are desperate to have him cloned so that one day he will stand before his surgeons in court and accuse them of his wrongful death. These parents will later withdraw their support under intense media and government scrutiny, complaining that Boisselier is a "publicity hog." But tonight she is away from all this. She shakes her head. And then she starts to dance again. I am amazed. I ask her, "How can you dance at a moment like this?" And she responds, "What can we do? We must dance." And as her smile returns the only word to describe her countenance is *beatific*. I realize then that I am dancing with a martyr. And, indeed, in the days to come Boisselier will announce at the morning assembly that she will take her lab offshore if need be, that she will not be stopped in her mission to clone a human being—to explore the frontiers of science as what she terms "an alternative ethicist." Later a member of the Valcourt audience will write:

> Did you see her move on the stage when she came to talk to us about the latest scientific news? She wasn't walking, she was floating, soaring . . . visibly from happiness! Who knows, in the future History books perhaps we will read something that goes like this: "And the spirit of Brigitte soared above them, and their eyes were opened and they knew they were like gods." . . . Brigitte states to whoever wants to listen, that she will fight until the end to see her projects come to light. (Terrusse, *Apocalypse* 2001: 31)

And who would doubt it? Expelled from France as a "cultist" and relinquishing legal custody of her children as a consequence, Brigitte Boisselier's is a lived political narrative of heroic self-sacrifice. And it will end, if all goes by script, as did Joan of Arc's, only when all hope for the bench-science practice of human cloning goes up in legal flames. Later, in a follow-up story to Baby Eve, an anonymous FDA official will tell the *New York Times* (Kolata and Chang 2003) that the lab was a nonsterile schoolroom in West Virginia where an unprepared graduate student worked with cow ovaries from a nearby slaughterhouse, using state-of-the-art equipment the sad couple of the ten-month-old child had purchased. Raëlians I queried shrugged off the story. Truth? Or a fiction of a hostile press? Or of a hostile government?

The open-air disco is winding down as the dancers spontaneously join in singing the refrain from Raël's song to the Elohim—arms raised toward the stars. I was later told, "We gave them a sign. They must have seen it. They must know that we love them." Which is also why Raël is raising money to build his embassy on Earth. Conceived as a civil space, complete with landing pads and rooms for conducting diplomatic exchanges with the alien Other who is Us, the embassy is the ultimate faith site of the movement, the optimistic countertextual artifact of Raël's vision of the apocalypse (Bull 1999). And at the time of this writing you can see it on the Rael.org website, in posters on sale at seminars, in a recent *New York Times* "Week in Review" section, and prominently displayed as a model at UFOland alongside the crop circle design that inspired its architectural floor plan.

It is nowadays something like common knowledge that crop circles are large geometrical designs impressed on fields of growing grain through a process in which the living shafts are unnaturally bent or flattened. Documentary specials on public television, limited-distribution films, and blockbusters such as M. Night Shyamalan's *Signs* (2002) (an alien horror film shunned by Raëlians) have broadened the audience for crop circle conjecture. But for many thousands in the UFO community, they are approached as trace evidence of extraterrestrial contact with Earth and can generate raging controversy among believers and skeptics alike. On one side are groups like the United Kingdom's Skeptics organization, which tends toward the view that "the burden of proof rests squarely with believers" since human intelligence is known and unknown intelligence is not. On the other side of the debate are groups such as the Centre for Crop Circle Studies, out of England, whose scientific inquiries include measurements of electromagnetic fields and have led it to state that only 3.5 percent are either hoaxes or created as earth art.

The importance of crop circles for Raëlians was apparent on my first tour of UFOland. The museum, now alas drastically reduced in scale and its space converted to condominiums, is billed as the "first UFO interpretive center in the world," and the exhibits are accessible only by guided tour. At the time organized thematically into rooms, the installations were striking and professional. So now I am following the tour guide, together with a few Americans visiting for the first time, into an airlock-style vestibule that opens through massive elevator doors onto a room dominated by an "exact replica" of the spacecraft that hosted Raël in 1973 and to the right of it "the largest model of DNA in the world," constructed out of hundreds of primary-color plastic balls (fig. 2).

From here, we move through the other rooms in sequence. They are dedicated to the life of the Prophet, the theme of genetics, the planets of the solar system, and, of particular interest to me, a "the history of the UFO phenomenon" in a setting designed to resemble a bunker.

As I enter the bunker room, I am entering common ground in the cultural imaginary of UFO believers everywhere in the world and one of the mysteries that unites them: the military secrets of Area 51 in Nevada and the site near Roswell, New Mexico, that are linked in popular imagina-

FIG. 2. Raël with DNA model. (From *U.S. News and World Report*. Special issue. July 9–16, 2001, 20.)

tion to the 1947 crash of a UFO, and not long ago overwhelmingly to *The X-Files* film and television series. Crop circles figure prominently in the UFOland bunker, and one inspired the floor plan of an architect's model of the dreamed of Embassy for alien-human exchange (figs. 3, 4). All such designs are to be understood in what Mary Poovey calls "the mode of the factual" (1998: xvi). As such, the bunker extends an invitation to engage crop circles and other signs of visitation not as mysteries but as "modern facts," with implicit grounds for claiming scientific legitimacy. Even the "ancient signs" components of the exhibition, which feature "Aztec

FIG. 3. Model of the Raëlian embassy. (Courtesy of Rael.org.)

prophecy" and Egyptian monuments, are presented here as *inscriptions for translation* rather than cryptic metaphysical essences or the sacred geometry of a space of mystical experience. Thus, while the crop circle exhibit of UFOland makes visible claims to an invisible truth that is "out there," always partially hidden (Bull 1999), it likewise renders Raëlians *visible to themselves* as a legitimate knowledge community. Given that "that which is invisible and that which is non-existent look very much alike" (McKown in MidNyte 2001), this is an instance of social visibility standing for itself; and as well, of it eliciting as it were its own future. Photographs and videotaped images of crops circles, many in black and white, produce a "reality effect" not lost on visitors, it would seem, as they pose their often technical questions to UFOland's scientist-guides—a McGill University postgraduate science student and an established nanotechnologist. In short, the sociality of UFOland cannot be understood only in terms of the social *effect* of a pseudoscience rhetoric, for the reason that the creative act of participating in ufological discourse is integral to and constitutive of sociality.

We depart UFOland, and I depart the seminar, in time to travel to a National Academy of Sciences (NAS) panel on the scientific and medical aspects of human cloning, where pro- and anticloning scientists, including

FIG. 4. Crop circle embassy design. (Courtesy of Rael.org.)

Boisselier, have been invited to engage one another before an NAS advisory board. The exchanges are heated, onstage and off, as one might expect. A wall of shoulder-to-shoulder video cameras representing all of the country's major news organizations separates the upper and lower galleries of the theater, and journalists follow panelists into the vestibule to engage them during breaks. A *Wall Street Journal* science writer approaches when he sees that I know the Raëlians there and offers his card. Do I have access to Boisselier? Do I have an opinion on whether the resistance to human cloning is a smoke screen for attacking stem cell research and, further down the road, assisted reproduction?[12] Returning home, I open my e-mail and find a message—one of the many daily postings to Raëlian science group subscribers. The message, embedded in articles and summaries detailing the latest advances in mainstream scientific news, proclaims that "The Mother of All Crop Circles" appeared on July 4 near Stonehenge in Wiltshire, England, in a shape resembling the Raëlian spiral. Interested readers should go to cropcircleconnector.com for further images (fig. 5).

The "photo" on my computer screen looks so obviously fake that I take it as a joke. I decide not to go there. But later an article will appear in the special summer edition of the Raëlian magazine *Apocalypse*, with better photographs and firsthand commentary on the Raëlian star formation by

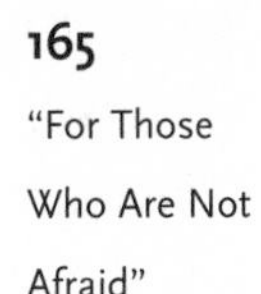

FIG. 5. Spiral crop circle. (From *Apocalypse International* 124 [summer 2001]: 31.)

one Stuart Dike: "This formation has taken everyone's breath away," he writes, "and is without a doubt, the greatest formation since the crop circles began! It . . . covers an area of nearly 700,000 square feet! Whatever numbers you find within the sheer scale of this formation, it will certainly have a lot of numbers behind it." He continues: "You really can't appreciate the size of this formation, without being inside it. . . . Standing in any part of it, and witnessing circles all around you, is quite extraordinary" (2001:31).

This being late summer and the "cerealogy" season, there follows a report by the Raëlian bishop-guide in Britain, Marcel Terrusse, of two other formations near Chilbolton in England—one, "a reverse cryptography of zeros and ones" and the other a "digitized" image of an anthropomorphic face. Unlike hoax crop circles, these two are "authentic," Terrusse explains, because their geometry is "mathematically accurate." He continues: "One of the challenges the Elohim face is to not provoke a reaction of fear among humans. . . . the Crop Circles are certainly a step in a global strategic plan to prepare us for contact. They incite humans to question themselves on the authors of these short-lived works . . . and prepare them psychologically for an official and peaceful contact. . . . 'Life is a movie' and we are right in a scenario of *Contact*" (2001: 33).

The communicative value of images, so deeply interesting to Raëlian artists, reminded me of something I had read on a website about genuine circle makers, that, although "anyone can, using simple equipment, flatten crops into any shape or design they wish, the genuine circle makers, whoever they are, always add an extra dimension to their creations, one of aesthetics. It's something you know when you see it but cannot easily explain because it touches everyone differently. It has to do with proportion and balance, clarity and accuracy, and the ability to communicate at a level that *transcends wonder*" (Allen 1994, emphasis mine).

How different from those who would locate the sources of religion at reason's limits (e.g., Derrida 2002).

Toward an Anthropology of Visits

Whereas ufology holds a respectable place in political theories of democratic culture (Dean's *Aliens in America* [1998] paved the way) and the sociology of religion (Denzler's *The Lure of the Edge* [2001] and Partridge's UFO *Religions* [2003] most recently), anthropology has only recently begun to consider the "outerspaces" of ufological discourse as legitimate locations for exploring historically and culturally contingent social relations. Anthologies of new religious movements offer mainly objectivist accounts and useful qualitative and quantitative data, specifically for Raëlians in Susan Palmer's extensive investigations.[13] Indeed, she was quoted recently in the *Atlantic Monthly* as saying "If you're interested in studying religion, NRMs [New Religious Movements] are a great place to start. Their history is really short, they don't have that many members, their leader is usually still alive, and you can see the evolution of their rituals and their doctrines. It's a bit like dissecting amoebas instead of zebras" (quoted in Lester 2002: 41). (Many Raëlians I know would like that analogy.) This literature in many ways sets the stage for ethnography such as Harding's important study of New Christian fundamentalists (2000; see also Brown 1997 on New Age communities), her work with Kathleen Stewart on the intertwined narratives of conspiracy theory and therapeutic culture (2003), and Lepselter's groundbreaking ethnography of abductee support groups and UFO believers in the American Southwest (1997). Studies such as these are creating new horizons of reflexivity for the *critical* cultural study of technoscience spirituality. Thus, while participatory ethnography of alien knowledge communities is extremely rare, to use a Raëlian metaphor drawn from sensual meditation, ethnography is "oxygenating" the discourse of new religious movements, supplying the "supplement" of intersubjective knowledge exchange. Accordingly, we find ethnographic visits fueling the abduction of broadly familiar terms of reference of science culture debate, and landing them in the discursive realms of subjects' spiritual networks, alternative bioethics, self-narratives, and ideologies of personhood.

Conversely, ethnography is "grounding" the literature of the so-called parasciences or pseudosciences that would categorically pathologize alien and UFO beliefs. Much of this literature consists of insider accounts of "contact" experiences, characterized by dense descriptive texts (see especially Bryan 1995; and Hamilton 1991) that often reveal fear-driven abduction narratives and conspiracy scenarios. Taken collectively, these accounts can read as a psychopathological critique of contemporary American values, and as analyzed in their connection to power relations they provide primary source material for arguing that "ufology is political" in an anxious "alien age" (Dean 1998). Ethnography can unsettle this construct also by revealing the diversity and *achieved ambiguity* (as distinct from anxiety) of subject positions in the social networks that qualify monolithic constructions of an "American Society" or, for that matter, of a paranoid alien age.

Here I have tried to present an experience-near rendering of some of the spaces that orient Raëlian sociality—spaces that draw the ethnography to diverse cultural documents, textual artifacts and performances, and the exchanges that produce them. In these spaces, claims to truth and legitimacy for the heteroknowledges of UFO networks are collectively manifested and witnessed, and evidence of a loving humanity is proffered to the off-world creators whom Raëlians seek to welcome. It is this value for "the visit" that draws Raëlian practice into relation with other so-called UFO religions and into the range of spiritual and science culture conversations generally speaking. Thus, for example, Bruno Latour's value for "propositions," which consist of "offers made by an entity to relate to another under a certain perspective" (2000: 372), relate in turn to the offer inherent in Raëlian users' contingently linked cultural spaces, including cyberspaces: *invitational sites* for sojourners, who may or may not be counted among the "committed" (including ethnographers) but who participate in exploring, interrogating, and inscribing social connections, and disconnections, in the course of their spatiotemporally discontinuous physical and/or virtual visits. I like the idea of an anthropology of visits for Raëlian research because it prescribes a cultural value specifically for hospitality—and for the host. Hosting is the armature of Raëlian religious narratives and ideology. Recall that Raël hosted and was hosted by extraterrestrials on his home planet and also, later, on theirs; his embassy embodies a space for legitimating hosted contact and exchange. Too, Raëlian Internet hosting creates an open invitation to religious engagement and participation in the market in human cloning through its Clonaid "brand name," an act of externalization of the bodily person that mocks the Roman Catholic host, internalized by the faithful as the body of Christ. Indeed, an anthropology of visits—its invitational sites—offers an appropriate map of and for any cultural anthropology of contingency that is open to examining the historicity of reflexive ethnographic engagement in light of the "never innocent" transparency (Strathern 2000: 309) of both public and academic markets for knowledge.

Where, then, does or should the ethnographer stand in all this? For my part, I know that the intoxicating rhetoric of Brigitte Boisselier's vision of reproductive cloning, and other Raëlians' unconditional embrace of intelligent design creationism, are precisely the conditions of my ethnographic distance on the Raëlian philosophy—in some sense not unlike the space that Susan Harding finds for herself as a witness to fundamentalist Baptists when she states "I began to acquire the knowledge and vision and sensibilities, to share the experience, of a believer. . . . This space between belief and disbelief, or rather the paradoxical space of overlap, is also the space of ethnography" (2000, 58).

But what to do in my case, which was not so clearly the betwixt and between of Harding's interlocutory "third space," in part because I was working on one level in relation to Clonaid's opaque publicity agents and on another level, one not reducible to the Clonaid brand name, in relation to the transporting radical democracy of the movement's identity politics. "These are sweet people," as Randolfe Wicker put it in a conversation with me before going on to explain why he had distanced himself and his Gay Cloning Rights organization from Raëlians he had once embraced as kindred spirits. "You know, they are very pro-gay and they talk a lot about emotions" he went on. "They even have cross-dressing dances at the seminars . . . and they gave me a standing ovation when I gave a talk there. I almost joined." But when the crucial time came, he had felt compelled to speak out against Clonaid to a U.S. congressional committee, offended, he told me, by the "media circus" the Raëlians had made of the cloning debate, and a beauty-pageant-style display at one of the seminars of women, known as Angels, who had offered their wombs to human cloning and for human-alien reproduction with the extraterrestrial Designers.

For my part, I could accept that my professional connection to and knowledge of Raëlian subjects could only be "partial"—a point Marilyn Strathern (1991) has of course established as a fact of ethnographic life. But it was and is more difficult to accept that, unlike any certain and stable third space of interlocution, my process of engagement would have an uncertain historicity: to use Raëlian value categories, I was "committed" in some respects, "closed" in others, and furthermore awkwardly positioned with regard to being among the "awakened"—an *emergent* consciousness category that distinguishes committed Raëlians from those who do not yet recognize themselves as the "open" subjects they actually are. I would hear time and again in their conversion narratives how someone "had always lived this way," for example, as a rebel opposed to corporate values, religious dogma, or dominant-culture social institutions such as monogamous marriage, without knowing that he or she was living the Book of Raël. Raëlism had offered a collective identity, and several persons I knew were graciously willing to extend this identity option to me. These were persons with whom I shared many cultural and personal values and with whom I would have been closer if living The Book were not a practical guiding commitment for one of us only. It is these gaps by degrees of separation that produced the felt effect of more or less distance between realms of shareable reality within "the field," the situation of being at a comfortable remove in some spaces and so completely distant in others that I not only experienced myself as alien vis-à-vis subjects for whom this space is "home" but found myself out of view of the moral horizon of possibility for doing fieldwork by anything other than an uncertainty-based directive for ethnographic practice and, homologously, representation.

Yet this is precisely the point: that this condition of creative tension—this active gappiness—can be hospitable for writing culture while conscious that "Ethics, politics, and even responsibility . . . will only ever have begun with the experience and experiment of the aporia" (Derrida 1992), that this gap is our natural habitat, although it comes with a warning to "Mind the Gap" (Baudrillard 1988).

And I would take the point even further for the outer third spaces of fieldwork with UFO-linked social networks and claim these as exemplary invitational sites of ethnography, based precisely on this *uncertainty principle of the subject position*—and the history of achieved ambiguity (as distinct from anxiety) that it generates for ethnographers, in congruence with subjects and media profiling of cloning news. In her ufological ethnography, Susan Lepselter approaches the problem of writing the unheimlich, or "uncanny" spaces of subjects who find each other through their narratives of alien abduction, by asking "What would it mean to stake out a storied home in the realm of the not-at-home? To make one's bed in the unheimlich [she references Freud] . . . a space both familiar and strange, at once as densely naturalized as one's home ground, and as alien as that same ground appears when its hidden gaps begin to show?" (1997: 198). I would simply put the question to ethnography in the same terms, which are the pragmatic terms, I argue, of a shared *logic of abduction*.

"Abduction" in a New Key

> Someone asked Rael what he should say to friends who called Rael a paranoid schizophrenic, a dangerous man. Rael told us: And what if this were all just a beautiful dream? Isn't it better than the horrors of the world we're now living in?—A Raëlian subject

I am aware that it could seem almost weird to propose recovering the concept of abduction from pragmatic philosophy, specifically Charles Sanders Peirce's writings on "abductive reasoning" (particularly as discussed by Hans Joas [1996]) to talk about abduction in its connection to aliens, including ethnographers. But, returning to Latour's "propositional" model, I would argue that pragmatism is precisely the place to look for the missing element in Latour's construction: the leap of faith that propels Raëlians in their search for kinship in the outerspaces of ufology, as its does science practice, namely, the creative act. For Peirce, abductive reasoning entails "the production of a new hypotheses *in the creative act*" (Joas 1996: 135, emphasis mine). As such, it presents a third form of logic, separate from induction, in which a general law is inferred from particular facts "torn up by the roots," as Francis Bacon put it (in Poovey 1998: xvii), and separate from deduction, which proceeds from universal laws to particular cases. Abduction, standing for Peirce precisely "between merely passive absorption of sensory impressions and communication with others about explanatory hypotheses" (Joas 1996: 135), is thus "the only logical operation which introduces any new idea" (134), since in the act of abduction, to quote Joas's summation, "the scientist frees himself from the yoke of former perceptions and received interpretations and creates a free relationship to both. . . . *Self-control and experience are used for the purpose of liberation to enable the free play of ideas and perceptions to take place*" (135, emphasis mine). Hypotheses, in this logical mode of "hopeful suggestions," are thus always and optimistically "on probation" (Peirce [1883] 1982–2000). This *inherently relational* form of action is so strikingly a signature of Raëlian rhetoric and cultural discipline—and so central a condition of writing Raëlian ethnography—that not to enter into its play of discourse, to resist ethnography's ludic dimension or solemnize its intersubjective journeys of discovery, would be tantamount to misrepresentation.

This brings me to a question that had intrigued and bothered me from the start of the Raëlian fieldwork, concerning a conspicuous absence among Raëlians "on the ground" of what Jodi Dean (2003) calls "abduction recollections." Given that people were eager to talk about their journeys through life and how they had found the Raëlian movement, what for Raëlians was doing the work that abduction accounts were doing for—and to—so many other "true believers" in an extraterrestrial presence?

Just coming to this question gave me pause, since I had asked a version of it once before, far away, in a remote region of Melanesia. I asked a Sabarl Islander whether there were any "stories" (*lihulihu*) about the ritualized mortuary exchanges called *segaiya* that my fieldwork has been focused on. The person I was talking to paused, then responded, "We don't need stories of *segaiya*. Because we do it all the time." Now, what Sabarl people did "all the time" was a ritual process ordered into a scripted sequence of exchanges. Raëlians were doing something else all the time, something more fractured into event time and lost time to everyday routines, in line with the E.T. effect of abduction—and postmodernity. In their logic of feeling, and in their hypothetical idea play and often sketchy, unsystematically executed interpretative leaps of faith in technoscience spirituality; in their faith in the outerspaces of sociality and self-expression; in unexpected seminar disconnects and connections; and in their imaginative dance with the specter of the alien returning their gaze heavenward, they were habitually *ab*ductive. Raëlians practiced abductive reasoning all the time—a practical *abduction in the key of optimism*. Thus, The Messages could positively transport actors out of their everyday habits of thought and conventional settings and sweep them away on the wings of conjectural connections between empirical facts and received knowledge into new, sometimes risky or scary, sometimes enlightening arenas of social experimentation and *embodied* self-prospecting.

In this regard, Raël and Boisselier are, to quote a journalist from *The Times of London*, "playing with fire." Radically performative anti-Catholic demonstrations; Raël's blatant letters to world leaders, warning them to resist escalating violence or to support gay and lesbian rights or genetic research; or his disrobing protests, in which, one woman told me, somewhat surprised, "all the cameras were pointed at my breasts"—all of these risk exposure to "anticult" violence, as when a local protestor crashed a truck into the walls of UFOland following the Baby Eve announcement. When I queried Raël's tactics, I received this response from a Raëlian friend and social science colleague in Toronto, by e-mail.

> I'm feeling more and more that the world is in such a terrible mess that the kind of shaking up that Rael is doing through the media with Clonaid, attacking the Church, and now support of GMO's [genetically modified organisms], is necessary to get over the suicidal course we're on now. He's challenging the culture of fear that has been promulgated by the churches, governments and now the media—the most powerful means of social control—by getting people to evaluate their assumptions, their values and habits. Just what we're encouraged to do at the seminars (this past one was especially powerful in that regard—you would have loved it). Agreeing or disagreeing with any aspect of it (I'm no lover of Monsanto's hypocrisy) doesn't alter the need for self questioning, determining the provenance of our deeply held beliefs, and deciding whether they are suitable or not—within the context of a long-term vision of what the world could be like if we manage to survive. Whew! Where did that come from?

By stressing hospitable exchange over us-them boundary maintenance, Raëlians see themselves as opening pathways to new expressions of social activism, just as they open channels to new forms of encounter with "another who is us," at a reflexive remove. It is ironic that the movement's most successful publicity campaign rests on the marketing vision of Clonaid—a vision that, taking replication for reproduction, contains the seed of the evil twin of Raëlian "genius," namely, a totalizing, commodified, human personhood.

This is structurally ironic—but is it surprising? In *Playing God?* John Evans (2002) has recently argued that the debate over human genetic engineering suffered a takeover by bioethicists because it failed to retain the public as the ultimate decision maker. Referring to herself as an "alternative ethicist," Brigitte Boisselier confounds mainstream bioethics, on the one hand, by keeping the human cloning debate alive in the public realm and, more consequentially perhaps, in the realm of religious ethical debate—albeit in antimainstream religious terms—that bioethicists have historically sidelined. On the other hand, Clonaid commits in the extreme to the value of autonomy that is a central goal of mainstream bioethicists; while they cloak themselves in the rhetoric of disinterested public good, she exposes autonomy, in the image of the pro-choice designer baby, as an easy companion of the values and practices of late capitalism.

The Culture of the Rush

Social documents such as films and television specials, not to mention video and card gaming, graphic novels, and Internet sites, have elaborated a strongly felt ambivalence toward the intentionally manufactured human double (see Hillel 1996). The multimediatized story of the divinely engineered Baby Eve puts a finer point on this cultural ambivalence, revealing the dimensions not so much of a global media culture of copy as of a "landscape of point-for-point ad hoc settlements" brokered by specific interests in science, sacred or secular (Saussy 2001: 179). "Unstable, suspenseful, loosely related to facts, and latently contradictory," the story articulates a model of and for mediation as situated social practice "that addresses everybody all the time *but cannot wait to integrate all the responses*" (179, emphasis mine). While noting the "heavy reliance of narrative in the PR of the new [mediatized] religiosity" (Bal 2001: 262), it is this *protentive* model, I propose, that explains the "natural" attraction of contemporary media to new religious movements that specifically highlight faith in technoscience; at the process level, new science and new religion share media's impatient embrace of the breaking moment over solid grounds. Because of Clonaid, Raëlians have become emblematic of the shaky science culture of "the rush."

I could give dozens of examples of Raëlians quoted as instances of "the edge" that E.T. culture represents for mainstream science but none quite as succinct as the story of responses to the cloning enterprise of Advanced Cell Technology (ACT), which hit the news in 2002 when its scientists cloned the first human embryos and hit the wall of conservative moral approbation when they extended their experiments to cow-human embryos. Commenting from the private biotech sector, one corporate head imagined religious fundamentalists thinking "My God . . . these people are going to make chimeric creatures—mixing cows and humans" and went on to condemn ACT's "publication by press release." Then he added: "It's not in the same category as the Raëlians, because there are certainly legitimate scientists at ACT trying to do this work, okay? But from the perspective of the regulatory bodies, they are in the same spaceship" (quoted in Dunn 2002: 40).

In short, the basis of the affinity of the media and technoscience spirituality—as practiced by scientists or those who are "deeply religious" or both—is the armature they share of "prosthetic supplementarity." That is, as an "extension of human capacities," mediatization, like the Raëlian or ACT's cloning programs, "simultaneously distances and undermines what it extends, exacerbating the vulnerabilities of the finitude it seeks to alleviate and protect" (Weber 2001: 52). This finitude being the human condition of (catastrophic) mortality that defines Raëlians' ultimate goal for science—a goal they happen to share with ACT's founder Michael West, whose interest in cloning began with the question of how science could "cure" old age—small wonder that the movement both guards itself against the media that abducts its message and threatens its "ensoulment" (as Talal Asad [2001] has termed embodied spirituality) and at the same time actively encourages media intercourse toward the goal of propagating the faith. Human reproductive cloning turns on repetition as action "recollected forward" (Weber 2001 from Kierkegaard), with results that are the opposite of a nostalgic replay of the past or, for that matter, of dwelling in a static present: it is "news." Productively or otherwise, mediatized faith-based cloning must, as creative social action, get well and truly carried away.[14]

Postscript: Brigitte/"Brigitte"

> News Flash: April 29, 2003. South Hadley. Bioethics Panel to visit introductory biology class at Mount Holyoke College. Introductory students in Bio 200 will have the opportunity to interact with 9 prominent experts* in the field of human cloning and stem cell research. Many of them serve on

President Bush's Council on Bioethics, and others include a United States Senator and the first scientist to announce the creation of a human clone. *Experts will be portrayed by members of MHC Bio 321 Cloning Seminar Class, who have spent the entire semester learning about these prominent national figures.—*THE BIO 200 TIMES*

Before the big event was "advertised" to Mount Holyoke College (MHC) students in Professor Rachel Fink's "news flash" to her introductory biology class, I arranged to interview "Brigitte Boisselier," a member of the bioethics panel performance and the senior class. She has, she tells me, used the Internet for research, mostly, and some television interviews and Dr. Boisselier's taped interview for Congress, and that the Internet work was a little confusing because the Clonaid site would change and links would disappear. The cloning issue for the Raëlian movement seemed to become more important when the news of Baby Eve broke and the website was about Raël's vision of eternal life, but today it seems more focused on the extraterrestrials that created humans and advancing science in general than about human cloning. Now she's not sure what the relation between Raëlianism and Clonaid is about.

Then "Brigitte" read her prepared statement in the first person. It included her "belief that human cloning is about creating a scientific inquiry and defending the freedom of human reproductive choices. . . . Clonaid has been an advocate of couples wanting to have genetically related children using science, couples that are unable to produce children in the traditional way with other assisted reproductive technologies. . . . Many people have criticized my work but I cannot understand their position. How can a baby cause so much fear and so much disgust and so much aversion? What we are talking about is pro-Life to the highest degree. Cloned children are created out of the greatest love. . . . All these procedures can and should be regulated to avoid abuses."

"BRIGITTE" CONTINUED: The most interesting thing that I have gotten from this research is that she [Boisselier] has this amazing sense of confidence. Her presentation as a character always comes across, which was kind of refreshing in a way. It is easy to critique her but you have to wait and see that she wouldn't take much notice of it.

ME: When you are in the role of "Brigitte," you will try to portray her sense of

FIG. 6. Oceanic Raëlians. (From *Apocalypse International* 123 [fall 2001]: back cover.)

confidence. Did it change you as you were doing the research and getting a sense of her? Did it alter your ideas about either reproductive or therapeutic cloning?

"BRIGITTE": Last semester I was assigned to a pro-reproductive rights side of the argument in a debate. It was something I didn't agree with at the time. I thought it would be difficult to convince someone else of something I didn't believe in. But she is amazingly articulate and amazingly believable. I mean, the Raëlian movement aside, her ideas about love and her argument about cloning's relationship to other reproductive technologies that had developed years ago and how those were first perceived . . . I thought that that was an interesting comparison that made sense to me. So I found myself persuaded by her argument and probably by her confidence too.

ME: She is so sure that human reproductive cloning is not only going to happen but that it should happen. Did you ever think that you might like to attend a Raëlian seminar?

"BRIGITTE": I would love to! I would be fascinated. I check the website every week because of this class topic and I find it very interesting.

ME: Do you believe her? About Baby Eve?

"BRIGITTE": I think I do, and yet I don't. It is really hard for me to be able to say she is lying. . . . I think that when I first got into the research it was more about

> Clonaid, and then I learned that there is this big movement behind it that is deeply involved and organized, and now I look more at her, the person, and her work.

To be continued . . .

Notes

I am indebted to my friends and members of the Structure of the Raëlian movement for their hospitality during my visits online, in Quebec Province, and in Boston. I also thank the authors of this collection for remarkable conversations that expanded my horizons and Jodi Dean and Kathleen Stewart for insightful critical readings of this essay. Finally, I am grateful to my colleagues and the Dean of Faculty at Mount Holyoke College, Donal O'Shea, for their generous support.

1. Raël's texts refer to the creators as practitioners of human cloning, and he has often detailed a vision of a future in which a person's personality could one day be "downloaded" into her or his cloned body. However, one scientist within the movement commented that *genetic engineering* or *biotechnology* would be more accurate terms with which to describe the Raëlian project, as "we are not anyone's clone." Indeed, Raëlians vary considerably with regard to how literally they take the cloning imagery and how important science is to them as a matter of faith in the movement's goals for enhanced personhood.

2. In Raël's published work, especially regarding the "geniocracy" of new world leaders that he envisions after the apocalypse (he contrasts these explicitly to George W. Bush), and likewise as applied to the human cloning eugenic vision of Clonaid, *genius* corresponds to Johann Gottfried von Herder's "Higher geniuses" who serve humanity. However, in common usage Raël's, and many Raëlians' exegesis on *genius* is more along the lines of Herder's broader definition of inner potential: "Whatever human nature has brought forth in genius manner, be it science or art, an institution or action, is the work of the *genius*, and *any* ability to awaken human gifts and encourage them to fulfill their purpose is precisely *genius*" (quoted in Joas 1996: 84).

3. Borrowing Benedict Anderson's insight on charisma in Indonesia ([1972] 1990: 27) that power is vested in persons and things by others (see also Keane 1997: 10)—indeed, that its objects may need to mask any intention to seek power—I would qualify the *categorical* use of the term *charismatic* to describe Raël's spiritual effect on his followers on several grounds. First, the degree of power vested in Raël varies considerably across the Raëlian network: members and others, including me, frequently take him privately to task on some aspect of his teaching and afterward find their views incorporated in his public addresses (without attri-

bution). Too, his "aura" varies across cultural settings. While I was told that Raël is "revered" in Europe and East Asia and greeted as the Pope might be, in Australia, much as I saw him in Quebec, he is regarded more like a wise and beloved uncle, an Oxbridge don, a sports or entertainment celebrity, or a chief executive officer (CEO). He could be seen lawn bowling in an area removed from common use, mixing freely on social occasions dressed in casual whites, and chatting with those who had gathered for a meal as if a personal host. As a religious leader, the title of His Holiness was employed only recently to send a message to the press that he should be approached with respect, "like the Dalai Lama," I was told (though he fashions himself as a peace leader explicitly in the mold of Mahatma Gandhi, and film clips from the film *Gandhi* are strategically placed elements of his seminar lectures). Meanwhile, his followers refer to him by his first (and only) name with familiarity, not awe. For them, his effect is legitimated by his special knowledge of "the truth" of alien contact rather than vested in spiritually charged symbols. The book he wrote and published as testimony to his vision is possessed of no particular aura for most persons I know. And also, like a CEO, he has a succession plan in place, he explained, and an executive committee authorized to vote him out of office if he loses his reason with age or for any reason no longer commands trust.

Having stated this, Raël and Boisselier are together the only "natural signs" of authority and sites of faith across the movement's dual commitment to techno-science and the spirituality of the senses, and their physical presence does have a compelling effect. If we accept that meaning resides between the subject receiving a message and its producer, Raël's and Boisselier's unclaimed charisma leaves the movement open to becoming a location of unbounded anxiety by the "closed" outsiders of official culture. As has been persuasively argued by Barkun (1994), Docherty (2001), and Richardson (1995) for the Branch Davidians' tragic apocalypse, it is not Raël's guidance or Boisselier's "alternative ethics" but totalitarian responses to their publicity images that Raëlians should reasonably fear, responses arguably fanned by the Structure's occasional opacity to outsiders, and its generally discouraging position on critical exchange and debate with those outside the Raëlian movement (see Chryssides 2003 on this point).

4. An important discussion of this debate can be found in Franklin, Lury, and Stacey's *Global Nature, Global Culture* (2000).

5. Rushkoff continues: "Media is saying something in the way it finds its stories, churns them out, swallows them again, redigests them, and spits them out once again. This is more than a simple cultural bulimia. This is a complex but, on some level, effective form of mass catharsis and self-observation that our society employs to monitor and then modify itself" (1996: 20).

6. My thanks go to Julia Jean for this thoughtful gift.

7. It was originally published as *The True Face of God* (1998).

8. A Raëlian reader commented that it was "a little unfair to pass by so easily" the Elohim concept, given that this was not only central in Raëlian philosophy but a three-thousand-year-old concept in all Judeo-Christian-Abrahamic religions. "(Anonymous, personal communication, 2001).

9. For a fascinating discussion of the relationship between journalism and religious secrecy, see Derrida's "Above All No Journalists!" (2001).

10. It is irresistible to note comparisons with Ignatius of Loyola, the late-medieval Catholic reformer whose "shockingly concrete" *Spiritual Exercises* employed somatic imagery to work against "loss of the body" in acts of piety. While trained on hell, the meditative images, Burcht Pranger argues, being without narrative, leave the reader "at liberty to fill in (the gaps between) the points raised by The Spiritual Exercises and to make up his own story . . . [provided with] "salient points" out of which places can be composed in order to be filled up with images." This is "how memory should work: it is through concentrated and brief flashes rather than extensive and comprehensive narratives that scenes from the past can be brought to mind and the senses revived" (2001: 189–91). The relevance of the Ignatian method for understanding the process of abduction "recollections" is striking.

11. Of course, this exchange gave me pause. Were Raëlians sending spiritual messages to themselves about themselves in their sensual meditations or is the Structure selling a spiritual commodity that would channel persons' needs, as Raymond Williams argues ([1962] 1980), and their desires, through Raël?

12. For full discussion of "behind the scenes" and "behind the screens" media ethnography, see Ginsburg, Abu Lughod, and Larkin 2002.

13. See especially Lewis 1995; Palmer and Hardman 1999; Palmer 1994; Partridge 2003; and Robbins and Palmer 1997.

14. For published research on Raëlian sociality out of the sociology of religion, see especially the work of Susan Palmer (1994, 1995, 1997a, 1997b, 1999, 2004) and, out of England, George Chryssides (2003).

Intertextual Enterprises: Writing Alternative Places and Meanings in the Media Mixed Networks of Yugioh

MIZUKO ITO

In the late 1980s and early 1990s, during a renaissance in Japanese *anime* (animation), outer space provided the otherworldly context for disrupting narratives of the ordinary. The outer space genre of anime juxtaposed old technologies with new and integrated the fantastic with familiar and everyday social dramas. In *Space Cruiser Yamato* a World War II battle cruiser is reborn as a spaceship. In *Urusei Yatsura*, Lum, a sexy space alien, falls in love with an Earthling and becomes a vortex of spiraling chaos in his formerly mundane life. In *Galaxy Express 999*, a young boy travels between distant planets in an otherworldly steam locomotive. Other anime genres dealt with the everyday dramas of romance, sport, and school life. In contrast, the fantasy genre needed a distanced spatial canvas on which to render narratives of escape and difference, and space became one of the most compelling staging grounds for this imaginary of childhood fantasy.

In more recent years, cyberspace and inner space have come to occupy a similar role in the imaginary of Japanese popular culture. We don't need to travel vast physical distances to encounter the uncanny but can find it close to home, in the near future, in multiple-personality, psychological narratives in an everyday world visited by alien beings and supernatural creatures of uncertain origin. As fantasy has become a well-established element of run-of-the-mill media-enhanced reality, narratives of space exploration have imploded, becoming part of a pastiche of reference that sees little need to differentiate between aliens, mythology, the supernatural, and the virtual, all of which are inseparable from everyday and familiar worlds. Narratives of otherworldly experience persist in technologically and phantasmagorically enhanced versions of our everyday world as goddesses, angels, monsters, aliens, and virtual creatures inhabit the homes and psyches of children. In *Digimon*, chosen children are able to enter the DigiWorld through their computers, and Digimon wander into our world through their relations with children. In *Corrector Yui*, the heroine battles forces of evil by donning her virtual reality helmet and transforming into a cyborg superhero. In *Angelic Layer*, young girls participate in a competitive sport in which they manipulate fighters in virtual space. Most famously, in *Pokémon* otherwise uremarkable children develop intimate relationships with monsters with special powers, adventuring in a pastoral world that may be Earth or another planet. The distance between here and elsewhere has been rendered inconsequential.

One focus of my work has been on *Yugioh*, a *manga* (comic) and anime series that also relies on a blend of the real and virtual and the interpenetration of the Other world of multireferential fantasy with the everyday social lives of children. In this essay, I describe how the fantastic and otherworldly characters and narratives of the *Yugioh* pantheon are part of the everyday constructions of identity and social relations among children, adult fans, and media industries. First, I frame this work as an effort in the ethnographic siting, or locating, of the virtual. Then I describe the cultural politics of a linked but heterogeneous imaginary of *Yugioh* as it ties together people, commodities, and images in a complex media mix. In addition to making the fantasy of *Yugioh* manifest across a wide range of settings, the practices that I track also have the effect of rendering different versions of childhood, gender, and economic relations.

The Ethnography of "Other" Space

Like the ethnographies of alien encounters described in the other essays in this volume, I am interested in tracing how people in "our world" experience and produce intimate narratives of distant and strange worlds. What are the concrete locations and materials through which alternative realities are inscribed and subjectified, the contact points where we encounter and identify with the virtual Other? How do marginal and fantastic imaginaries function as sites of alternative cultural production and performance? Finally, how can we translate an anthropological commitment to the study of difference and everyday practice to virtualized narratives of the uncanny?

My fieldwork in Japan and the United States examines popular culture as material through which consequential difference, alternative realities, and differentiation from the mainstream are produced and performed. Unlike traditionally exotic anthropological objects, these sites of inquiry display difference as a product of partial, selective, and self-conscious performance rather than as an outcome of preinscribed and holistic cultural distance. This is a move that complements efforts to tease apart the isomorphism between peoples, places, and cultures (Gupta and Ferguson 1997) and transnational and diasporic studies in particular (Clifford 1997; Ong 1999), stressing cultural difference and heterogeneity within and across national boundaries. Unlike studies that take national identity or ethnicity as the key objects to be analyzed and deconstructed, however, my work looks at forms of affiliation such as gender, age, and social status and how they are "placed" by new media networks rather than geographic boundaries. These exoticisms are part of the intimate and everyday workings of "our societies" and commodity capitalism, a response to a proliferating palette of identifications and imaginaries that flow within and across national borders.

Otherworldly discourses and images of cyberspace and media space are built through the real, mundane, and material networks of commodity capitalism and everyday social practice, and anthropological practice involves first tracing these networks of spatially distributed relations. Methodologically, this has meant following *Yugioh* content across multiple sites of production and consumption and looking at how media content is mobilized in practice by people in a wide range of social locations. To borrow from Arjun Appadurai (1996), this is an effort to look at "the imagination as a social fact" rather than a set of referents to be examined independent of practice and material relations. This has meant analyzing how *Yugioh* content is a product of particular material relations in new forms of commodity capitalism. The production of virtualities "out there" is also about the production of realities "at home." In contrast to contextualization in a geographic area, George Marcus has argued that "within a multi-sited research imaginary, tracing and describing the connections and relationships among sites previously thought to be incommensurate is ethnography's way of making arguments and providing its own contexts of significance" (1998: 14).

The innovation of the ethnographer as well as the informant is less in rendering the unfamiliar intelligible than in tracing unconventional readings of and linkages between familiar but dispersed objects, in producing and performing the everyday as a site of phantasmic creativity. In the case of children's popular culture, and *Yugioh* in particular, these networks extend beyond the texts themselves, the creators of the texts, and the intended consumers to include a wide range of social actors that repackage, appropriate, and perform *Yugioh* in often unexpected ways.

Childhood, Fantasy, and the Media Mix

At least since the rise of television in the 1950s and beyond, children's popular culture has been a haven for imagining alternative realities, ghettoized and (partially) contained by the "naturally" imaginative and phantasmic life stage of childhood. Even before the advent of mass media, childhood provided a repository of difference both intimate and strange, but recent years have seen childhood fantasy becoming both a more fantastic and capitalized site of cultural production in Japan and elsewhere. Children's play is cloistered in the domestic space of the home, controlled by the institution of the family. And yet, particularly since the advent of the television, and more so with the advent of the Internet, kids are also getting "out" more, in virtual and imaginary spaces produced through media networks. The imaginary spaces of children's media are also moving "in" to structure the subjectivities of children, domestic micropolitics, and a growing industry. Morphing from the *Mickey Mouse Club* to *Teenage Mutant Ninja Turtles*, children's popular culture is becoming more fantastic, more culturally hybrid, and more "far out" even as it is becoming an utterly unremarkable aspect of everyday life for children (Cross 1997) and increasingly for adults as well.

The production of a space of childhood as a uniquely innocent space, deserving of protection, has gone hand in hand with increasing adult engineering of childhood, ranging from formal schooling to the proliferation of media designed for children. *Yugioh* and other contemporary media mixes in children's content need to be located within this production of childhood as a distinct social arena and market. Popular culture has become a mechanism for defining a distinct life stage of childhood and articulating a counterhegemonic subculture of children in opposition to hegemonic adult values. In *Sold Separately*, Ellen Seiter (1993) writes about how commercials depict children's products as a vehicle for critiquing and escaping adult worlds and accountabilities.

> Anti-authoritarianism is translated into images of buffoonish fathers and ridiculed, humiliated teachers. The sense of family democracy is translated into a world where kids rule, where peer culture is all. Permissiveness becomes instant gratification: the avid pursuit of personal pleasure, the immediate taste thrill, the party in the bag (117–18).

Much as the counterculture of the 1960s and 1970s provided powerful advertising tropes in creating a new youth-oriented market (Frank 1997), the growth of the children's culture market has rested on differentiation from adult sensibilities and everyday accountabilities. In Japan, antagonistic discourses between children and adults are somewhat less pronounced (White 1994), but children's popular culture has reflected a similar escapist and fantastic element. Japanese anime has provided a unique vision of childhood as charmed and cute but not innocent, an imaginary that has proved compelling both in Japan and overseas (Allison 2004; Kinsella 1995). This particular imaginary has been increasingly integrated into international media markets, particularly in the past decade, when anime became a major international commodity.

In the later years of the 1990s, Japan stole center stage in transnational marketplaces of children's media by innovating in media forms that create a hybrid relation between analog and digital media, a merging of the strengths of broadcast media with the communicative and performative power of the Internet and video games. *Pokémon* revolutionized the workings of media technology. By linking content in multiple media forms such as video games, card games, television, film, manga books, toys, and household objects, *Pokémon* created a new kind of citational network that has come to be called a "media mix."

The media mix of *Pokémon*, and subsequent series such as *Digimon* and *Yugioh*, creates a virtual world that manifests itself in multiple media forms and through which consumers can craft their own narrative trajectories through play with video and card games (Allison 2002; Tobin 2004a). This is a networked world of expanding reference that destabilizes the prior orthodoxy of children's media (Tobin 2004a). Rather than spoon-feed stabilized narratives and heroes to a supposedly passive audience, *Pokémon* and *Yugioh* invite children to collect, acquire, recombine, and enact stories within their peer networks, trading cards, information, and monsters (Buckingham and Sefton-Green 2004; Yano 2004) in what Sefton-Green has called a "knowledge industry" (Sefton-Green 2004, 151). These media mixes challenge our ideas of childhood agency and the passivity of media consumption, highlighting the active, entrepreneurial, and technologized aspects of children's engagement with popular culture. They also create a proliferating set of contact points between practice, media, and imaginings, as players perform and identify with media characters in multiple and often unexpected ways.

Yugioh

Yugioh was the most popular media mix content among elementary age boys in Japan in the years from 2000–2002. Launched in 1996, the *Yugioh* manga series has also spawned a television animation, its own immensely popular card game, over ten different video game versions, and character goods ranging from T-shirts to packaged curry to pencil boxes. One survey in 2000 of three hundred students in a Kyoto elementary school indicated that by the third grade every student owned some *Yugioh* cards (*Asahi Shinbun* 2001). The *Yugioh* animation was released in the United States in 2001, and now the card game has overtaken *Pokémon* in popularity there.

The hero of *Yugioh*, Mutou Yugi, is a high school boy with a split personality. Yugi's original personality is one of a small, weak, skinny, and unpopular kid, whose one strength is his skill in playing games. One day he solves a complex ancient Egyptian puzzle and unlocks a hidden spirit of an Egyptian pharaoh within it, who becomes a second personality for him, Yami Yugi (Yugi of darkness), powerful, secure, decisive, and ruthless. The two Yugis use their game expertise to combat forces of greed and evil, battling adults as often as other children. The series pivots around the rivalry between two master duelists, Yugi and Kaiba, with Yugi representing one pole of kindness and fraternity and Kaiba representing an opposing pole of ruthless individualism. Occasionally the two find themselves united against the forces of evil, such as the shadow corporation the "Big Five" or a group of "Card Hunters" that uses cheating and counterfeiting to rob others of their rare cards.

The series focuses on a card game, Magic and Wizards, a thinly veiled reference to Magic: The Gathering, the card game that swept the United States in the early 1990s. In the manga and animation, players engage in lengthy duels, where they pit monster, magic, and trap cards against each other in dramatic play, often involving technologies that render the dueling monsters in 3D. The monsters include creatures derived from an entire spectrum of fantasy genres: outer space, medieval, occult, mythological, cartoon, and magical. Red-eyed dragons blast robot warriors, and a Venus on a half shell casts spells on penguin soldiers and carnivorous hamburgers. These fantastic creatures are rendered in the everyday world with more and more fidelity through advancing virtual reality technologies. The series began by mapping a contact point between the world of the monsters and the human characters in the threat of psychological horror; Yami Yugi's special powers could hurl his opponent into a "world of darkness" inhabited by the monsters depicted in the playing cards. Eventually, the (fictional) creators of the card game develop technologies that render the monsters in fully interactive 3D inflicting real-life pain as their monsters attack each other and the players. The anime depicts real and virtual worlds in constant and dynamic contact. In current renditions, duels becomes vividly lifelike through "duel disks" worn on the players' arms, which project the monsters in vivid holographic 3D.

Yugioh is similar to the media mixes of *Pokémon* and *Digimon* in that they involve human players that mobilize otherworldly monsters in battle. Unlike *Digimon* and *Pokémon*, however, the monsters in *Yugioh* inhabit the everyday world of Yugi and his peers in the form of trading cards, which the players carry with them in their ongoing adventures. The "other world" of the monsters is in intimate relationship with the everyday; the human players in the manga mobilize monsters in their everyday world, and kids in "real life" mobilize these same monsters in their play with trading cards and game boys. The activities of children in our world thus closely mimic the activities and materialities of children in Yugi's world. They collect and trade the same cards and engage in play with the same strategies and rules.

Scenes in the anime depict Yugi frequenting card shops and buying card packs, enjoying the thrill of getting a rare card, dramatizing everyday moments of media consumption in addition to the highly stylized and fantastic dramas of the duels themselves. Trading cards, Game Boys, and character merchandise create what Anne Allison has called "pocket fantasies," "digitized icons . . . that children carry with them wherever they go" and "that straddle the border between phantasm and everyday life" (2004: 42).

Just as in the anime, the focus of dramatic action for kids is moments of card play. The boys that I encountered in the course of my fieldwork engaged with *Yugioh* at multiple levels. Most owned versions of the game boy game, read the manga at least periodically, and watched the TV show. Some participated in Internet groups that exchanged information and *Yugioh* goods. But the most popular is the card game. All of the boys I encountered had some kind of collection of cards that they treasured, ranging from kids with large boxed collections and playing decks in double-encased sleeves to kids with a single, dog-eared stack of cards held together by a rubber band. The standard process of game play is one on one, where duelists pit monster, magic, and trap cards against one another. Each player makes a playing deck of forty or more cards that reflects a personal style of play. Children develop certain conventions of play among their local peer groups and often make up inventive forms of game play such as team play or play with decks mimicking the characters in the manga series. Rules are negotiated locally, among peers, who acquire knowledge through extended peer networks, television, and manga.

Yugioh was a ubiquitous fact of life for kids in Japan during the years that I was conducting fieldwork in Tokyo. Boys would appear at playgrounds with their favorite cards displayed in cases worn around their necks. As I pick up my three-year-old daughter from day care, I see two tots wielding dominoes striking a characteristic duelist pose. "Time to duel!" one of them announces. Conversations about dark witches and white dragons peppered talk that I overheard on trains and on the street. At a McDonalds, I see a little girl, maybe five years old, excitedly tearing open a pack of new *Yugioh* cards under the supervision of her puzzled parents. "What do you do with these?" they ask. "They are just cool." Even children not old enough to play the card game enjoyed the anime series and were energized by the palpable electricity of competitive play that coursed through the networks of kids' play and imaginings. *Yugioh* was truly a mass phenomenon, creating an alternative imaginary and exchange economy that alternately alarmed, perplexed, and amused older generations.

In the remainder of this essay, I describe three uncommon contact points between the fantasy worlds of *Yugioh* and the worlds of child and adult players, sites that direct some of this electricity into more concentrated spectacles of the *Yugioh* imagination. I illustrate some of the ways in which the other world of *Yugioh*, embedded in a variety of media technologies such as trading cards, the Internet, and anime, become mobilized as concrete material and symbolic resources in the lives of committed *Yugioh* players and fans. These sites of translation between fantasy and reality are sites of consequential subject formation, social negotiation, and the production of childhood as a particular cultural domain.

Siting 1: Yugi Incarnate

In the course of my fieldwork, I had the good fortune to meet Yugi incarnate, an eleven-year-old *Yugioh* expert. I will call him Kaz. My research assistants and I had been frequenting one hobby shop in central Tokyo that hosted weekly *Yugioh* tournaments. We are usually the only female participants in these events, which are dominated by guys in their teens and twenties. Kaz was one of the regulars at this event, generally beating the adults that competed regularly and taking home the weekly gift certificate prize. It was unusual to see elementary-aged kids that frequented these mostly adult-oriented spaces, and Kaz stood out even more in being the most skilled *Yugioh* player of the bunch. This was despite a substantial financial handicap compared to the adult players, who could afford to buy all the cards they needed to play. He lived in a single-parent household headed by his father and had an unusual amount of freedom in traveling throughout the city after school and on the weekends.

Kaz's play with the older duelists in the tournaments had overtones of Yugi that other players remarked on. A leader of one of the powerful adult gaming teams called him a prodigy of immense talent. Another player described how he was "like Yugi" in that he always managed to draw the right card at just the right time. Another player explained to me that Kaz did not always have the best strategy but he was fearless in his attacks and relied on his intuition, having "the heart of the true duelist" often ascribed to Yugi. I often marveled at his composure as he trounced older players in duel after duel. He was a ruthless player, and after defeating his opponents he would often rub it in with an understated but cocky self-confidence.

Nobody was surprised when Kaz won the Tokyo regional junior championship hosted by Konami, the company that makes *Yugioh* cards. Konami sponsors separate tournaments for adults and children, and Kaz was just below the cutoff for the junior category. I was among the small group of his fans that followed Kaz to this event and the subsequent national championship, which was held at the Toy Show. Upon entering the huge hall of the trade show, we quickly spotted the *Yugioh* booth. It is dedicated to the national championship, and the center of the booth has a large enclosed structure that spectators enter from one side. It is a replica of the stage that was the setting for the second duel between Yugi and Kaiba. The center of the space has a glass box containing a table and just enough space for two duelists. Along the periphery is seating for the spectators and a booth with two commentators, who give blow-by-blow descriptions of the play.

Before long, the final duel of the junior "King of Duelists" tournament is announced. Of course, Kaz has made it to the finals, and his name is trumpeted together with his opponent's. The two boys walk through a set of double doors that open with clouds of smoke to announce their entry. In contrast to the spectacle of Plexiglas and smoke being produced on the corporate side, the players and spectators are strikingly mundane. Kaz is dressed in the same black Puma jogging suit that I see him wearing almost every time I see him, and even his close friends alternate between watching the duel and chatting and playing with their Game Boys, barely attentive to the action on center stage. As is typical of the duels of more experienced players, there is little dialogue between players, and all the action is understated. In contrast to younger children, who might mimic the turns of phrase of the anime characters and boast about the cards they are playing, professional duelists communicate with gesture and expression more than verbal bravado, making the emotional undercurrents of the duel detectable only to the experienced observer. Kaz wins, and his friends are blasé, declaring that it was "a foregone conclusion." In the award ceremony that follows, the press snaps pictures of a grinning Kaz and he appears in the next edition of *Shonen Jump Comics* together with the next installment of *Yugioh*.

Kaz's relationship to Yugi is less surface mimicry than performance of a resonant subjective and social location. Kaz's virtuosity at the card game and the grudging respect of his adult opponents mirror the narrative of *Yugioh*. Like Yugi, too, Kaz had two faces, the face of the ruthless duelist and the childish persona of a sixth grader. My research assistants describe in their field notes how they think he is adorable, and I feel the same. He has pink cheeks and an embarrassed and shy smile that appears when he is talking about anything other than *Yugioh*. After winning the national championship with his characteristic swagger, he blushes beet red when one of my research assistants congratulates him and gives him a small gift. For Kaz and his cohort, performing Yugi means performing in competition; persona, age, dress, and language are secondary to proficiency at the game. Yugi is a role model for a practice bounded by the parameters of a form of game play.

Kaz channels the narrative of *Yugioh* into the referents of our world, making them consequential and meaningful in the competitive negotiations between children and children and adults. Kaz, like Yugi, inverts the power dynamic between adult and child within the virtual world of *Yugioh* play. He is a figure of a child, elevated to heroic proportions in a national cultural imaginary and backed by an immense media apparatus that provides the cultural resources for his performances. Kaz provides an example of engagement with *Yugioh* that demonstrates the agentive potential of children when they are given the resources to compete with adults, as well as evidence of the growing appeal of "child's play" in the world of adult recreation. Although Kaz's precocious performances challenge some of the power hierarchies between adult and child, his play also reinscribes the domain of play as authentically childlike, a domain bracketed from the "real" consequentiality of work and mainstream achievement.

Siting 2: Card Otaku and the Resignification of Value

Unlike Kaz, who is an uncommon but legitimate subject in the narratives of *Yugioh* and the competitive spectacles produced by game industries, many adult gamers are in an uneasy relationship with the dominant narratives of *Yugioh*. Adult game and anime fans are often described at times by the pejorative term *otaku*, which roughly translates as "media geek," with hints of connoisseurship associated with the American term *cult media* (Greenfeld 1993; Kinsella 1998; Okada 1996; Tobin 2004b). Otaku are often objects of suspicion because of what are perceived as dangerous boundary crossings between reality and fantasy, adult and child. Unlike children, who compose the "normal" audience for animated content, the cultural category of otaku has regressive, obsessive, erotic, and antisocial overtones for the cultural mainstream. Recently the term has migrated to Euro-American contexts as a way of celebrating forms of media and technofetishism associated with Japanese popular culture and technology. Key to its popularization in the United States, the premier issue of *Wired* described otaku as "a new generation of anti-social, nihilistic whiz-kids" or "socially inept but often brilliant technological shut-ins" (Greenfeld 1993). In Japan, the terms gets used more broadly to refer to individuals or specific groups, as well as a certain cultural style, *otaku-kei* (otaku-like) events, fashions, magazines, and technologies that may or may not be shunned by the mainstream.

Like most popular forms of anime content, *Yugioh* has an avid following of adult fans. Adult otaku communities are the illegitimate offspring of the *Yugioh* media empire and are in an uneasy relationship with the entertainment industries that create *Yugioh* content. They exploit gaps in dominant systems of meaning and mainstream commodity capitalism, mobilizing tactics that are a thorn in the side of those relying on mass marketing and distribution. Card otaku, who buy and sell cards through alternative networks, even to the extent of creating counterfeit or original cards, are considered a threat to normalized capitalist relations. Let me give you one example of the tension between mainstream industry and otaku, how they intervene in the flow of symbolic and monetary capital between producers and consumers.

Yugioh cards have been released in a variety of forms, including ready-to-play packs, vending-machine versions, and limited-release versions packaged with Game Boy software in books and distributed at trade shows. The most common form of purchase is in five-card packs costing 150 yen. A new series of these five-card packs is released every few months. When purchasing a pack of cards, one doesn't know what one will get within the fifty or so cards in a series. Most card packs have only "normal," run-of-the-mill cards, but if you are lucky you may get a "rare," "superrare," "ultrarare," or perhaps even "ultimate rare" card in one of your packs.

One kind of otaku knowledge is known as *sa-chi* (searching), which are methods with which card collectors identify rare card packs *before* purchase. Collectors meet with each other on rounds of convenience stores, sharing tips and techniques. Now these tips are posted on numerous Web sites soon after the new packs hit the shelves. These websites post detailed photos highlighting and describing minute differences in packaging such as the length of the ridges along the back of the card pack or slight differences in printing angle and hue.

I find myself out at 1:00 A.M. with a group of card collectors, pawing through three boxes of just released cards. The salesperson is amused but slightly annoyed, and it takes some negotiating to get him to open all three boxes. My companions pride themselves on their well-trained fingertips, which enable them to identify the key card packs. They teach me a few tricks of the trade, but clearly this is a skill born of intensive practice. After identifying all the rare, superrare, and ultrarare cards in the store, they head out to clear the other neighborhood shops of rare cards before daybreak, when run-of-the-mill consumers will begin purchasing.

Single cards, often purchased in these ways, are sold at card shops and on the Internet. In city centers in Tokyo such as Shibuya, Ikebukuro, and Shinjuku, there are numerous hobby shops that specialize in the buying and selling of single cards, and they are frequented by adult collectors as well as children. These cards can fetch prices ranging from the equivalent of pennies to hundreds of dollars for special edition cards. Street vendors and booths at carnivals will also often have a display of single-sale *Yugioh* cards that children flock to. The Internet, however, is probably the site that mediates the majority of these player-to-player exchanges. The total volume is extremely large. One collector I spoke to said he purchases about six hundred packs of *Yugioh* cards in each round of searches and could easily make his living buying and selling them.

Some of these adult traders are in it for that money, but all that I encountered in the card shops that I frequented proclaimed their love for *Yugioh*, and their commitment to the game. They would face off with Kaz and each other in high-tension competition, groaning in frustration at their losses. They organize themselves in regional teams that compete in official competitions in which Kaz and other kids would participate. They generally associate with each other with pseudonyms such as Yellowtail or White Moon, which they use only in the context of card game play, bracketing their more mundane identities in the moments when they sit at the duel table. The Internet sites for these *Yugioh* teams are the primary site for affiliating, with chat rooms, bulletin boards, card trade areas, and virtual duel spaces. Their real life meetings are called *offukai*, or "offline meetings," a term similar to what U.S. virtual communities call "flesh meets"

Children share the same active and entrepreneurial stance, cultural fascinations, and interests as the adult gamers, but they lack the same freedom of motion and access to money and information. The rumor mill among children is very active, though often ill informed. All the children I spoke to about it had heard of search techniques, and some even had some half-baked ideas of how it might be done. Children create their own microeconomies among peer groups, trading, buying, and selling cards in ways that mimic the more professional adult networks. Despite adult crackdowns on trading and selling between children, it is ubiquitous among card game players.

Konami has been rumored to have tried, unsuccessfully, to pressure some card shops to stop the sale of single cards. They have also tried to exclude the members of at least one adult gaming team from the official tournaments. Konami makes its money selling card packs to regular consumers through mainstream distribution channels. At the same time, Konami appeals to multiple markets by mobilizing mass-oriented strategies as well as fodder for otaku and entrepreneurial kids. They have both an official and unofficial backchannel discourse. They continue to generate buzz and insider knowledge through an increasingly intricate and ever-changing set of rules and the release of special edition cards and card packs. The market for media mix content is becoming organized into a dual structure, where there are mainstream, mass distribution channels that market and sell to run-of-the-mill consumers and an otaku zone of exchange that blurs the distinction between production and consumption, children and adults.

This backchannel discourse of the card otaku is the mostly unsung but often performed story of *Yugioh* as a case of new-economy commodity capitalism and an entrepreneurial and wired childhood. Unlike the spectacular narratives told at official tournaments and on the TV screen, the furtive rounds of collectors in the shadow of the night and the flow of cards through Internet commerce and street-level exchange point to alternative material realities in the symbolic exchange of *Yugioh* cards. These are entrepreneurial narratives involving forms of virtuosity and negotiation that are morally complicated and subversive, in contrast to the heroic narrative of good versus evil and spectacular competition gracing the pages of the manga series and official tournaments. The symbolic capital of *Yugioh* refuses to be contained within the sanctioned networks and contact points of mainstream industrialists marketing stabilized narratives to masses of children.

Siting 3: Appropriating Yugi

In December of 2002, I made one of my yearly pilgrimages to Comic Market, the largest trade show in Japan and the epicenter for a certain brand of manga-otaku. The show occupies the Tokyo Big Site twice a year, an immense convention hall located on a new landfill in the plastic port entertainment town of Daiba near Tokyo Bay. As usual, I arrive in the late morning and miss the crowds of fans that camp at the site at the crack of dawn to purchase manga fan zines, or *doujinshi*, the self-published manga, videos, and game software that reshape mainstream anime and manga narratives. The site is always packed, and millions of yen exchange hands as fans purchase magazines ranging in price from a few U.S. dollars to thirty for the high-end glossy publications. Up to three hundred thousand fans attend this event and are kept in line by an organizing team of militaristic precision that shoos throngs away from fire zones with megaphones, distributing flyers on how photos are or are not to be taken, issuing press badges, selling telephone-book-sized catalogs for the equivalent of twenty U.S. dollars. Magazines by the most popular writers are always in short supply, and buyers line up for hours in the cold and heat to purchase copies, scarce commodities that are often resold at shops and on the Internet. Unlike events catering to video game or other forms of technology otaku, the Comic Market is dominated by young, working-class women, although there is a respectable male contingent as well (Kinsella 1998: 289). Children are rarely present at this event, which is dominated by teens and young adults. There are an estimated twenty to fifty thousand amateur manga circles in Japan (Kinsella 1998; Schodt 1996: 37).

Unlike prior years, when there were only a handful of booths devoted to *Yugioh* renditions, this year *Yugioh* content dominated four long rows in the main convention room. The most popular theme is the romance between Yugi and Kaiba, the two rivals, but some also depict liaisons between Yugi and his best friend Johnouchi, Kaiba and Johnouchi, or other, less central characters. In a somewhat different vein, some artists render Yugi as a girl, with the enormous doe eyes typical of girl characters, in sexy but childlike poses. I wander through the aisles, purchasing a few magazines, some *Yugioh* letterhead, and postcards. Like most content featuring *bishounen* (beautiful boys), *Yugioh doujinshi* are generally created and consumed by women and follow the "June" genre of erotic manga featuring male homosexual relationships (named for the magazine, *June*, which popularized this genre).[1] I don't see any men on either the buying or selling end of the *Yugioh* booths. Some women avoid my gaze as I browse through their manga. Others I hear chatting openly and gaily about the liaisons between characters in the latest works.

More striking than the orderly rows of booths selling doujinshi are the cosplay (costume play) participants, who are decked out in wigs, plastic spacesuits, and other trappings of their favorite manga and anime characters. Doujinshi, video game, and anime events are all occasions for cosplayers to strut their stuff, striking poses for conventioneers toting professional camera equipment specifically for cosplay shots. The cosplayers are like Digimon and Pocket Monsters warping into our real world, colorful but routine additions to every event related to manga and anime. I spot three different groups of *Yugioh* cosplayers in my meandering through the convention halls. All groups have the central figure of Yugi, a cosplay challenge with red, black, and blonde hair spiked out in all directions. Kaiba is the second favorite, generally in his signature floor-length leather jacket with dark hair swept over his eyes. Jounouchi rounds out the basic trio, though more dedicated groups will also feature peripheral characters such as Kaiba's brother Mokuba or Yugi's girlfriend Anzu. These characters are performed by women, as is the case with most cosplay acts. Websites of cosplayers often have front pages with a warning: "This site is devoted to otaku content and gay content for women. Don't enter if you don't like this kind of stuff." Or, more simply: "Men keep out!" Favorite photos are posted of cosplayers at events such as the Comic Market or smaller, *Yugioh*-only fan events.

Like the zine artists, cosplayers vary in their openness about their alternative identities. Most conceal their cosplay activities from classmates, family, and workplace colleagues, seeing their cosplay lives and friends in high tension with the normalcy of their everyday lives. On these cosplay Web pages, and in the halls of the Comic Market, I encounter another incarnation of *Yugioh*, but one with strikingly different properties from Kaz and his cohort of card addicts. These are women otaku resignifying a series of imaginings coded as competitive, male, and child-oriented in the cultural mainstream, taking pleasure in claiming it for a woman-dominated space of desire, camaraderie, and play. With their bodies and their pens, these cosplayers and artists reinscribe *Yugioh* as a different form of play than the status economy of duels and card collecting. This is fantasy made manifest in places devoted to alternative identities and practices resolutely differentiated from the mainstream cultural imagination.

The Symbolic Economy of *Yugioh* and Children's Media

In this essay, I have described some of the heterogeneous networks of narrative and materiality that produce the imaginary of *Yugioh* as a social fact. *Yugioh* achieves its status as otherworldly fantasy manifesting itself in everyday reality through the complicated interplay among competitive play, exchange, and media production and connoisseurship. The trajectories between representation, practice, meaning, and value are by no means direct; the dominant narrative of corporations marketing culture to receptive masses of child consumers is only the beginning of the webs of relationships built with the materials of popular culture that enmesh the everyday and the fantastic.

Children's media provide repositories of the value, signification, and exoticized imagining that morph across multiple regimes of value (Appadurai 1986). In the mainstream but ghettoized regime of sanctioned children's media, *Yugioh* becomes a vehicle for children to imagine and sometimes perform greater competence than adults at complex games. The penumbra of these mainstream spectacles is the gray market of trading-card exchange that unites the ludic with real-life economies in a regime of value that threatens mainstream forms of capitalist exchange. In a radically different domain, female artists and cosplayers inhabit parallel lives that invert the dominant regimes of age as well as gender identity. These are plays between multiple marginalities, the marginal status of children, gray markets, and adult subcultures that mobilize mass culture in particular ways.

One important aspect of the relationship between our world and the other world of *Yugioh* is the role of children as the literal and symbolic mediums for translation. *Yugioh* and the majority of anime content are still *coded and marketed* as children's culture despite adults' role in their creation, consumption, and resignification. Just as Yugi's immature frame harbors the spirit of a powerful adult pharaoh, *Yugioh* content is a celebration of the triumphs of childhood over adult norms of responsibility, deferred gratification, discipline, work, and academic achievement. Sharon Kinsella (1995) suggests that one reason for the popularity of child-identified and cute products among young adults is that they represent resistance to mainstream adult. Yugi is representative of the depiction of children in anime as pure and uncorrupted and having unique powers, the ability to cross between mundane and otherworldly realities. Children engage with this culture as a form of peer identification and empowered immersion in a world where "kids rule." Youth and young adults engage with this culture as a way of deferring their entry into adult subjectivity or maintaining a parallel life of child-identified play even as they lead professional lives. I often saw salarymen at card shops pulling their neckties off as they sat down at the duel table. They would often self-deprecatingly talk about themselves in infantilized terms. As one adult gamer told me, "You're probably wondering why an adult like me is wasting all his money on kid stuff like this." Attributes associated with childhood, their commitment to play, and their fusion of fantasy and reality become ideals for a disaffected counterculture of young adults.

The symbolic separation of childhood as a unique cultural and subjective space is a cultural obsession in Japan as elsewhere, even as it is being challenged by the practical intersections between adult's and children's worlds. Only when the object of childhood is reified and idealized can we experience a sense of that object in violation and at risk. Childhood is becoming a compelling transnational cultural export outside of the domain of actual children precisely because of the value placed on an uncorrupted sphere of childhood. Otaku culture, associated with the Japanese media mix of children's media, has become a prominent adult subculture in other parts of Asia, Europe, and the United States. A media fan culture has existed in the United States around certain types of adult-oriented content such as *Star Trek*. But the Japanese otaku culture has unique characteristics, with children playing the starring roles, as well as more mainstream appeal among children. The international spread of Japanese otaku culture is normalizing adult consumption of children's media even as it continues to depict childhood as a uniquely gifted life stage.

Recent articulations of childhood studies have posited that the category of "child" is produced and consumed by people of all ages, within the power-laden hierarchies of child-adult relations (James, Jenks, and Prout 1998; James and Prout 1997). Following on this, I argue that adults are increasingly not only mobilizing tropes of childhood in political and personal arenas but are also consuming childhood as an alternative identity formation. In his study of advertising images in the 1960s and 1970s, Thomas Frank (1997) describes what he calls the conquest of cool, the appropriation of hip, youthful, countercultural images in selling commodities that broadcast resistance to the square mainstream of work and discipline. I believe we are seeing a similar process in the conquest of cute in the commodification of images and products of childhood. Childhood play is becoming fetishized and commodified as a site of resistance to adult values of labor, discipline, and diligence, as well as a site for alternative forms of symbolic value and economic exchange. It becomes a receptacle for our dissatisfactions about rationalized labor, educational achievement, stabilized economic value, and mainstream status hierarchies. For adults, these images of childhood are a colorful escape from the dulling rhythms of salaried work and household labor.

I began this essay by positing similarities between the otherworldliness of outer space and media space, but differences are also worthy of note. As with the other essays in this volume, I have worked to describe the concrete locations and discourses through which alien worlds manifest themselves in our everyday practices and identifications. In *Yugioh*, we have a world of fantasy made manifest through the workings of people, practices, technologies, and representations. I have described people in a variety of different social locations insisting on child's play as more authentic and valuable than everyday life, embodying certain truths and ideals corrupted by mainstream and adult society. Yet what distinguishes *Yugioh* is that it is more about the "fugitivity of reality" or the "fugitivity of value" than the "fugitivity of truth," which Dean describes as central to ufological discourse. Cosplayers, kids, and card addicts see themselves constructing and performing alternative realities rather questing for a greater truth "out there." What unites these discourses, whether alien or fantastic, is a shared suspicion of the ordinary as a site of mystification and a commitment to finding truth in an intimate but irreducibly exotic Other.

Notes

This research was funded by a postdoctoral fellowship from the Japan Society for the Promotion of Science, the Abe Fellowship, and the Annenberg Center for Communication at the University of Southern California. It has benefited from the comments of Debbora Battaglia, who organized the session at the American Anthropological Association meetings where this essay was first presented, as well as comments by the discussants, Jodi Dean and Susan Harding.

1. In an interview in Frederik Schodt's *Dreamland Japan*, *June* founder Toshihiko Sagawa explains the appeal of this genre for women. "The stories are about males, but the characters are really an imagined ideal that combines assumed or desired attributes of both males and females. Thus the heroes can be beautiful and gentle, like females, but without the jealousy and other negative qualities that women sometimes associate with themselves" (1996: 122). Although these works are similar to the "slash" genre of fan fiction in the United States (Jenkins 1992; Penley 1991), Japanese doujinshi take even greater creative license in repackaging established content, sometimes even changing characters' gender and often ignoring the mainstream plot entirely.

Close Encounters of the *N*th Kind: Becoming Sampled and the Mullis-ship Connection

RICHARD DOYLE

Reference Abducted

On any ordinary day—to the extent that there are such things—I see an awful lot of aliens. Most are Greys, and their olivine, inky eyes make it hard to notice their egged, practically ovulating, faces. Come to think of it, most of them are nothing but face, transplanted ocelli alighting on back-packs, skateboards, bumper stickers, tattoos. And none of them move. Not even a little. Are my eyes themselves arrested here? These aliens are, strictly speaking, liquid, conforming to the space of their containers, miming the rhythm of their vehicles, veritably bouncing from one signifying surface to another: news wire report becomes retracted becomes rumor becomes Area 51 becomes TV series: *Roswell*.[1] When I am not looking, or, I guess, even when I am, they seem to replicate. I mean, how else did so many of them suddenly, yet unmistakably, arrive?

Unless you have been in a coma since 1947—and, perhaps, even if you have—you have seen them too. Don't pretend. I know, it's a bit embarrassing. I can't remember the first time I saw one, if there was a first time. It's as if they have always been there and I simply have no memory of them. Do they, like any fit object of a paranoid narrative, remove evidence of their past existence, wipe our memories clean even as we gaze on, through them? From early childhood, I recall an enormous hypodermic, the sudden arrival of needle and plunger at the age of three, an incident with a broken leg. I can flash back to the taste of orange soda in a can at the age of five, a creamsicle, picnics gone awry, kisses and anguish, a buffet lunch from weeks ago. Why can't I remember the first time I saw an alien?

Maybe it is only now that these uncanny guests are literally able to appear, to become stickers, film images, patches, T-shirts, bongs . . . Perhaps, even, there is something about the present that forces them to appear, that flushes them out of the sky and onto an icon that replicates across our increasingly networked infoscape. Less beings of representation than proliferation, aliens arrive with news of a massively global, evolutionary transformation: the Earth become citational network.

Of course, the biologist Lynn Margulis, in recuperating and buttressing the work of early-twentieth-century researchers such as Vernadsky, has demonstrated that the Earth has long been such a mesh of connections, but it is only relatively recently that this interconnection has again become an object of scientific consciousness. Through processes both technological and social in nature, the Earth has become less globe than mesh, each and every location of which is liable to sprout an alien. If the "Big Blue Marble" images of the Earth from space were extraterrestrial citations that provoked a sense of unity, then the proliferating icons of the alien image—Look, there's another one!—renders a networked ubiquity.[2] The movement from Gaia to the alien is topological in effect, as the Big Blue Marble goes inside out, imploding into itself as every surface on the Earth becomes, in principle, interconnected with any other, ready for an alien sticker or maybe a Starbucks . . . It is in this sense that the alien presents an impossible vision: the visualization of an always mobile and differentiating network, our increasingly informatic biosphere.

The effects of these cross-connections cannot be captured by terms as simple as *globalization* or *information*, but even a crude quantitative analysis of the production of information is instructive. According to a recent study, it took humans approximately three hundred thousand years to produce twelve exabytes of information, and since the year 2000 we have likely doubled that output.[3] One may and should argue the premises of any such calculation, but the study is nonetheless instructive; something like an infoquake is taking place, a massive increase in symbolic activity that renders usual understandings of context and boundaries into non sequiturs. Indeed, it would be surprising if such a transformation of the human ecology *didn't* present unusual symptoms, and it is my contention that, along with mountains of spam, the alien is one of them: *essentially* out of context, the alien is perhaps deterritorialization itself, our spacey and spatial rendering of the strange and uncertain proximities of the increasingly networked Earth. As veritable artificial life forms sprouting in the massively networked ecology of Terra, aliens perhaps augur a change in consciousness whose only cosmological analogue is Copernican. A new and altogether uncanny vision of the human can be glimpsed in the alien: *Homo sapiens* is less "Man the hunter" than a receiving station for an uncanny Other. In this context, the vision of the alien is one of profound and unexpected hope: humans become unexpected sites of hospitality, a sudden proximity to a (transhuman) network: *Homo experimentalis*.

Sample Example

Do we have any witnesses to this event, this becoming icon of the alien, the alien's abduction by the image? What would prevent a witnessing of such a becoming?

We need, of course, more than one witness, and in this segment we will be listening to some complicated and implicated testimony about this entrance of the alien into our networks of replication. For before it became iterable enough to appear, literally, anywhere, the image of the alien was attached to a series of ecstatic bodies, bodies that were probed, abducted, instructed, forced to speak, and even subject to sudden fits of ideas.[4] Some of these bodies lived in and off the discourse we call, out of habit, science fiction. Others found themselves on a couch, on drugs, hypnotized, or speaking out of the pages of a popular book. But all of them, as witnesses, testify to the sampled quality of abduction.

By sampling, of course, I am referencing the heterogeneous chains of sound and/or image that have composed hip-hop and new music performance for three decades. Sampling—the grafting of one sequence of sound or image onto another—relies in its conceptualization and practice on an abstraction of sound and image as information, information whose major effect emerges less from a production of meaning than from a capacity to be networked, hooked up with new contexts and moments. By this I do not mean the music, video, or text that samples seek to *inform* in the CNN sense of the term, although that may also be true. Rather, the emergence of the practice of sampling is coincident with the capacity to manipulate sound and images as sequences, a citationality amplified by the digital media, whose very substrate is discontinuity. So, for example, when DJ Spooky operates through the syntheses of disjunctive sound—a track from a stereo album used to test high-fidelity equipment that enunciates the words "stereophonic sound" is blended and refrained through percussion, horns, jet engines, and various styles of noise—he treats the entire audio universe as an immense informatic palette.

> The Subliminal Kid moved in and took over bars, cafes and juke boxes of the world cities and installed radio transmitters and microphones in each bar so that the music and talk of any bar could be heard in all his bars and he had tape recorders in each bar that played and recorded at arbitrary intervals and his agents moved back and forth with portable tape recorders and brought back street sound and talk and music and poured it into his recorder array. (DJ Spooky, *Necropolis*, liner notes, sampling from Burroughs, *Nova Express*)

As the sampled liner note copy suggests, the emergence of sampling as a technique is conjoined with the continual possibility of *being sampled*. Not merely a manipulative technique of an informatic medium, sampling describes an ontological condition—the continual and structural possibility of sampling, of one chunk of information being copied and networked with another, "street sound and talk and music . . . poured into his recorder array." Crucial to this tactic is the prima facie aleatory character of the act of transduction itself—"recorded at arbitrary intervals"—which suggests an unfathomable origin, a continual differentiation that puts the very agency of creative production into disarray. Hence the importance today of the DJ as a figure who is everywhere transforming our vision of the artist, the author, the researcher.

Indeed, this ontological exposure is registered on at least two intertwined strands: hope and terror. Hope fathoms the capacities for transformation complicit with being sampled. New surface areas of embodiment and deterritorialization are constantly exfoliating as technologies of informatic sampling blur the very landscape of "human" consciousness, rendering practices of autonomy, privacy, and propriety into entropic conceptual formations good mostly at propagating themselves. Contemporary privacy technologies such as PGP (Pretty Good Privacy) cryptography and voice encryption seek to reduce the possibility of such media citations—such as a digital photograph of an abused prisoner—and their subsequent high-velocity propagation through the mediascape. Here information economies seem to enable little more than the acceleration and amplification of that most ancient of media: the rumor.[5] Information technology's habit of replication threatens to make secrecy extinct.

This amplification has nonetheless induced a qualitative difference in the experience and scope of our ecology of rumor, to the extent that the entire Earth becomes subject to what Jung called the "UFO rumor" in the ubiquitous visualization and narration of the alien. Abduction's difference pertains to its demand for an identity to *host* the alien—abduction is the (re)appearance of the transhuman on subjectivity's radar. In this sense, the global village exists only to the extent that global gossip can be said to circulate, a connective tissue of rhetorical practices, including images of massively parallel events whose function is less to communicate than to *inform*—and this provides a talismanic avatar or heuristic for the translation of a massively parallel system into a serial one.

Becoming parallel, as the mathematician Brian Rotman has put it, is a most plausible and even adaptive response to this infoquake. SETI@home, for example, is a data-processing tentacle of the search for extraterrestrial intelligence. Data collected by the Arecibo 305-meter diameter radio telescope is cut into .25-megabyte sections and distributed over a network of computers connected via the Internet. These computers—in basements, dens, labs, Starbuckses—"crunch" the raw data and search for patterns along the hydrogen spectrum, 1,420 MHz. The unused computer time of millions is harnessed and organized into an investigation of the cosmos. While a serial computation of this sort would be prohibitively expensive and take an enormous amount of time, this parallel solution makes the computation of even computationally "hard" problems (such as the traveling salesman or P = NP problems) plausibly tractable. In this context, SETI@home "customers" sample the cosmos and troll, with sympathy, for the alien: "Upon completion (typically after several days) of the data analysis for each chunk, a short message reporting candidate signals is presented to the customer and also returned to Big Science and to the University of Washington for post-processing" (http://setiathome.ssl.berkeley.edu). Faced with an unknown and enormous quantity of information, SETI@home reconceptualized its work, shifting from the concept of the individual listener (e.g., radio astronomer Frank Drake's "eureka" moment in 1959, which helped launch the field) to that of a collective or at least distributed intelligence. Still, such a distributed approach has its downside. When it comes to the *interpretive control* of the project, for example, SETI@home is essentially leaky—expectant "customers" are likely to evolve their own interpretative practices and become convinced that they are about to achieve contact. Indeed, without such an expectation, one wonders why anyone would download the software at all, save the pleasure of being part of a collective intelligence grappling with a cosmic question and thereby, just possibly, achieving contact with each other. Hence the licensing agreement accepted by each "customer" of SETI@home contains the unusual request that he or she not contact the media.

> Strong signals will occasionally be detected and displayed by SETI@home software during the course of data analysis. Please do not call the press when such signals appear, as thousands of signals have so far all proven to be due to interference (human made artificial signals) or test patterns used to test the hardware and software. (SETI@home licensing agreement)

Given this context, it might be asked what "use" a serial practice such as "identity" is to an ecology of massive information amplification. Ought we not jettison the very practice of the self in this new ecology of massive information? Just who is it that can "accept" this licensing agreement and promise not to panic?

Jung suggested that the disc figure of the UFO, while not exhaustively explained as a purely psychological problem, was in fact a mandala, a visual figure for the navigation and imagination of totality. Simultaneously open and closed, the mandala offers a way of organizing the massive multiplicity of the cosmos. Robert Thurman goes further in his analysis of the Tibetan Buddhist deployment of the mandala, arguing that these forms offer nothing less than an "architecture of enlightenment," veritable media technologies for the transformation of serial subjects into the massively parallel beings and bodhisattvas of enlightenment. Perhaps the self itself is such an avatar, a useful handhold on the enormous complexity of newly amplified and highly redundant information. In this context, the self is a veritable filter, as well as a "cipher," for organizing the sudden apprehension of information.

Yet this self can never, in principle, manage all of this information even as it emerges from it: "A seller on eBay tried to auction off a cough drop that Gov. Arnold Schwarzenegger allegedly used, then tossed into a trash can, listing the item under the heading Schwarzenegger's DNA. But the ad posted on the popular Web site was quickly yanked after eBay decided it fell into the category of body parts, which the Web site will not list for sale."[6] As this example of a thwarted eBay transaction makes clear, the thoughts and practices of the "informational universe" are hardly confined in their effects to our usual understandings of media. They are also an aspect of a larger panic—an encounter with the exo-biological character of an informational universe, what funkster George Clinton (perhaps the most sampled man on the planet) has dubbed in another context "the Mothership Connection," a connection among and between bodies that is less about cognition than funk—an "interplanetary" affective transmission. In such an informatic universe, evolution and its distribution function less according to a logic of incorporation than proliferation, a universal ecstasy that thrives on the copy (DNA adrift) even more than it eats away at an interiority or organism: World become Kazaaa.

For musical sampling is merely one site of the deterritorializing effects of informatics. Informatic capture enables an unpredictable movement: moving sounds from one site to another, the high resolution tweaking of a sample differentially repeats transformations in practices of the life sciences. With the emergence of a digital molecular biology organized around the manipulation of traits or alleles as information, the "organism" or even "life" no longer serves as a delimitable object of biological inquiry. Instead—as with DJ Spooky's sonic universe—molecular biology operates on an immense informatic interface. The new citationality of molecular biology enables an emerging remix among species and phyla. The contours of the human body are being virtually reorganized, as the alleged "essence" of the body, DNA, becomes mobile, a movable and thus removable script of oneself that is constantly available to an alleged "outside" that we cannot master. It is perhaps little wonder, then, that one of the most consistent and problematic reports of the abduction narrative is that a subject's DNA has been sampled.[7]

Pitches are given to venture capitalists, initial public offerings are floated, living systems begin to coevolve with the stock market. As a result, unprecedented life forms arrive and refuse their policy of biocontainment: Taco Bell finds itself subject to an invasion by alien DNA, as Starlink Corn, a genetically modified organism not intended for human consumption, ends up in its taco shells and on its menus. Indeed, "Life finds a way" (*Jurassic Park*).

It is, of course, crucial that such novel life forms arrive first as nearly transparent commodities available for universal exchange, dissipative structures literally becoming machines for the production of selective wealth. Beyond "speaking" as commodities or transforming our ecology into an allegedly dead zone of "things," such novel life forms augur new forms of leaky deterritorialization that are quite literally ecstatic, an allopoiesis that overtakes the self-propagation of autopoietic systems. Autopoietic systems —such as ourselves—evolve as renderings of a sturdy but dynamic distinction between "inside" and "outside," a scar of Darwinian natural selection, while allopoiesis names those practices of momentary breakdown—such as abduction?—coincident to massive and sudden transformation.[8] Darwin's lengthy and delirious treatments of sexual selection—such as his discussion of birdsong, itself a recombinant act of allopoiesis—is perhaps most instructive for the present. We are, as the evolutionary psychologist Merlin Donald might put it, out of our heads, increasingly distributed beings whose cognitive and evolutionary insides are becoming outsourced, folded into and across a network like so much Starlink Corn in so many crunchy fast food simulacra of Mexican cuisine. Donald wrote of the effect that external storage device "writing" had on the emergence of thought and interiority, but he only hints at the forms of consciousness cultivated by a much more amplified and differential ecology composed by this most recent encounter between capital and evolution, biotechnology—the new capacity to copy and express aspects of living systems.

Citing Sightings: Close Encounters of the *N*th Kind

> Once upon a time called "Right now!"—George Clinton, *The Mothership Connection*

If this recombinant universe of incessant sampling is the ever shifting context for the emergence of an identity subject to abduction—"I'm abducted, therefore I am"—it is all the more striking that one of the key technologies of informatic replication should itself repeat motifs of an abduction event. Kary Mullis, the chemist who received the Nobel Prize for the invention of polymerase chain reaction (PCR), usually gives at least partial credit for the discovery of PCR to his use of LSD, an attribution I have treated seriously and at some length elsewhere.[9] But in *Dancing Naked in the Mind Field*—Mullis's 1998 autobiography—he also writes with great humor and insight about an experience with a glowing raccoon.

While familiars and other animals make frequent appearances in the burgeoning literature on abduction, Mullis's encounter with a glowing mammal is striking in its formulation and resonance with the biotechnologies that his invention—a veritable Xerox machine for DNA—would enable. While space, time, and audience credulity constrain my account of Mullis's abduction event and its possible importance to the context of PCR's emergence, I would like to offer a schematic treatment of his account of this "encounter with aliens" as a way of foregrounding the persistence and consistency of the sampling symptom sketched out above.

In 1985, Mullis drove out to his Mendocino, California, cabin, a place he dubbed the Institute for Further Study. Less than two years earlier, Mullis had covered the interior of the cabin with scrawled reactions that traced out the simple idea for a polymerase chain reaction. As Mullis describes it, PCR is a technique for extracting a sample of DNA using a "find" sequence—a short segment of DNA that would stick to its mirror image—then iterating this process with a shorter "find" segment of DNA, and so on in "further study" until he had located the site (cite?) he sought to amplify. In yet further study, as Mullis puts it, "I could make that sequence of DNA between the sites where the two search strings landed reproduce the hell out of itself" ([1998] 2000: 6).

Suffice to say that in both its conceptualization and its effects, PCR is a sampling device, a recipe for replication. Mullis's algorithmic approach to DNA treats genomic information less as a "book of life" to be "read" than as a program to be hacked. In addition, the hack Mullis deploys is itself citational in action: it seeks merely to extract and copy.

And it is precisely as a citation or sample that Mullis describes what occurred in 1985 at the Institute for Further Study.[10] Heading to the outhouse, Mullis stumbles onto some weird shit, indeed: "I walked down the steps, turned right—and then at the far end of the path, under a fir tree, something was glowing. I pointed my flashlight at it anyhow. It only made it whiter where the beam landed. It seemed to be a raccoon. . . . The raccoon spoke. 'Good evening, doctor.' It said" (Mullis [1998] 2000: 131). Mullis thinks he said something in response, but he isn't sure what, and a discontinuity in his memory followed: "The next thing I remember, it was early in the morning. I was walking along a road uphill from my house. What went through my head as I walked toward my house was, 'What the hell am I doing here?' " (131). I will pass over the ways in which Mullis's testimony itself has recourse to a sample—he cites himself in the context of his own story, told in the first person—but suffice to say that this veritable cutting and pasting, deterritorialization and reterritorialization, is familiar enough to anyone who has perused the literature on abduction. Such a cutting and pasting is often itself told in informatic terms—"The forces involved in the implanting, storage, and recovery of information remain among the central mysteries of the whole abduction phenomenon"—and relies on an extraction and recontextualization of memory as well as a spatial deterritorialization and reterritorialization, an extraction whose find sequence appears to be "Good evening, Doctor."[11]

Now Mullis had some interesting and apparently effective therapeutic ideas about how to respond to the panic he incurred from this experience—it involves an AR 15 assault rifle, an enormous flashlight, and a good deal of shouting—but crucial to the account Mullis offers is another sampling, the experience of being a citation in the literature of abduction, which of course he now (precisely right now) is. Here Mullis describes an encounter in a bookstore: "Some time later I was in a bookstore in La Jolla. I noticed a book on display by Whitley Strieber called *Communion*. On the cover was a drawing that captured my attention. An oval shaped head with large inky eyes staring straight ahead" (Mullis [1998] 2000: 135). "Captured" by the inky eyes, themselves possible citations of a raccoon's "mask," Mullis veritably falls into the book. He finds in it confirmation of his own symptoms—the cabin in the woods, a speech act to an animal with exaggerated eyes (an owl), the lost time and memory—when the phone rings, interrupting one sample with another: "While I was reading this book my daughter, Louise, called from Portland. 'Dad, there's a book I want you to read. It's called *Communion*' "(135). The convergence of citations here functions as a kind of evidence for Mullis, evidence that *something* was going on in this massive interconnection of stories of people whose attention has been captured in a way Mullis can only dub "weird." If it is indeed a "communion," it is a communion of a network. More crucial than any first-person testimony, the connection of a phone call and a book with a short segment of experience testifies to the effect of sudden interconnection associated with being sampled.

But *what* did Mullis experience? It is provocative to map the connections between his way of being in his cabin and ways of thinking and feeling associated with his transformation into a sample and his invention of a sampling technology. But of course Mullis invented PCR almost two years *before* his experience with the glowing raccoon. His first published article *was* on time reversal, so perhaps this question deserves further study. But why the glowing raccoon? Mullis writes that he can't publish any scientific papers on the experience with the raccoon because he "can't make glowing raccoons appear. I can't buy them from a scientific supply house to study" ([1998] 2000: 136). Well, it was certainly dark that night, and flashlight or no it could be that the "masked" eyes of the raccoon were indeed a mask and that in a citation of his very own paper on time reversal Mullis saw a little bit of the future, a future in which PCR enables glowing mammals indeed.[12]

Sampling DMT "with His Pony Pal Pokey Too"

> . . . the thought came to me with certainty that they were manipulating my DNA, changing its structure.—DMT volunteer, University of New Mexico, 1991[13]

Six years after Mullis's encounter with a (possibly bioluminescent) raccoon, Dr. Richard Strassman began human subject trials with N-N-Dimethlytryptamine (DMT), a potent psychedelic compound endogenously produced by the human brain. When injected, smoked, or ingested in combination with an MAO (mono oxidase) inhibitor such as *Syrian rue* or *Banisteria caapi*, DMT consistently produces visions that are among the most compelling in the human archive. Psychonauts regularly describe their experiences in ballistic terms, a kind of psychedelic "shock and awe": "I can only say it is like being shot out of a cannon into space and coming onto a 20 hit acid peak in about 10 seconds. User beware. Approach this with the utmost respect."[14]

Perhaps the truly remarkable thing about Strassman's study is that he was able to carry it out. In the midst of an intense War on Drugs, Strassman legally administered an extremely potent psychedelic to human volunteers. Compared to this extraordinary act of knowledge production, the reports of the DMT volunteers perhaps risk banality—a kind of tripper's "Penthouse Forum." Yet it is worth noting that some of the most persistent and consistent reports produced by Strassman's volunteers concerned alien contact, as in the alien biotechnologists narrated in this section's first sample from an (apparently) transgenic tripper.[15]

Ubiquitous, indeed, "Greys" show up even in a realm persistently described as an alternate dimension. Familiars of deterritorialization, these aliens are primarily informational beings: "Many volunteers' encounters with life-forms in these non material worlds involved the powerful sense of an exchange of information. The type of information varied widely. Sometimes it concerned the biology of these beings."[16] At once biological and informatic, this "powerful sense" is indeed sensory and packs a paradoxically informatic wallop. San Francisco Bay Area psychonauts Gracie and Zarkov write that for an interval of one to five minutes after smoking DMT, "For all practical purposes, you will no longer be embodied. You will be part of the intergalactic information network."[17]

But if amateur psychonauts and Strassman's volunteers experience DMT as a veritable password into a encrypted network of information, they nonetheless insist that the beings are no mere simulacra: "This is not at all a metaphor. It is an independent constant reality" (Strassman 195).[18] And, while the volunteers repeatedly parried attempts to highlight the rhetorical nature of their encounters—definitively differentiating the DMT experience from, for example, a dream—they nonetheless narrated their experiences in the terms and characters of a space topologically, if not ontologically, other than ordinary reality: "A high-tech nursery with a single Gumby, three feet tall, attending me. I felt like an infant. Not a human infant, but an infant relative to the intelligences represented by the Gumby" (193).

What exactly are "the intelligences represented by the Gumby"? Gumby, as many readers are no doubt aware, was the claymation character created by Art Clokey who could "jump into any book with his pony pal Pokey too." Gumby was thus a three-dimensional, interdimensional traveler whose very vehicle was intertextuality—a capacity to be spliced into any other text. Gumby: familiar of a world enmeshed.[19]

This mesh yields an experience of reality that is both deeply participatory and hardly subject to individual control. On the Usenet newsgroup alt.drugs.psychedelics, the appropriately handled "Twitchin" sums it up after an experience smoking DMT's legal (and more potent) chemical cousin, 5-MEO-DMT.

> DMT Aliens are there. . and they are not purpleheaded beasts! (unless you want them to be!) What is reality? It is what WE as humans make it. . its impossible for ALIENS to see it the same. . I mean, our senses. . we make it. . that's what makes OUR reality. . THEY will be different. . information highway. . hyperspace. . that's where things MERGE. . that's when ALL are ONE. . live through it. . experience it. . its temporary. . 30 Mins later. . Im back (?)—I love this space where you try to "recover."—

While this posting would seem to lean toward a solipsistic recuperation of human agency—"What is reality? It is what WE as humans make it . . .", Twitchin negotiates the ontological conundrum of the alien by simultaneously affirming human participation in the emergence of our reality and entangling us with a thoroughly differential and densely interconnected informatic Other. The encounter with the alien becomes fundamentally unknowable—"THEY will be different"—and palpably involved with human experience, the experience of experiment and ordeal characteristic of the "MERGE" into information: "that's when ALL are ONE . . . live through it . . . experience it. . . ."

Crucial to these encounters is that they must be experienced to be communicated or understood; as with the simple algorithms of the physicist Stephen Wolfram's *New Kind of Science*, no shortcut exists between the informatic encounter and the patterns they yield. These are encounters of the *n*th kind, unknowable in advance even as they are thoroughly informational.[20]

How to navigate such an enmeshed ecology? How can we, with Twitchin, "try to 'recover' "? For if allopoiesis—the dynamics of becoming Other, even, perhaps, alien—must be folded into our amnesiac theories of life, so, too, do we continue to dwell fitfully within the egoic and all-too-human ecologies of heredity, labor, and value *extraction*—the autopoiesis of self-propagating capitalism. These practices of compression (more product, less time)—and deterritorialization (information shrinks and kinks space, enabling the sudden proximity of the alien) tell a very truncated story of the future, a telos whose vanishing point into nanotechnology augurs what one website calls the "big scrunch," a reductionist apocalypse. How can a highly distributed and increasingly allopoietic open-source infosphere continue to sustain beings so addicted to encrypted, privatized, and entropic forms of life? I would suggest that abductees are early adopters of a transitional, transhuman identity precipitated by our intensified and amplified ecologies of information. Can the identity practices of the last century—citizen, soldier, human—survive the infoquake that abduction records?

In short, no. If they are to do so, these identity practices must avoid the algorithmic bottleneck presented by a regime of verification—it is a computationally intense labor, for example, to sort out an experience of DMT or abduction into categories of true and false, categories that may be non sequiturs in a world of information constantly subject to change. Indeed, as Strassman found out, it is even difficult to differentiate between DMT experience and abduction events themselves. In place of verification, we need tools that can help us "live through it" even as it transforms us.

Philip K. Dick, a veritable psychonaut of Gaia's newly informatic mesh, wrote incessant exegesis of his experience being transformed into information in the early 1970s. Dick wrote until his death in 1982, finding an adequate response to his alien, informatic contact only in graphomaniacal autobiographical fiction that claimed to be telling the truth in at least four novels and a handwritten, unnumbered manuscript at least nine thousand pages long. "Nailed by information," Dick rendered a name and an outburst of information—VALIS, the Vast Active Living Intelligent System. VALIS—or, as he sometimes called it, Sophia, firebright, the AI (artificial intelligence) voice—was symptomatic of Dick's perception that the universe was composed entirely of information. Fittingly for a novelist who felt that he had "fallen" into one of his own novels, VALIS told Dick the same thing it told one of his characters, Nicholas Brady: He had tuned into an intergalactic network.

Dick's response is instructive. It was only by jettisoning his sense of an autonomous self—he became a character in one of his books, though his books were fiction—that he was able to manage the ontological shock of nonlinear time and alien contact.[21] But his turn toward fiction was not a retreat into illusion but a disciplined treatment of the world (not unlike Gumby's) as both "intertwingled" with metaphor and irreducible to it, a practice that experiences fiction as differential to reality, not opposed to it.[22]

Roland Fischer, a psychologist at Ohio State University in the 1960s, offered a model of what he called the "perception-hallucination" continuum as a "multi-valued logic" for navigating the differences and distinctions between "ordinary" states of consciousness and "altered" ones provoked by (scientifically administered) psilocybin. Fischer sought to move beyond an oppositional understanding of hallucination (or fiction) and reality, but in so doing he crafted not a perspectivalism but a deeply participatory ontology wherein states not subject to 3D verification palpably exist for the subject. Thus, "hallucination and dream experiences may not only be 'true' or 'false' but also 'as-if true' and 'as-if false,' while the subject is playing an actor's role and is, at the same time, a captive audience of his own drama. It is like the experience of alternating figure and ground while being included in the change" (1969: 166).[23] This fluctuation of figure and ground is entangled with the subjective experience of the investigator: an attempt, and failure, of verification: "What needs to be specified is the inability of the hallucinating subject to *verify* through *voluntary motor* performance in *Euclidean three dimensional physical space* the phenomena experienced in the *conceptual and sensory* dimension" (Fischer 1969: 161).

This disjunction between motor performance and sensory stimuli is, for Fischer, the very kernel of hallucinatory phenomena, as his research suggests over and over that a high sensory to motor ratio provokes hallucinatory experience in human subjects. Perhaps today we are witnessing the manifestation of a similar mismatch, as human consciousness undergoes a figure-ground fluctuation as it becomes transhuman: beings of evolution and PCR wielding hackers of it, the Mullis-Ship Connection, whose very image is the cartoon made flesh of the Grey. The twofold expansion of information—both a quantitative increase and its technical expansion into new domains—is not matched by any significant increase in voluntary motor performance (e.g., judgment or deliberation), but it can perhaps be modeled by the rush of information in a DMT session and the avatars of Greys that apparently enable the replication of DMT reports. If so, these citations of the alien are most certainly hallucinations, not (yet) subject to verification in "*Euclidean three dimensional physical space*." Yet these hallucinations announce the difficult truth of their own existence, signatures of a transhuman condition enmeshed with the dynamics of information, the reception of an uncanny, proliferating, and uncertain Other: close encounters of the *n*th kind.

Notes

1. If Google is understood in the oracular tradition, properly treated as an offshoot of the *I Ching*, then it yields something like the following queried "Roswell?": www.crashdown.com. Accessed May 12, 2005.

2. See, for example, the Apollo 14 astronaut Edgar Mitchell's experience with the view from his cockpit window at www.edmitchellapollo14.com/bookexcerpt .htm#), as well as James Lovelock's experience with the Big Blue Marble pictures in Lovelock, *Gaia: A New Look at Life on Earth*.

3. Google, "How much information 2000," http://www.sims.berkeley.edu/research/projects/how-much-info.

4. *Ecstasis*: the state of being beside oneself.

5. For a treatment of gossip and rumor as an origin story for language, see Robin Dunbar's *Grooming, Gossip and the Evolution of Language*.

6. See http://www.hindustantimes.com/news/181_775574,00030010.htm/.

7. In recent years, DNA has also become the principle medium for the investigation of alien abduction accounts. See www.theozfiles.com/anomaly_investigation _group.htm. The Johnson Space Center is operating an alien DNA collection station—a hyperclean "hospitality" room ready to be dusted by alien DNA, which, some argue, continually dusts the Earth. See "Keeping Alien Samples Safe for Study," at www.space.com.

8. Allopoiesis emerges out of the work of Humberto Maturana and Francisco Varela, Chilean biologists whose theory of "autopoiesis" was an influential postcybernetic model of living systems and a potent response to the molecular reductionism of ascendant molecular biology. *Autopoiesis* names the dynamic systemic production of an organization by itself, while *allopoiesis* invokes such a system rendering something other (i.e., other than itself). The concept of allopoiesis functions as a rhetorical adjunct to a definition of *autopoiesis* in Maturana's and Varela's work, as well as in the wider literature on autopoiesis. The *Web Dictionary of Cybernetic Systems* notes in its definition of *allopoiesis* that "The primary value of the concept of allopoiesis is that it contrasts with autopoiesis" (Dunbar 1998). This "contrast" often suggests that biological systems function as fundamentally autopoietic systems—organisms capable of "autonomy"—and that allopoietic systems somehow "lack" autopoiesis. This is at best half the story of living systems, a story

about life's habits of territorialization that forgets the continual implication of deterritorialization with living systems: reproduction is fundamentally allopoietic, yielding entities even in genetic drift that differ from generation to generation. And evolution itself exudes novelty that recursively alters its own dynamics—the evolution of photosynthesis pumped the atmosphere with oxygen, enabling the emergence of aerobic life, enabling the emergence of hominids busy pumping the atmosphere with hydrocarbons. For more on the dynamics of deterritorialization and territorialization at play in allopoiesis, see Doyle 2003.

9. Doyle 2002.

10. Here Mullis's institute samples from another space of psychedelic investigation—the Merry Pranksters school bus, "Further."

11. Mack 1994: 52.

12. This is, of course, Eduardo Kac's transgenic bunny, Alba, in digital raccoon drag. Alba was created by splicing a gene from a bioluminescent jellyfish (the GFP gene) into her genome. She glows only under the proper wavelength of light. See www.ekac.org.

13. Quoted in Strassman 2001: 206. See also Narby 1999.

14. Thorn's report is available at http://lycaeum.org.

15. Jim DeKorne's excellent *Psychedelic Shamanism: The Cultivation, Preparation and Shamanic Use of Psychotropic Plants* (1994) offers a lengthy and instructive discussion of the connection between shamanic practice and abduction. DeKorne was a volunteer in Strassman's study.

16. Strassman 2001: 190.

17. This is available at http://www.nepenthes.lycaeum.org/GandZ/gandz.dmt.html.

18. This refusal of the metaphorical nature of the DMT vision is perhaps the most consistent symptom of its ingestion, both in Strassman's reports and the more anonymous media of the Internet trip report: "It wasn't a planet that 'kind of looked like a lion', it absolutely WAS a lion's head so immense as to be a planet" (http://www.dmt.lycaeum.org/reports/reports/thorn.txt).

19. This is available at www.feetofclay.brokentoys.org. See also Kaplan and Clokey 1986. *Gumby: The Authorized Biography*.

20. See Wolfram's A *New Kind of Science*, available at www.wolframscience.com/nksonline/page-739.

21. For all intents and purposes, Dick was Gumby, damn it: "This brings me to my frightening premise. I seem to be living in my own novels more and more" (Fischer 1969).

22. *Intertwingled* is sampled from the work of Ted Nelson.

23. Fischer notes that these "as-if" experiences are kin to both hallucinated states

and dreams in the difficulty they pose for interpretation: "The symbolic metaphorical language and logic is labeled by reference to the very context within which it is expressed which makes the interpretations as difficult as, for instance . . . learning English in English" (1969: 166). This is of course precisely the situation of the human infant.

"Come on, people . . . we *are* the aliens. We seem to be suffering from Host-Planet Rejection Syndrome": Liminal Illnesses, Structural Damnation, and Social Creativity

JOSEPH DUMIT

> From: CC
>
> This sounds like an X-File, BB {grin} I bet Mulder would believe you . . .
>
> SCULLY: Mulder, all the blood work and tests have come back normal. I understand these people are suffering, but there's nothing quantifiable here.
>
> MULDER: This has been seen through history, Scully, and called by many names: hysteria, neuralgia, post-viral encephalopathy, Epstein Barr virus . . .
>
> SCULLY: Yes, but how do we prove to the medical establishment what these people are experiencing? We have no reliable evidence.
>
> MULDER: The truth is out there, Scully . . .
>
> ok, that's just some grins for all the *x-files* fans out there . . .
>
> —Newsgroup message posted to alt.med.cfs

This joking message parodying an X-*Files* conversation is poignant because chronic fatigue syndrome (CFS) sufferers are too often the subject of such conversations. When a CFS sufferer goes to a medical professional, he or she is faced with inconclusive diagnoses with depressing regularity. Those who suffer from CFS *are* the aliens in the conversations, the ones who cannot be explained by the current medical system but cannot be explained away either. Yet they persist, in between the lines, and online they try to figure out more mundane matters: how to obtain some kind of care, how to keep their friends, how to understand why they cannot keep anyone's attention long enough to make a difference.

Chronic fatigue syndrome is an illness that enters the established medical lexicon by way of substantial impairment of daily life involving loosely articulated and widely variant symptoms that include crushing physical exhaustion; the sense of being "like an empty shell," unable to muster social interaction and lacking energy to focus, hold onto, or "track" thoughts; a crashing response to recreational or otherwise relatively benign drugs; and so on.[1] Not surprisingly, CFS is often linked to social rejection and medical exclusion, in part because it is characterized by great uncertainty as to its nature, cause, and social course. Overall, then, CFS can be profoundly alienating personally, within the sphere of medical discourse, and politically as well.

My focus here is on chronic fatigue syndrome as one in a set of invisible or emergent illnesses and the social movements that surround them —illnesses, that is, which seem to challenge the norms of contemporary technoscience and biomedicine. These illnesses include multiple chemical sensitivity, repetitive strain injury, and Gulf War syndrome (GWS). My interest here is not what science, medicine, and intellectuals do or should make of people with these illnesses but with what sufferers have collectively done with science, medicine, and social science in the name of their afflictions. Based on interviews, fieldwork, and extensive analysis of online discussions, I have come to call these collective afflictions *illnesses you have to fight to get* (Dumit, forthcoming). Each one has an intense, unique history and is often extremely different from the others symptomatically and otherwise. Further, each has been the recent subject of ethnographic work, and, indeed, the anthropology of these disorders is growing (Brown et al. 2004; Ware and Kleinman 1992; Fortun 2001; Young 1995).

In this essay, I first provide an overview of the social forms of these illnesses, of contradiction and liminality, and how these shape the subjectivity and uncertain community of sufferers. Next, invoking the work of Alberto Melucci, I trace how and why these uncertain communities become social movements whose aims are not to reform society but to join it. I argue that these movements are tactical and not strategic, aiming in a most mundane way to be assimilated by having sufferers become patients in a system that currently refuses to accommodate them. Finally, I take up some situations in which CFS sufferers are targeted as conveniently repugnant because they do not fit in and are turned into exemplars of what is wrong with society. "Host-planet rejection syndrome" is an ironically apt description of their ongoing predicament.

Despite their very different histories and meanings, "illnesses you have to fight to get" share some important characteristics that should, on one level, be separated and studied and on another level be analyzed together as structurally (in part) produced by culture and the political economy. In brief, and with every intention of being provocative, the ways in which these illnesses have similarities are listed below.[2]

1. *Biomental.* Their nature and existence are contested as to whether they are primarily mental, psychiatric, or biological. In contrast to analyses of the genome project populations, for example, these people are not "at risk" or "presymptomatically ill." Rather, they are the opposite: symptomatically nonill by any existing diagnostic criterion (Dumit 2000; Nelkin and Tancredi 1989). Thus, instead of biology preceding symptoms the symptoms precede biology.
2. *Causally undetermined.* Their etiology is likewise contested as to social, genetic, toxic, and personal possibilities. They are also therapeutically diverse: the nature and reimbursement of competing therapies, including alternative medicine, is wide open. And they are cross-linked: each of these conditions has been linked to the other ones as subsets, mistaken diagnoses, and comorbid conditions.
3. *Legally explosive.* Each condition is caught up in court battles, administrative categories, and legislative maneuvers. Disability status, for instance, is haphazardly applied to all of these illnesses.
4. *Biosocial.* Persons having these conditions are organized and coordinated and feel a kinship based on their shared illness experience.

The level of medical, social, legal, scientific, and economic disorder implied by these characteristics and their undecidability must not be underestimated. Each of these conditions is a serious matter not only for the persons afflicted but also for the thousands of physicians, families, researchers, corporations, insurance companies, and administrative agencies having to deal with them.

Those who, in one way or another, have one of these illnesses come to inhabit or embody a particularly liminal space.[3] Victor Turner derived the concept of liminal from the work of Van Gennep as a transition phase between two states of social order. In its first meaning, the liminal is a period or area of ambiguity with few attributes of either state, defined negatively as neither one nor the other. But, Turner observes, this threshold nature of the limen, or margin, can itself be protracted and prolonged into a tunnel, into a positive status of its own, neither one nor the other *and both one and the other* (1982).

Rereading the characteristics of these illnesses in light of liminality invites consideration of how together they structure an antisocial space opposed to biomedical categorization—neither mental nor biological nor even psychiatric and yet all of them, neither social nor environmental nor personal and so on. And most significantly in the American medical system they are neither healthy nor diagnosable, insurable nor disabled. Socially this renders them silent and without representation in the political sense and unrepresentable in an objective, scientific sense. As a result of the overdetermined ambiguity and contestability of these illnesses, there are endless delays possible with diagnoses. Decisions can be bureaucratically and structurally deferred for years, periods that are on time scales equal to the illness and the sufferer's life and livelihood.

Among the many compelling personal reasons for collective action around these illnesses is the fact that sufferers have usually had repeated bad experiences in obtaining a diagnosis or treatment from the medical establishment and getting compensation from insurance companies. Despite experimentation with alternative medicines, most sufferers are still ill. Therefore, they must *learn* to live with their symptoms as chronically ill persons. And they must come up with some form of explanation as to "what is going on," an explanation that does not end with the idea that one is going crazy. Many try to maintain an open, rational attitude toward the inherent incompleteness of science, the fact that new discoveries are constantly challenging previously held notions.

From: RR

Of course, what it boils down to is that we can speculate til hell freezes over [about chronic fatigue syndrome], but until the data is in, we simply won't know. It's simple intelligence to be open to possibilities, especially in the world of research, but beyond that. . . . For all we know, this IS a job for Scully and Mulder {G} (alt.med.cfs).

Struggling with an actively contested illness can be analyzed as a form of individualization, a specific form of domination in the United States today in which each specific encounter with the system has its own rationale. A CFS sufferer, for instance, might be faced with a sympathetic doctor who nonetheless can't treat him or her for CFS because a managed care contract won't allow it. In the words of one doctor, quoted by a sufferer: "We don't even have a code for this disease, so we're not going to pay you."[4] It might be possible to track down the specific history of that contract, the administrative policy meetings, computer algorithms, industry practices, and medical claims used over time to produce the denial. But even then it might not be possible to assign blame easily. For the sufferer, it is not this one instance, possibly glossed as a glitch, but rather the *cumulative history* of "glitches," "arbitrary judgments," "interpretations," "stereotypes," and so on that wears down the individual and constitutes a very real form of what Melucci calls "symbolic" domination—domination by information and symbols, categories and bureaucracies—in which the very inability to receive a fair hearing constitutes a social and cultural judgment of repugnance.[5] What aids the perpetuation of this domination is the fact that it is more or less invisible except through personal narratives. Such narratives take time to listen to, and time is scarce in bureaucracies.

In this case, the standard critiques of the contemporary information society, which argue about the evacuation of meaning and reduction of experience, are inverted. My argument is that in the absence of care and institutional help folks with these illnesses are left with too much experience, excessive meaning, and suffering.

The combination of these factors, which structure the symbolic domination and frame the undecidabilities of these illnesses, produces a decidedly liminal space-time that I call "decompensation psychosis." Inverting the legal-psychiatric classification of "compensation neurosis" in which a patient is accused of being sick only in order to get paid for it, I'm interested in the fact that many people with these sociomedical disorders often cannot get even a psychiatric diagnosis. In other words, they are neither healthy nor ill nor even mentally ill; they are. in the colloquial phrase, "just plain crazy."

Being just plain crazy is a fully repugnant, prolonged liminal status produced at the moment when mental illness has gained some legitimacy within sociomedical circles. The categorical bureaucratic ability to be just plain crazy points to the collapse of medical care onto suffering in general: if you are suffering, you are in need of medical care. If you then can't get medical care or insurance or disability status, then there is an assumption that you probably aren't really sick or suffering. This chain of associations is, I think, relatively new, and it is worth considering because we all produce it at one time or another. It points, perhaps, to a cultural situation in which we have become dependent on the verification of suffering by third parties.

Most sufferers come to CFS as a definition by default. They have been diagnosed and treated unsuccessfully for depression and other psychiatric conditions. They have tried self-help, alternative therapies, and just pulling it together, and none of these have helped. In the process of failing to find any of these socially acceptable explanations for themselves, they become socially unacceptable.

> . . . because of CFS I am a total outcast. And that's not to mention the physical and mental pain CFS causes.
>
> If your friends and family are treating you as an outcast, you need to educate them about CFS. If they can't be educated, then you need different friends.

Online they find a community of outcasts, of those who understand that because science and medicine are considered the definition of rationality to fight them allows one to easily be designated irrational, crazy, and even paranoid. Timothy Melley defines *paranoia* as "a condition in which one's interpretations seem unfounded or *abnormal to an interpretive community*" (2000: 17). Discovering shared experiences and frustrations online becomes the making of an alternative interpretive community, though a fragile one, because it is founded on the practical desire to integrate.

Aliens Unite

> Here we may have a loving union of the structurally damned pronouncing judgment on normative structure and providing alternative models for structure.—Turner 1982: 51

There are many important critiques of contemporary technoscience and society that hint at how difficult everyday life is getting: Lyotard's notion of the collapse of master narratives in the postmodern condition, Habermas's colonization of our life world, David Harvey's dissection of our work economy, Thomas Szasz's analysis of the reduction of experience to categories, and Kenneth Gergen's account of the evacuation of meaning. Each, like Ulrich Beck's *Risk Society* analysis, asserts that "More and more people are slipping through normalized gaps in the social safety network . . ." (Beck 1992; Gergen 1994; Harvey 1989; Lyotard 1984; Szasz 1996). Yet these analyses almost exclusively proceed at the level of policy and reaction. They ask: what are corporate-science rationality, informatics and networking, surveillance and diagnostics doing to us, what is being lost, and how can this be challenged? They provide precious little help in figuring out how people actually make their way within and make lives out of the institutions of our brave new world order.

A few, like Alberto Melucci, *are* specifically concerned with the processes of meaning making within and alongside technoscience (as I explain further below). But there are a great deal of structural—and by that I mean historical, social, cultural, and political economic—reasons why the current conflicts emerge in the forms that they do.

For instance, given the tremendous uncertainty in characterizing these illnesses, and given the set relations to biological uncertainty outlined above, we can begin to understand why it might be *necessary* that sufferers from certain kinds of illnesses must organize into movements and intervene in both diagnostics and venue in order to get any sort of help or understanding.

Even the public stature of the illness movement, its appearances in the media, functions socially as a message: the existence of a movement around individual suffering makes health care system problems more visible, puts them on the public agenda, and opens the space for dialogue about the meaning of suffering from something like CFS.[6] Without these movements, CFS and other "invisible illnesses" would be unintelligible.[7]

These "gray zone sufferers" offer a set of systemic critiques, or critiques of the biomedical system, meant to enable sufferers to make shared sense of their personal histories of seemingly haphazard troubles. *The networks also continually experiment with and offer new forms of social relationships for sufferers and the public at large to inhabit* (Beck 1992: 135). These include the idea of illness as a lifestyle (such as a person with CFS), which requires cultural respect for differences caused by otherwise invisible illnesses, and, in the case of other relationships, the notion of the patient as an expert, a survivor, and a communicator.

Ulrich Beck and others describe living in contemporary society as requiring a reflexive "do it yourself" approach to one's biography. What these social movements aim to do, I am arguing, is to provide just such "construction kits of biographical combinations." For example, Mary Katzenstein describes important work being done by women in women's movements as "rewriting, through language and symbolic acts, their own understanding of themselves in relation to society" (quoted in Taylor 1996: 6–7). One place where we can directly see this active, reflexive theorizing of society and undiagnosable illness sufferers' place in it is on the Internet, where these illness movements have websites and Usenet discussion groups. Such websites, in addition to books and articles, include creative attempts by sufferers to inform the general public as to how they should be talked to. These include letters that they desire others to write to them. These letters provide the syntax, form of respect, appreciation, and understanding that cannot be captured except from the voice of the Other. Turner formulates the role of this liminal, free, ludic recombination of cultural factors into new forms of symbols precisely: "Symbols instigate action by saturating goals and means with affects and desire" (1982: 23). Through these biographical rewritings, sufferers enable a new way of life to become socially shared.

These issues and resources provide the basis for the networks of small groups, Internet communities, and mass media sharing that make life more livable for sufferers. As a social movement, sufferers and others committed to helping them provide a community and offer alternative personal narratives, strategies for surviving, and emotional support. In the words of William Gamson, there is a big difference between individual resistance and "being part of the Resistance" (quoted in Taylor 1996: 15).

These social movements are in part organized around intervening in the choice of venues, the kind of research, and the kind of metaphors used to characterize the resulting uncertainty. They are also engaged in the production of alternate metaphors, venues, and sciences.

Victor Turner locates the generation of meaning at the interfaces between established cultural subsystems (1982: 41). In attempting to change the venue where decisions regarding illnesses are made, these movements use the undecidability of the illnesses against the institutions that otherwise defer and delay. By making courts decide medical matters, Congress decide scientific ones, and the media decide political questions of research agendas, these new social movements help generate new meanings.[8]

From: WW

Re: Why us?

I'm of the opinion that every night, after I go to bed, I am abducted by aliens who perform torturous experiments. Such as pulling my body apart, and then putting it together a little differently. That's why I'm always tired and in constant pain. I think they also take my brain out to experiment and I am missing a few brain cells.

Sounds more plausible than I have this mysterious illness that is life long with no known cause and no cure.

Clueless

From: OO

Oh, well—THAT explains it!

LOL

From: JJ

Sounds like you've been reading Elaine Showalter . . . except she's *serious* about those aliens and the connection to FMS/CFS!

JJ

—Newsgroup message posted to alt.med.cfs

In 1997, a mothership abducted the CFS community. Elaine Showalter, feminist and literary historian of hysteria, deployed a new book, *Hystories*, in which she attacked CFS directly. Rather than showing how sufferers were positioned like women in a patriarchal society, deprived of rights and marginalized, Showalter instead threw in the towel on hysteria and chronic fatigue syndrome, claiming them to be nothing other than mental illnesses and really just a kind of psychosocial fad. She also threw in what popular culture considers the kitchen sink—alien abductions and satanic ritual abuse—declaring all of these, including chronic fatigue syndrome, to be the cultlike products of manipulative, glory-seeking therapists. It seems safe to say that without the inclusion of chronic fatigue syndrome (and two pages on Gulf War syndrome) the book would have been boring and unnoticed. The fights over alien abduction, for instance, had settled into communities of believers, gawkers, and those annoyed that the topic still haunted the front page. Chronic fatigue syndrome, however, was and is a highly contested illness category, defined and studied by the Centers for Disease Control, with a string of court decisions in its favor and acceptance in some insurance and disability cases, though exclusion in others. Showalter's inclusion of CFS alongside alien abductees ensured that the CFS community, which had been slowly gaining recognition for the illness, would respond with surprise and anger. Her book thus ensured her presence on talk shows and in the news, where she could promote it through displays of this anger.

"The Actively Sick"

> As it happens, disagreeing with the [CFS sufferers] about their views on this non-fatal affliction can get them really riled up. That's what Professor Elaine Showalter learned after the appearance of "Hystories: Hysterical Epidemics and Modern Media," a book from Columbia University Press. In stressful times, she suggests, some people devise different coping mechanisms and methods of escape. Sometimes they take comfort in the interest of nosy aliens who come from so far away to visit them or find excuses for their problems in recovered memories of childhood trauma long suppressed and of course hard to document.
>
> Chronic Fatigue is second on her list of six modern psychological epidemics, along with alien abduction, ritual satanic abuse, recovered memory, Gulf War Syndrome, and Multiple Personality Syndrome. She doesn't deny [that persons with CFS] are feeling poorly, but thinks they are suffering from what Freud called neurasthenia and what many therapists and doctors today would call depression in any of its many varieties. But psychologically grounded ailments still carry a prevalent stigma outside the therapeutic paradises of say, New York. So to explain their symptoms, people look, even yearn, for some physical problem, an exotic virus or maybe a little brain lesion.
>
> —*Wall Street Journal*, August 26, 1997

The *Wall Street Journal*'s response to CFS in this and a number of other articles and editorials is to impugn sufferers with malingering, suggesting that they are faking their symptoms to get a free lunch on the welfare state. The argument is actually aimed at the welfare state apparatus itself—social security and worker's compensation in particular. Chronic fatigue syndrome is singled out as if it were a perfect exemplar of purely evil manipulation of capitalism's generosity.

Showalter's book enabled this use of CFS in a particularly malicious way. She claimed that she is really on the side of sufferers who are *really* suffering from a mental illness (such as depression), and if only the world would stop stigmatizing mental illness then everything would be fine. I discuss this rhetorical maneuver at length elsewhere, but note here that the claim is counterfactual: U.S. society remains extremely biased against mental illness, and Showalter's and the *Wall Street Journal*'s use of *psychological* rather than *psychiatric*, reinforces this bias (Dumit 1997; Dumit, forthcoming).

In discussion groups online, CFS sufferers found this all to be an incredibly bad joke told at their expense. They were already alienated enough; now they had been abducted again. One sufferer discussed a government hearing on Gulf War syndrome that was aired on TV.

> The host felt GWS was half AIYH [all in your head], half real.
>
> The thing that struck me the hardest was one reporter shouting at the top of his lungs; "It's all a hoax!"
>
> If he'd have stood up, I bet Showalter's book would have fallen out of his lap!
>
> Showalter is getting plenty of attention from the media. (Newsgroup message posted to alt.med.cfs)

The level of attack on a personal level that sufferers' experience (being told by doctors that there is nothing that can be done, they are stuck between a rock and a hard place) is heightened here. Whereas first they are ignored and excluded by the medical system and treated as outcasts by friends and family, now they are accused of being part of a conspiracy, one that involves aliens.

One form of response to this accusation was to take the connection seriously. In 1998, Max Burns found a coincidence between one group of U.K. sufferers and the experiences of alien abductions. He proposed a study to determine whether there was any real connection. But he also engaged in a lengthy series of hypotheses of possible forms of relationship between alien abductions and CFS.

> In the interests of not jumping to conclusions. It could be that: The abduction scenario is a direct symptom and brain disorder and part of the many parts of "Myalgic Encephalomyelitis" (Chronic Fatigue Syndrome) and that all people

who are claiming abduction have this illness, but the symptoms in some abductees are minute compared to others and that they do not know that they have the illness.

However if that were the case it would open up the question? Why do sufferers of "Myalgic Encephalomyelitis" (Chronic Fatigue Syndrome) all claim to have been abducted by Aliens?

That Alien abduction is yet another symptom to this illness, a symptom which can manifest its self in the human brain as a memory, the same memory, This in its self if true, would for me anyway, be quite an astounding discovery.

Or perhaps that "Myalgic Encephalomyelitis" (Chronic Fatigue Syndrome) is a direct result of the alleged alien implants, which it has been claimed by a large number of abductees to have been placed inside of their heads, and in some way be causing the illness because of the implants interruption by proximity to certain areas of the brain, causing the brain to send out incorrect signals to the body and the cause effect of this is the human body receiving the incorrect information to function normally, causing the multi faceted symptoms of "Myalgic Encephalomyelitis" (Chronic Fatigue Syndrome).

There is even a hypothesis that these aliens are in some way feeding off the human life force draining energy from the alleged victim of these abductions, and the symptoms after these alleged incidents, do bear a striking resemblance to the symptoms of "Myalgic Encephalomyelitis" (Chronic Fatigue Syndrome).

Or that the abductions scenario is all in the minds of the abductees and that "Myalgic Encephalomyelitis" (Chronic Fatigue Syndrome) in the cases where abduction is also being claimed, is a direct result of the depression being caused by believing that they are being abducted by aliens.

Or perhaps it is something all together different from the from above? We will have to wait and see what information, if any, the investigation reveals. (Newsgroup message posted to alt.alien.research)

The response to Burns's request for a study by persons with CFS was mixed. Many could not figure out whether he was serious or not. Some posted his hypotheses online as a joke perhaps gone too far. They found this collision between what they thought of as absurd (aliens) and what they experienced everyday (alienation because of their uncertain condition) to be nonetheless an occasion for anxious humor.

From: MM
Subject: Re: Symptoms: Dizzy when laying down

[VBG] So glad people are getting some humor and grins from this . . .

See, my theory has always been that we *are* the aliens. This is what Showalter missed in her "tome"—she could have tied it all up in a neat little package, and made literary—oops!—I mean scientific, history. heeheehee . . .

MM

". . . take me to your doctor . . ."

From: LL

That's it MM! We have all been abducted by aliens and given this mysterious disease.

This is FUNNY! The odd twist to this is my sister is convinced her and I were abducted by aliens, and she suffers from a lot of the same things as myself, yet hasn't been diagnosed with this DD [dreaded disease].

Sufferers of CFS and other uncertain emergent illnesses often feel as if their bodies are alien to them. If they were aliens, at least their heretofore inexplicable problems would make some sort of sense. But, contrary to the conspiracy theorists described by Melley, these sufferers do not actually imagine systemic explanations for their problems. They only joke about them. They spend their time discussing the specifically political features of their social world in order to imagine how to navigate it better.

Jokes about being aliens recur among CFS sufferers, yet the connection between CFS's great uncertainty and the vehemence of the attacks against the sufferers eluded me until I investigated the very meaning of being alien.

The term *alien* has a disjointed entry in the *Oxford English Dictionary* (OED).

Alien, adjective

1. Belonging to another person, place, or family; strange, foreign, not of one's own . . .
3. a. Foreign in nature or character; belonging to something else; of foreign or other origin.

   b. Science Fiction. Of or pertaining to an (intelligent) being or beings from another planet; that derives from another world.
4. Of a nature or character differing from, far removed from, inconsistent with.

This passes imperceptibly into:

5. Of a nature repugnant, adverse or opposed to.

The slide between definitions four and five is eerie, as it appears in a dictionary dedicated to distinctions. The two definitions seem so far apart: a factual description of difference versus an extremely negative emotional reaction. Yet the guardian of definitions, the OED, describes their relationship as one of uncanny similarity, foreign difference passing imperceptibly into repugnance.[9] Here at least there is the germ of a theory of an alien logic to help us understand (but not become comfortable with) the rejection of sufferers whose fate it is to not have a clearly defined illness to go with their symptoms. This alien logic is of course straightforward to many sufferers:

> come on, people . . .
> we *are* the aliens.
> we seem to be suffering from host-planet rejection syndrome.
> GG
> HA HA HA HA HA HA HA HA HA HA HA HA HA HA
> (you may have something there!).
> (Newsgroup message posted to alt.med.cfs)

The grinning comment here is a precise analysis of the imperceptible shift whereby a suffering that no one denies imperceptibly becomes a suffering that must be denied. Just who does own and speak for the planet? In another *Wall Street Journal* editorial, published the year after the one discussed earlier, the editors assert on the one hand: "There can be no doubt that some real disorder affects people suffering from what's known as Chronic Fatigue Syndrome. The question is what. The struggle between the cadres out agitating for official recognition of their ailment and the medical skeptics has run on for some time" (Dec. 23, 1998).

But they lead off their editorial with the following statement.

> The campaign to legitimate the status of the mystery ailment known as chronic fatigue syndrome may soon be bearing fruit—a kind likely to line the pockets of lawyers and the physicians now specializing in the treatment and diagnosis of CFS.
>
> A specialist within the Social Security Administration tells us that the Chronic Fatigue activists now attempting to establish the syndrome as a federal compensatory disability are a highly talented lobby. . . . If the activists are any measure, this source says, "there is a very strong obsessive component to this disorder."

The editorial concludes by impugning CFS patients as having a "deranged sense of victimization." It is as if the current unknown nature of CFS ("the question is what") justifies the accusations, suspicion, and alienation. The argument seems to be that until it can be understood it should be ignored and criticized. Here is a different sort of response by a sufferer.

> The problem is: what do you want doctors to DO with a disease they cannot test for, which does not seem to fit any known epidemiological patterns, and which presents in so many varied ways, but consistently co-occurs with psychiatric symptoms? Nobody is rounding up CFS or MCS patients and locking them up in concentration camps. But without a positive hypothesis—and a *specific* one—what is to be done?
>
> 1. Believe it exists before objective biomarkers are found to prove that they exist.
> 2. Help the patients who have the condition to help them cope with this disease.
> 3. Support research initiatives.
> 4. Do NOT label the condition as psychiatric, just because MEDICINE does NOT understand it, and it's a convenient face-saving measure for the local MD.
>
> (They don't have to say "I don't know" and reveal that they really are NOT God, after all.) The deficiency lies within the field of MEDICINE. The deficiency does NOT lie within the PATIENT. (Newsgroup message posted to misc.health .alternative)

Here the fight reaches this point: if there is no evidence and no cure, what then? The response is key: First accept the suffering and help people to cope. Second, do the research, and, third, do not accuse the patient. Psychiatry comes out on the losing end of things, not because of who psychiatrists are today but rather because of their structural position in other systems. In health care, they are "undercovered": mental illnesses do not have full parity in insurance. This means that insurance companies profit from shifting people out of physical and into psychiatric categories. In workers' compensation cases, psychiatric conditions may be seen as physical, but then precisely to that extent they are seen as non-work-related; therefore, producing them as "psychiatric" excludes people from the system of care and help altogether. In the case of the Social Security Administration and disability, psychiatry is responsible for both malingering/faking and mental illnesses, and this doubling (and psychiatry's refusal to give up the faking niche) forces people away from the diagnosis (Dumit, forthcoming; Walsh 1987).

We thus must raise a question similar to Verta Taylor's in her book *Rock-a-by Baby* on postpartum depression self-help groups. She asks, "What events have led women over the past decade to embrace psychiatric understandings and [scientific] resources as tools for social change?" Part of the answer that Taylor suggests is that the biological is also a way of "clinging to normality" (1996: xv, 134–35). If we accept the argument that there is no clear way to settle our current relation to biological uncertainty, then the venue matters as much as or more than the data. Clinging to normality requires locating the biological in one site and not another. Sufferers of CFS understand that they are in the uncertain position of the alien who does not conform to current understandings of illness and disease.

Interestingly, they are not primarily trying to persuade scientists; instead they are staking claims and changing situations by *means of* science and scientists. These groups as new social movements are in fact asserting their right to *be not subjects* but *objects* of science. They are arguing that the resources and the symbolic and curative powers of science, technology, and medicine should be directed toward them.

I am here inverting the moral critique of technoscientific power in everyday life, suggesting that this power is also a resource to mobilize within collective lives. These sufferers desire, in other words, to become patients—and therefore members of the mainstream American community of the medically validated, "licensed" sufferers (see Lepselter in this volume). This is a form of what Jacques Ranciere defines as "the logical schema of social protest" as "Do we or do we not belong to the category of men or citizen or human being, and what follows from this?" (1995: 66). In the case of these illnesses, the protest is: "We are humans suffering and yet we are not treated with any of the care or compassion that should follow." The need to claim human status emerges precisely from being rendered aliens.

Notes

I would like to thank the Susan Harding, Anita Chan, Debbora Battaglia, Sylvia Sensiper, and an anonymous reviewer for many helpful comments on earlier drafts of this essay. Initial work on it was made possible by an NIMH (National Institute of Mental Health) Postdoctoral Fellowship and a Humanities and Social Science Grant from the Massachusetts Institute of Technology.

1. According to he official Centers for Disease Control definition: "Clinically evaluated, unexplained chronic fatigue cases can be classified as chronic fatigue syndrome if the patient meets both the following criteria: (1) Clinically evaluated, unexplained persistent or relapsing chronic fatigue that is of new or definite onset (i.e., not lifelong), is not the result of ongoing exertion, is not substantially alleviated by rest, and results in substantial reduction in previous levels of occupational, educational, social, or personal activities. (2) The concurrent occurrence of four or more of the following symptoms: substantial impairment in short-term memory or concentration; sore throat; tender lymph nodes; muscle pain; multi-joint pain without swelling or redness; headaches of a new type, pattern, or severity; unrefreshing sleep; and post-exertional malaise lasting more than 24 hours. These symptoms must have persisted or recurred during 6 or more consecutive months of illness and must not have predated the fatigue" (Centers for Disease Control 2003: http://www.cdc.gov/ncidod/cfs/defined/defined2.htm, last accessed May 6, 2005).

2. This list is drawn from Dumit (forthcoming), and the topics are expanded on further in that article.

3. On the other hand, as Patricia Kaufert (1998) has pointed out, the word *liminal* has to some degree extended to everyday usage. Thus, it pays to revisit the term in its philosophic construction and application by anthropologists.

4. See Johnson 1996. This phrase and the uses of noncoding are discussed in Dumit, forthcoming.

5. See Melucci 1996a for a discussion of individualization and symbolic domination.

6. The very existence of self-help groups can be interpreted as developing a challenge to professional power (Klein 1983). Self-help groups empower members and challenge medical orthodoxy (Vincent 1992, quoted in Kelleher 1994: 111).

7. On the status of CFS and other social illness movements as invisible, see Barrett 1997.

8. See Dumit 2000 for an analysis of the change of venue as a temporary strategy and symptom of the shifting status of science.

9. This slip begs for an investigation of the alien hybrid via Homi Bhabha's analysis of hybridity, as well as Harding's analysis of repugnance (Harding 2000; Bhabha 1995).

REFERENCES

Agamben, Giorgio. 1999. *Remnants of Auschwitz: The Witness and the Archive*. New York: Zone.

Aharon, Y. N. Ibn. 1957. "Diagnosis: A Case of Chronic Fright." *Saucer News* 4(5):3–6.

Alexander, Chris. 1997. "An Interview with Chris Alexander." *Other Wise* 4:4–7.

Allen, Marcus. 1994. "Behind the Hoaxers—Physicists, Scientists, Stompers and the Secret History of Circle Faking." *Sussex Circular*, 33 (September). http://www.greatdreams.com/faking/htm.

Allison, Anne. 2002. "The Cultural Politics of Pokemon Capitalism." Paper presented at Media in Transition 2: Globalization and Convergence. Massachusetts Institute of Technology. Cambridge, Mass. 10–12 May.

———. 2004. "Cuteness as Japan's Millennial Product." In *Pikachu's Global Adventure: The Rise and Fall of Pokémon*, edited by Joseph Tobin. Durham: Duke University Press. 34–49.

Anderson, Benedict R. [1972] 1990. *Language and Power: Exploring Public Cultures in Indonesia*. Ithaca: Cornell University Press.

Anonymous. *Heaven's Gate*. 1994. Internet poster. http://www.press1.com/current/hgate/mirror/book/6-6.htm. Accessed March 10.

Anonymous [H. G. Wells]. 1893. "The Man of the Year Million: A Scientific Forecast." *Pall Mall Budget*, November 16. 1796–97.

Appadurai, Arjun, ed. 1986. "Introduction: Commodities and the Politics of Value." In *The Social Life of Things: Commodities in Cultural Perspective*. New York: Cambridge University Press.

———. 1996. *Modernity at Large: Cultural Dimensions of Globalization*. Minneapolis: University of Minnesota Press.

Arcturus Books. 1994. *Catalogue, 1994–12: December*. Port Saint Lucie, Fla.: Arcturus.

Arnold, Kenneth, and Ray Palmer. 1952. *The Coming of the Saucers: A Documentary Report on the Sky Objects That Have Mystified the World*. Boise, Idaho, and Amherst, Wisc.: The authors.

Aronson, Virginia. 1999. *Celestial Healing: Close Encounters That Cure*. New York: New American Library.

Asad, Talal. 2001. "Reading a Modern Classic: W. C. Smith's *The Meaning and End of Religion*." In *Religion and Media*, edited by Hent de Vries and Samuel Weber. Stanford: Stanford University Press. 131–47.

Asahi Shinbun (newspaper). 2001. "Otousan datte Hamaru." Tokyo. 24.

Baard, Erik. 2002. "Keeping Alien Samples Safe for Study." "Tech Wednesday." 13 February. http://www.space.com/businesstechnology/technology/astrobio_guards_020213.html.

Badley, Linda. 1996. "The Rebirth of the Clinic: The Body as Alien in *The* X-*Files*." In *"Deny All Knowledge": Reading* The X-Files, edited by David Lavery, Angela Hague, and Marla Cartwright. Syracuse: Syracuse University Press. 36–51.

Bakhtin, Mikhail. 1981. *The Dialogic Imagination*. Austin: University of Texas Press.

Bal, Mieke. 2001. "Mission Impossible: Postcards, Pictures, and Parasites." In *Religion and Media*, edited by Hent de Vries and Samuel Weber. Stanford: Stanford University Press. 241–68.

Balch, Robert W. 1980. "Looking behind the Scenes in a Religious Cult: Implications for the Study of Conversion." *Sociological Analysis* 41(2): 137–43.

———. 1982. "Bo and Peep: A Case Study of the Origins of Messianic Leadership." In *Millennialism and Charisma*, edited by Roy Wallis. Belfast: Queen's University. 13–72.

Balch, Robert W., and David Taylor. 1977. "Seekers and Saucers: The Role of the Cultic Milieu in Joining a UFO Cult." *American Behavioral Scientist* 20:839–60.

Barker, Eileen. 1984. *The Making of a Moonie: Choice or Brainwashing?* New York: Basil Blackwell.

Barkun, Michael. 1974. *Disaster and the Millennium*. New Haven: Yale University Press.

———. 1994. "Millenarian Groups and Law Enforcement Agencies: The Lessons of Waco." *Terrorism and Political Violence* 6:75–95.

———. 1998. "Politics and Apocalypticism." In *The Encyclopedia of Apocalypticism*, Vol. 3, edited by Stephen J. Stein. New York: Continuum. 442–60.

Barnes, Bloor, and John Harry. 1996. *Scientific Knowledge: A Sociological Analysis*. Chicago: University of Chicago Press.

Barrett, Deborah. 1997. "Seeing 'Invisible' Illness: Transforming the Medical Gaze through Lived Experience." Presentation at the Interdisciplinary Workshop at Emory University, Atlanta.

Barry, Dan. 2004. "Close Encounters." *New York Times Magazine*, April 25. 132.

Bates, Jonathan. 1998. *The Genius of Shakespeare*. New York: Oxford University Press.

Battaglia, Debbora. 1999. "Toward an Ethics of the Open Subject: Writing Culture 'In Good Conscience.'" In *Anthropological Theory Today*, edited by Henrietta Moore. Cambridge: Polity Press. 114–15.

———. 2001. "Multiplicities: An Anthropologist's Thoughts on Replicants and Clones in Popular Film." *Critical Inquiry* 27:493–514.

Baudrillard, Jean. 1988. *Xerox and Infinity*. London: Touchepas.

———. 1993. *Symbolic Exchange and Death*. Translated by Iain Hamilton Grant. London and Thousand Oaks, Calif.: Sage.

Bauman, Zygmunt. 2003. *Community: Seeking Safety in an Insecure World*. Oxford: Polity Press.

Beck, Ulrich. 1992. *Risk Society: Towards a New Modernity*. Translated by T. B. M. Ritter. London and Thousand Oaks, Calif.: Sage.

———. 1995. *Ecological Enlightenment: Essays on the Politics of the Risk Society*. Translated by Mark A. Ritter. Atlantic Highlands, N.J.: Humanities Press.

Beckley, Timothy Green. 1989. *MJ–12 and the Riddle of Hangar 18*. New Brunswick, N.J.: Inner Light.

Berger, Peter, Brigitte Berger, and Hansfried Kellner. 1974. *The Homeless Mind: Modernization and Consciousness*. New York: Vintage.

Berkhofer, Robert F., Jr. 1978. *The White Man's Indian: Images of the American Indian from Columbus to the Present*. New York: Vintage.

Berlitz, Charles, and William L. Moore. [1988] 1980. *The Roswell Incident*. New York: Berkley Books.

Besant, Annie. 1910. *The Changing World; and, Lectures to Theosophical Students: Fifteen Lectures presented in London during May, June, and July 1909*. Chicago: Theosophical Book Concern.

Besant, Annie, and C. W. Leadbeater. 1947. *Man: Whence, How and Whither—A Record of Clairvoyant Investigation*. Wheaton, Ill.: Theosophical Press.

Bethurum, Truman. 1954. *Aboard a Flying Saucer*. Los Angeles: DeVorss.

Bhabha, Homi. 1995. *The Location of Culture*. London: Routledge.

Bhatt, Chetan. 1997. *Liberation and Purity*. Berkeley: University of California Press.

Biagioli, Mario. 1995a. "Confabulating Jurassic Science." In *Technoscientific Imaginaries: Conversations, Profiles, and Memoirs*, edited by George Marcus. Chicago: University of Chicago Press. 399–430.

———. 2003. "Rights or Rewards? Changing Frameworks of Scientific Authorship." In *Scientific Authorship: Credit and Intellectual Property in Science*, edited by Mario Biagiolo and Peter Galison. New York: Routledge. 253–80.

Biagioli, Mario, ed. 1995b. *The Science Studies Reader*. New York: Routledge.

Biagioli, Mario, and Peter Galison, eds. 2003. *Scientific Authorship: Credit and Intellectual Property in Science*. New York: Routledge.

Blavatsky, Helena Petrovna. [1888] 1938. *The Secret Doctrine: The Synthesis of Science, Religion, and Philosophy*. 6 vols. Adyar, India: Theosophical Publishing House.

———. [1887] 1960. *Isis Unveiled: A Master-Key to the Mysteries of Ancient and Modern Science and Theology*. 2 vols. Pasadena, Calif.: Theosophical University Press.

Bowen, Charles, ed. 1969. *The Humanoids*. Chicago: Henry.

Bowler, Peter J. 1989. *The Invention of Progress: The Victorians and the Past*. Oxford: Basil Blackwell.

Brackett, D. W. 1996. *Holy Terror: Armageddon in Tokyo*. New York: Weatherhill.

Brenkman, John. 1979. "Mass Media: From Collective Experience to the Culture of Privatization." *Social Text* 1:94–109.

Bromley, David G., ed, 1998. *The Politics of Religious Apostasy: The Role of Apostates in the Transformation of Religious Movements*. London: Praeger.

Brown, Michael F. 1997. *The Channeling Zone: American Spirituality in an Anxious Age*. Cambridge, Mass.: Harvard University Press.

———. 1999. "The New Alienists." In *Paranoia within Reason*, edited by George Marcus. Chicago: University of Chicago Press. 137–56.

Brown, Phil, et al. 2004. "Embodied Health Movements: New Approaches to Social Movements in Health." *Sociology of Health and Illness* 26(1): 50–80.

Bryan, C. D. B. 1995. *Close Encounters of the Fourth Kind: A Reporter's Notebook on Alien Abduction, UFOs, and the Conference at M.I.T.* New York: Knopf.

Buckingham, David, and Julian Sefton-Green. 2004. "Structure, Agency, and Pedagogy in Children's Media Culture." In *Pikachu's Global Adventure: The Rise and Fall of Pokémon*, edited by Joseph Tobin. Durham: Duke University Press. 12–33.

Buck-Morss, Susan. 2000. *Dreamworld and Catastrophe: The Passing of Mass Utopia in East and West*. Cambridge, Mass.: MIT Press.

Bukatman, Scott. 1997. *Blade-Runner*. London: British Film Institute.

Bull, Malcolm. 1999. *Seeing Things Hidden*. London: Verso.

Bullard, Thomas E. 1987. UFO *Abductions: Measure of a Mystery*. 2 vols. Mt. Rainier, Md.: Fund for UFO Research.

———. 1989. "UFO Abduction Reports: The Supernatural Kidnap Narrative Returns in Technological Guise." *Journal of American Folklore* 102(404): 147–70.

Bulwer Lytton, Edward. 1871. *The Coming Race*. Edinburgh: W. Blackwood and Sons.

Butcher, Andy. 2001. "Aliens among Us." *Charisma* 26:46–60.

Campbell, Bruce F. 1980. *Ancient Wisdom Revived: A History of the Theosophical Movement*. Berkeley: University of California Press.

Cannon, Martin. N.d. [ca. 1992?]. "The Controllers: A New Hypothesis of Alien Abductions." Manuscript.

Carroll, Robert Todd. 2003. *The Skeptic's Dictionary: A Collection of Strange Beliefs, Amusing Deceptions and Dangerous Delusions*. Hoboken, N.J.: Wiley.

Carucci, Lawrence. 1997. *Nuclear Nativity: Rituals of Renewal and Empowerment in the Marshall Islands*. DeKalb: Northern Illinois University Press.

Centers for Disease Control. 2003. *Chronic Fatigue Syndrome: The Revised Case Definition*. Abridged ed. Atlanta: Centers for Disease Control.

Chalker, Bill. 2001. "The World's First DNA PCR Investigation of Biological Evidence from an Alien Abduction." http://www.theozfiles.com./anomaly_investigation_group.html.

"Chronic Disability Payments." 1998. Editorial. *Wall Street Journal*. 23 December.

Chryssides, George. 2003. "Scientific Creationism: A Study of the Raëlian Church." In UFO *Religions*, edited by Christopher Partridge. London: Routledge. 45–61.

Churchill, Ward. 1992. *Fantasies of the Master Race: Literature, Cinema, and the Colonization of American Indians*. Monroe: Common Courage Press.

Churchward, James. 1931. *The Lost Continent of Mu*. New York: Ives Washburn.

Cifali, Marielle. 1994. "The Making of Martian: The Creation of an Imaginary Language." Translated by Michael Munchow. In Flournoy [1994] 1901. 269–87.

Clark, Jerome. 2002. "The Trivialist." *International* UFO *Reporter* 27(1): 15–19, 29–30.

Clerc, Susan. 1996. "DDEB, GAJB, MPPB and Ratboy: *The* X-*Files*' Media Fandom Online and Off." In *"Deny All Knowledge": Reading* The X-Files, edited by David Lavery, Angela Hague, and Marla Cartwright. Syracuse: Syracuse University Press. 36–51.

Clifford, James. 1997. *Routes: Travel and Translation in the Late 20th Century*. Cambridge: Cambridge University Press.

Clifford, James, and George Marcus. 1986. *Writing Culture: The Poetics and Politics of Ethnography*. Berkeley: University of California Press.

Cocconi, G., and P. Morrison. 1959. "Searching for Interstellar Communication." *Nature* 184:844.

Collings, Beth, and Anna Jameson. 1996. *Connections: Solving Our Alien Abduction Mystery*. Newberg, Ore.: Wild Flower Press.

Collins, Harry M., and Trevor J. Pinch. 1982. *Frames of Meaning: The Social Construction of Extraordinary Science*. London: Routledge.

"Commander X." 1994. *The Controllers: The Hidden Rulers of Earth Identified*. Wilmington, Del.: Abelard Productions.

Conroy, Ed. 1989. *Report on Communion: An Independent Investigation of and Commentary on Whitley Strieber's Communion*. New York: Morrow.

Contact. 1997. Video disk, 150 minutes. Warner Home Video, Burbank, Calif.

Cook, Ryan. 2004. "Weather-workers, Saucer-seekers, and Orthoscientists: Epistemic Authority in Central Mexico." Ph.D. dissertation. University of Chicago.

Coon, Carleton S. 1962. *The Origin of Races*. New York: Knopf.

Cooper, Milton William. 1991. *Behold a Pale Horse*. Sedona, Ariz.: Light Technology Publishing.

Cowan, G. M. 1948. "Mazateco Whistle Speech." *Language* 24:280–86.

Crapanzano, Vincent. 1980. "Rite of Return: Circumcision in Morocco." In *Psychoanalytic Study of Culture*, edited by Warner Muensterberger and L. Bryce Boyer. New York: Library of Psychological Anthropology. 9.

———. 2003. "Reflections on Hope as a Category of Social and Psychological Analysis." *Cultural Anthropology* 18(1): 3–32.

Creighton, Gordon. 1969. "The Amazing Case of Antonio Villas Boas." In *The Humanoids*, edited by Charles Bowen. Chicago: Regnery. 200–238.

Cross, Gary. 1997. *Kids' Stuff: Toys and the Changing World of American Childhood*. Cambridge, Mass.: Harvard University Press.

Curran, Douglas. 1985. *In Advance of the Landing: Folk Concepts of Outer Space*. New York: Abbeville.

Däniken, Erich von. 1969. *Chariots of the Gods? Unsolved Mysteries of the Past*. Translated by Michael Heron. London: Souvenir.

Darlington, David. 1997. *Area 51: The Dreamland Chronicles*. New York: Holt.

Darwin, Charles. 1887. *The Life and Letters of Charles Darwin, Including an Autobiographical Chapter*. Edited by Francis Darwin. London: J. Murray.

Davenport, Marc. 1994. *Visitors from Time: The Secrets of UFOs*. Murfreesboro, Tenn.: Greenleaf. Revised edition. Newberg, Ore.: Wild Flower Press.

Davies, Paul. 2003. "E.T. and God." *Atlantic Monthly* 292:112–18.

Davis, John Jefferson. 1994. "The Search for Extraterrestrial Intelligence and the Christian Doctrine of Redemption." *Science and Christian Belief* 9:21–34.

Davis-Floyd, Robbie, and Joseph Dumit, eds. 1998. *Cyborg Babies: From Techno-Sex to Techno-Tots*. New York: Routledge.

Dean, Jodi. 1998. *Aliens in America: Conspiracy Cultures from Outerspace to Cyberspace*. Ithaca: Cornell University Press.

———. 2003. "Alien Doubts: Reading Abduction Narratives Post-Apocalyptically." In *UFO Religions*, edited by Christopher Partridge. London: Routledge. 239–55.

de Certeau, Michel. 1996. "Vocal Utopias: Glossolalias." *Representations* 56:29–47.

DeKorne, Jim. 1994. *Psychedelic Shamanism: The Cultivation, Preparation and Shamanic Use of Psychotropic Plants*. Port Townsend, Wash.: Breakout Productions.

Delafosse, Maurice. 1913. *Traditions historiques et legendaires du Soudan Occidental*. Paris: Publication de Comité de l'Afrique Française.

Delany, Samuel R. 1966. *Babel-17*. New York: Vintage Books.

Deloria, Vine, Jr. 1970. *Custer Died for Your Sins*. New York: Macmillan.

Denzler, Brenda. 2001. *The Lure of the Edge: Scientific Passions, Religious Beliefs, and the Pursuit of UFOs*. Berkeley: University of California Press.

Derrida, Jacques. 1992. *The Other Heading: Reflections on Today's Europe*. Translated by Pascale-Anne Brault and Michael B. Naas. Bloomington: Indiana University Press.

———. 2001. "Above All No Journalists!" In *Religion and Media*, edited by Hent de Vries and Samuel Weber. Stanford: Stanford University Press. 56–93.

———. 2002. *Acts of Religion*. Edited by Gil Anidjar. New York: Routledge.

Desjarlais, Robert. 1992. *Body and Emotion: The Aesthetics of Illness and Healing in the Nepal Himalayas*. Philadelphia: University of Pennsylvania Press.

de Vries, Hent. 2001. "In Media Res: Global Religion, Pubic Spheres, and the Task of Contemporary Comparative Religious Studies." In *Religion and Media*, edited by Hent de Vries and Samuel Weber. Stanford: Stanford University Press. 1–42.

Dick, Steven J. 1998. *Life on Other Worlds: The 20th-Century Extraterrestrial Life Debate*. New York: Cambridge University Press.

Dike, Stuart. 2001. "The Mother of All Crop Circles." *Apocalypse International* 124: 31–32.

DJ Spooky. 1996. Audio compact disc. *Necropolis: The Dialogic Project*. Knitting Factory.

Docherty, Jayne Seminare. 2001. *Learning Lessons from Waco: When the Parties Bring Their Gods to the Negotiation Table*. Syracuse: Syracuse University Press.

Douglas, Mary. [1966] 1978. *Purity and Danger: An Analysis of Concepts of Pollution and Taboo*. London: Routledge.

Dove, Lonzo. 1957. Review of *Other Tongues—Other Flesh*, by George Hunt Williamson. *Saucer News* 4(4): 6–8.

Doyle, Richard. 1997. *On Beyond Living: Rhetorical Transformations of the Life Sciences*. Stanford: Stanford University Press.

———. 2002. "LSDNA." In *Semiotic Flesh: Information and the Human Body*, edited by Philip Thurtle and Robert Mitchell. Seattle: Walter Chapin Center for the Humanities, University of Washington. 9–24.

———. 2003. *Wetwares: Theory Out of Bounds*. Minneapolis: University of Minnesota Press.

Drake, F. D. 1978. "The Foundations of the Voyager Record." In Carl Sagan, F. D. Drake, J. Lomberg, L. S. Sagan, A. Druyan, and T. Ferris, *Murmurs of Earth: The Voyager Interstellar Record*. New York: Random House. 45–70.

Druffel, Ann. [1988] 1980. "The Tujunga Milieu: Some Tentative Conclusions." In Ann Druffel and D. Scott Rogo, *The Tujunga Canyon Contacts*. New York: New American Library. 213–32.

Dumit, Joseph. 1997. Showalter's Hystories/Joseph Dumit Comments. Essay review posted on H-Women. 2 May. Archived at http://www.h-net.org/~women/threads/disc-dumit.html.

———. 2000. "When Explanations Rest: 'Good-Enough' Brain Science and the New Sociomedical Disorders." In *Living and Working with the New Biomedical Technologies: Intersections of Inquiry*, edited by M. Lock, A. Young, and A. Cambrosio. Cambridge: Cambridge University Press. 209–32.

———. 2001. "Playing Truths: Logics of Seeking and the Persistence of the New Age." *Focaal* 37:63–75.

———. Forthcoming. "Illnesses You Have to Fight to Get: Facts as Forces in Uncertain, Emergent Illnesses." *Social Science and Medicine*.

Dumit, Joseph, ed. 1997. *Cyborgs and Citadels: Anthropological Interventions in Emerging Sciences and Technologies*. Santa Fe: School of American Research.

Dunbar, Robin. 1998. *Grooming, Gossip, and the Evolution of Language*. Cambridge, Mass.: Harvard University Press.

Dundes, Alan, ed. 1991. *The Blood Libel Legend: A Casebook in Anti-Semitic Folklore*. Madison: University of Wisconsin Press.

Dunn, Kyla. 2002. "Cloning Trevor." *Atlantic Monthly* 289:31–52.

Dyke, Jose von. 1998. *Imagenation: Popular Images of Genetics*. New York: New York University Press.

Elgin, Suzette Haden. [1984] 2000. *Native Tongue*. New York: Feminist Press.

———. [1987] 2002. *The Judas Rose*. New York: Feminist Press.

———. [1994] 2002. *Earthsong*. New York: Feminist Press.

Ereshefsky, Marc. 2002. "Species." In *Stanford Encyclopedia of Philosophy*. http://plato.stanford.edu/entries/species/.

Estron, Tucker. 1996. "The Secret." *Other Wise* 1:4–5.

Evans, John. 2002. *Playing God? Human Genetic Engineering and the Rationalization of Public Bioethical Debate*. Chicago: University of Chicago Press.

Evans-Wentz, W. Y. 1911. *The Fairy-Faith in Celtic Countries*. London: H. Frowde.

Fann, K. T. 1970. *Peirce's Theory of Abduction*. The Hague: Martinus Nijhoff.

Feet of Clay: Confessions of a Tiny Tin God. 2003. http://www.feetofclay.brokentoys.org.

Feld, Steven. 1994. "Grooving on Participation: Further Comments." In Charles Keil and Steven Feld, *Music Grooves: Essays and Dialogues*. Chicago: University of Chicago Press. 181–94.

Fenster, Mark. 1999. *Conspiracy Theories: Secrecy and Power in American Culture*. Minneapolis: University of Minnesota Press.

Fernandez, Ramona. 2001. *Imaginary Literacy: Rhizomes of Knowledge in American Culture and Literature*. Austin: University of Texas Press.

Ferris, Timothy. "Voyager's Music." In Carl Sagan, F. D. Drake, J. Lomberg, L. S. Sagan, A. Druyan, and T. Ferris, *Murmurs of Earth: The Voyager Interstellar Record*. New York: Random House. 161–210.

Festinger, Leon, Henry W. Riecken, and Stanley Schachter. 1956. *When Prophecy Fails: A Social and Psychological Study of a Modern Group That Predicted the Destruction of the World*. Minneapolis: University of Minnesota Press.

Fischer, Roland. 1969. "The Perception-Hallucination Continuum (a Reexamination)." *Diseases of the Nervous System* 30:161–71.

Flammonde, Paris. 1971. *The Age of Flying Saucers: Notes on a Projected History of Unidentified Flying Objects*. New York: Hawthorn.

Flournoy, Théodore. [1901] 1994. *From India to the Planet Mars: A Case of Multiple Personality with Imaginary Languages*. Edited by Sonu Shamdasani. Translated by Michael Munchow. Princeton: Princeton University Press.

Fogelson, Raymond D. 1985. "Interpretations of the American Indian Psyche: Some Historical Notes." In *Social Contexts of American Ethnology, 1840–1984*, edited by June Helm. Washington, D.C.: American Ethnological Society. 4–27.

Fortun, Kim. 2001. *Advocacy after Bhopal: Environmentalism, Disaster, New Global Orders*. Chicago: University of Chicago Press.

Foucault, Michel. 1979. "What Is an Author?" In *Textual Strategies*, edited by Josue V. Harari. Ithaca: Cornell University Press. 141–60.

———. 1984. "On the Genealogy of Ethics: An Overview of Work in Progress." In *The Foucault Reader*, edited by P. Rabinow. New York: Pantheon. 340–72.

Fowler, Raymond E. 1979. *The Andreasson Affair*. New York: Bantam.

———. 1990. *The Watchers: The Secret Design behind UFO Abduction*. New York: Bantam.

Francis, Daniel. 1992. *The Imaginary Indian: The Image of the Indian in Canadian Culture*. Vancouver: Arsenal Pulp Press.

Frank, Thomas. 1997. *The Conquest of Cool: Business Cultures, Counterculture, and the Rise of Hip Consumerism*. Chicago: University of Chicago Press.

Franklin, Sarah, Celia Lury, and Jackie Stacey. 2000. *Global Nature, Global Culture*. London: Sage.

Freud, Sigmund. [1919] 1963. "The Uncanny." In *Studies in Parapsychology*, edited by Philip Reiff. New York: Macmillan.

Fry, Daniel W. 1966. *The White Sands Incident*. Louisville: Best Books.

Fuller, Jean Overton. 1988. *Blavatsky and Her Teachers: An Investigative Biography*. London: East-West Publications.

Fuller, John G. 1966. *The Interrupted Journey: Two Lost Hours "aboard a Flying Saucer."* New York: Dial.

Gabe, Jonathan, David Kelleher, and Gareth Williams. 1994. *Challenging Medicine*. London: Routledge.

Gabriel, Theodore. 2003. In *UFO Religions*, edited by Christopher Partridge. London: Routledge. 149–61.

Gadet, Françoise. 1989. *Saussure and Contemporary Culture*, translated by Gregory Elliott. London: Radius/Century Hutchinson.

Gamson, William A., and Andre Modigliani. 1989. "Media Discourse and Public Opinion on Nuclear Power: A Constructionist Approach." *American Journal of Sociology* 95:1–37.

Gamson, William A., David Croteau, William Hoynes, and Theodore Sasson. 1992. "Media Images and the Social Construction of Reality." *Annual Review of Sociology* 18:373–93.

Gergen, Kenneth J. 1994. *Realities and Relationships: Soundings in Social Construction*. Cambridge, Mass.: Harvard University Press.

Gerlach, Luther P., and Virginia H. Hine. 1970. *People, Power, Change: Movements of Social Transformation*. Indianapolis: Bobbs-Merrill.

Gilbert, James. 1997. *Redeeming Culture: American Religion in an Age of Science*. Chicago: University of Chicago Press.

Gilkey, Langdon. 1993. *Nature, Reality, and the Sacred: The Nexus of Science and Religion*. Minneapolis: Fortress.

Ginsburg, Faye D., Lila Abu-Lughod, and Brian Larkin, eds. 2002. *Media Worlds: Anthropology on New Terrain*. Berkeley: University of California Press.

Girard, Robert C. 1993. *Futureman: A Synthesis of Missing Links, the Human Infestation of Earth, and the Alien Abduction Epidemic*. Port Saint Lucie, Fla.: The author.

Godwin, Joscelyn. 1992. *Arktos: The Polar Myth in Science, Symbolism, and Nazi Survival*. Grand Rapids, Mich.: Phanes.

Goldberg, Steven. 1999. *Seduced by Science: How American Religion Has Lost Its Way*. New York: New York University Press.

Golding, William. 1964. *The Inheritors*. New York: Washington Square Press.

Gollon, John.1968. *Chess Variations: Ancient, Regional, and Modern*. North Clarendon, Vt.: Charles E. Tuttle.

Goodman, Heath, and Susan Lindee, eds. 2003. *Genetic Nature/Culture: Anthropology and Science beyond the Two-Culture Divide*. Berkeley and London: University of California Press.

Greene, John C. 1959. *The Death of Adam: Evolution and Its Impact on Western Thought*. Ames: Iowa State University Press.

Greenfield, Karl Taro. 1993. "The Incredibly Strange Mutant Creatures Who Rule the Universe of Alienated Japanese Zombie Computer Nerds." In *Wired*. March/April. 57–62.

Greenwald, Jeff. 1998. *Future Perfect: How* Star Trek *Conquered Planet Earth*. New York: Viking Penguin.

Gross, Larry, P., John Stuart Katz, and Jay Ruby, eds. 2003. *Image Ethics in the Digital Age*. Minneapolis: University of Minnesota Press.

Gross, Loren E. 1988. UFOs*: A History, 1947—a Minor Catalogue of* UFO *Reports and Notations on Various Unofficial Inquiries by Individuals and Privately Funded Organizations, as Well as Commentary on Military Investigations and Governmental Policies, Presented in Chronological Order*. Fremont, Calif.: The author.

Gupta, Akhil, and James Ferguson, eds. 1997. *Culture, Power, Place: Explorations in Critical Anthropology*. Durham: Duke University Press.

Gusterson, Hugh. 2003. "The Death of the Authors of Death." In *Scientific Authorship: Credit and Intellectual Property in Science*, edited by Mario Biagioli and Peter Galison. London: Routledge. 309–24.

Haight, Gordon S. 1958. "H. G. Wells's 'The Man of the Year Million.'" *Nineteenth-Century Fiction* 12(4): 323–26.

Haley, Leah. 1994. *Ceto's New Friends*. Tuscaloosa, Ala.: Greenleaf.

Hall, John R. 2000. *Apocalypse Observed: Religious Movements and Violence in North America, Europe, and Japan*. London: Routledge.

Hamilton, William F., III. 1991. *Cosmic Top Secret: America's Secret* UFO *Program*. New Brunswick, N.J.: Inner Light.

Haraway, Donna. 1991. *Simians, Cyborgs, and Women: The Reinvention of Nature*. New York: Routledge.

———. 1997. *Modest-Witness@Second-Millennium.FemaleMan-Meets-Onco Mouse: Feminism and Technoscience*. London: Routledge.

———. 2004. *The Haraway Reader*. New York: Routledge.

Harding, Susan Friend. 2000. *The Book of Jerry Falwell: Fundamentalist Language and Politics*. Princeton: Princeton University Press.

Harding, Susan Friend, and Kathleen Stewart. 2003. "Anxieties of Influence: Conspiracy Theory and Therapeutic Culture in Millennial America." In *Transparency and Conspiracy: Ethnographies of Suspicion in the New World Order*, edited by Harry G. West and Todd Sanders. Durham: Duke University Press. 258–86.

Harkin, Michael E. 1994. "Person, Time, and Being: Northwest Coast Rebirth in Comparative Perspective." In *Amerindian Rebirth: Reincarnation Belief among North American Indians and Inuit*, edited by Antonia Mills and Richard Slobodin. Toronto: University of Toronto Press. 192–210.

Harpham, Geoffrey Galt. 2002. *Language Alone: The Critical Fetish of Modernity*. New York: Routledge.

Harris, Roy. 1996. *Signs, Language, and Communication: Integrational and Segregational Approaches*. New York: Routledge.

Hart, Mitchell B. 2002. "Racial Science, Social Science, and the Politics of Jewish Assimilation." In *Science, Race, and Ethnicity: Readings from Isis and Osiris*, edited by John P. Jackson, Jr. Chicago: University of Chicago Press. 99–128.

Harvey, David. 1989. *The Condition of Postmodernity: An Enquiry into the Origins of Cultural Change*. Cambridge, Mass.: Blackwell.

Hawkins, John A. 1994. *A Performance Theory of Order and Constituency*. Cambridge: Cambridge University Press.

Hayakawa, Norio F. 1993. "UFOs, the Grand Deception, and the Coming New World Order." Revised and expanded version. Manuscript.

Heard, Gerald. 1950. *The Riddle of the Flying Saucers: Is Another World Watching?* London: Carroll and Nicholson.

Heffernan, Virginia. 2004. "Our Prospective Neighbors from the Galaxy Next Door." Review of the television program *Naked Science: Alien Contact*. *New York Times*, November 24. B12.

Heidmann, Jean. 1995. *Extraterrestrial Intelligence*. Translated by Storm Dunlop. New York: Cambridge University Press.

Heinlein, Robert A. 1961. *Stranger in a Strange Land*. New York: Putnam.

Helmreich, Stefan. 2001. "After Culture: Reflections on the Apparition of Anthropology in Artificial Life, a Science of Simulation." *Cultural Anthropology* 16:612–27.

Henry, Victor. [1901] 1987. *Le Langage Martien*. Paris: Didier Érudition.

Herman, Judith Lewis. 1992. *Trauma and Recovery*. New York: Basic Books.

Herrnstein, Richard J., and Charles Murray. 1994. *The Bell Curve: Intelligence and Class Structure in American Life*. New York: Free Press.

Hesemann, Michael. 1996. *The Cosmic Connection: Worldwide Crop Formations and ET Contacts*. Bath: Gateway.

Hesemann, Michael, and Philip Mantle. *Beyond Roswell: The Alien Autopsy Film, Area 51, and the U.S. Government Coverup of UFOs*. London: O'Mara.

Hexham, Irving. 1997. "UFO Religion." *Christian Century* 114:439–41.

Hexham, Irving, and Karla Poewe. 1997. *New Religions as Global Cultures: Making the Human Sacred*. Boulder: Westview.

Hill, Betty. 1993. Letter to the editor. *Saucer Smear* 40(3): 7.

———. 1995. *A Common Sense Approach to UFOs*. Greenland, N.H.: The author.

Hoagland, Hudson. 1969. "Beings from Outer Space, Corporeal and Spiritual." *Science* 163:1.

Hofstader, Richard. 1965. *The Paranoid Style in American Politics, and Other Essays*. New York: Knopf.

Hopkins, Budd. 1981. *Missing Time*. New York: Random House.

———. 1987. *Intruders: The Incredible Visitations at Copley Woods*. New York: Random House.

Hubback, Andrew. 1996. *Prophets of Doom: The Security Threat of Religious Cults*. Occasional Paper no. 67. London: Institute of European Defense and Strategic Studies.

Icke, David. 1997. *And the Truth Shall Set You Free*. San Diego: Bridge of Love.

Ivy, Marilyn. 1995. *Discourses of the Vanishing: Modernity*. Chicago: University of Chicago Press.

Jackson, John P., Jr. 2001. " 'In Ways Unacademical': The Reception of Carleton S. Coon's *The Origin of Races*." *Journal of the History of Biology* 34:247–85.

Jacobs, David M. 1992. *Secret Life: Firsthand Accounts of UFO Abductions*. New York: Simon and Schuster.

———. 1998. *The Threat*. New York: Simon and Schuster.

Jacobson, Matthew Frye. 1998. *Whiteness of a Different Color: European Immigrants and the Alchemy of Race*. Cambridge, Mass.: Harvard University Press.

Jakobson, Roman. 1960. "Concluding Statement: Linguistics and Poetics." In *Style and Language*, edited by T. A. Sebeok. Cambridge, Mass.: MIT Press. 350–77.

James, Jenks, and Alan Prout, eds. 1997. *Constructing and Reconstructing Childhood: Contemporary Issues in the Sociological Study of Childhood*. Philadelphia: Routledge Farmer.

———. 1998. *Theorizing Childhood*. New York: Teachers College Press.

James, William. 1975. *Pragmatism*. Cambridge, Mass.: Harvard University Press.

Jameson, Fredric. 1981. *The Political Unconscious*. Ithaca: Cornell University Press.

Jenkins, Henry. 1992. *Textual Poachers: Television Fans and Participatory Culture*. New York: Routledge.

Jho, Zoev. 1990. *E.T. 101: The Cosmic Instruction Manual*. Santa Fe: Intergalactic Council.

Joas, Hans. 1996. *The Creativity of Action*. Chicago: University of Chicago Press.

Johnson, Hillary. 1996. *Osler's Web: Inside the Labyrinth of the Chronic Fatigue Syndrome Epidemic*. New York: Crown.

Jordan, Debie, and Kathy Mitchell. 1994. *Abducted! The Story of the Intruders Continues*. New York: Carroll and Graf.

Kac, Eduardo. 2000. "GFP Bunny." http://www.ekac.org/gfpbunny.html.

Kafton-Minkel, Walter. 1989. *Subterranean Worlds: 100,000 Years of Dragons, Dwarfs, the Dead, Lost Races, and UFOs from Inside the Earth*. Port Townsend, Wash.: Loompanics Unlimited.

Kaplan, Lois, Scott Michaelsen, and Art Clokey. 1986. *Gumby: The Authorized Biography*. New York: Harmony.

Kaufert, Patricia A. 1998. "Women, Resistance, and the Breast Cancer Movement." In *Pragmatic Women and Body Politics*, edited by Margaret Lock and Patricia A. Kaufert. New York: Cambridge University Press. 287–309.

Keane, Webb. 1997. *Signs of Recognition: Powers and Hazards of Representation in an Indonesian Society*. Berkeley: University of California Press.

Keel, John A. 1975. "The Flying Saucer Subculture." *Journal of Popular Culture* 8(4): 871–96.

———. 1989. "The Man Who Invented Flying Saucers." In *The Fringes of Reason: A Whole Earth Catalog*, edited by Ted Schultz. New York: Harmony. 138–45.

Kehoe, Alice B. 1990. "Primal Gaia: Primitivists and Plastic Medicine Men." In *The Invented Indian: Cultural Fictions and Government Policies*, edited by James A. Clifton. New Brunswick, N.J.: Transaction. 193–209.

Kelleher, D. 1994. "Self-Help Groups and Their Relationship to Medicine." In Jonathan Gabe, David Kelleher, and Gareth Williams, *Challenging Medicine*. London: Routledge. 104–17.

Kelleher, D., J. Gabe, and G. Williams. 1994. "Understanding Medical Dominance in the Modern World." In Jonathan Gabe, David Kelleher, and Gareth Williams, *Challenging Medicine*. London: Routledge. xi–xxix.

Keller, Catherine.1996. *Apocalypse Now and Then: A Feminist Guide to the End of the World*. Boston: Beacon.

Keller, Evelyn Fox. 1995. *Refiguring Life: Metaphors of Twentieth Century Biology*. New York: Columbia University Press.

Keyhoe, Donald E. 1950. *The Flying Saucers Are Real*. New York: Fawcett.

———. 1955. *The Flying Saucer Conspiracy*. New York: Holt.

Kinder, Gary. 1987. *Light Years: An Investigation into the Extraterrestrial Experiences of Eduard Meier*. New York: Atlantic Monthly Press.

Kinney, Jay. 1989. "Déjà Vu: The Hidden History of the New Age." In *The Fringes of Reason: A Whole Earth Catalog*, edited by Ted Schultz. New York: Harmony. 22–30.

Kinsella, Sharon. 1995. "Cuties in Japan." In *Women, Media, and Consumption in Japan*, edited by L. Skov and B. Moeran. Honolulu: University of Hawaii Press. 220–54.

———. 1998. "Japanese Subculture in the 1980s: Otaku and the Amateur Manga Movement." *Journal of Japanese Studies* 24(2): 289–316.

Klass, Morton. 1995. *Ordered Universes: Approaches to the Anthropology of Religion*. Boulder: Westview.

Klass, Philip. 1985. "Radar UFOs: Where Have They Gone?" *Skeptical Inquirer* 9(3): 257–60.

———. 1989. *UFO Abductions: A Dangerous Game*. Updated ed. Buffalo: Prometheus.

Klein, R. 1983. *The Politics of the National Health Service*. London: Longman.

Kolata, Gina, and Kenneth Chang. "For Clonaid, a Trail of Unproven Claims." *New York Times*. June 1. A-13.

Kossy, Donna. 2001. *Strange Creations: Aberrant Ideas of Human Origins from Ancient Astronauts to Aquatic Apes*. Los Angeles: Feral House.

Kottmeyer, Martin S. 1990. "Entirely Unpredisposed." *Magonia* 35:3–10.

———. 1994. "Why Are the Grays Gray?" *MUFON UFO Journal* 319:6–10.

Kraut, Alan. 1994. *Silent Travelers: Germs, Genes and the "Immigrant Menace."* New York: Basic Books.

Kristeva, Julia. 1991. *Strangers to Ourselves*. New York: Columbia University Press.

Laclau, Ernesto. 1996. *Emancipation(s)*. London: Verso.

Latour, Bruno. 2000. "The Well-Articulated Primatology: Reflections of a Fellow Traveler." In *Primate Encounters: Models of Science, Gender, and Society*, edited by Shirley C. Strum and Linda M. Fedigan. Chicago: University of Chicago Press. 358–81.

Latour, Bruno, and Steven Woolgar. 1986. *Laboratory Life: The Construction of Scientific Facts*. Princeton: Princeton University Press.

Lavery, David, Angela Hague, and Marla Cartwright, eds. 1996. *"Deny All Knowledge": Reading* The X-Files. Syracuse: Syracuse University Press.

LaVigne, Michelle. 1995. *The Alien Abduction Survival Guide: How to Cope with Your ET Experience*. Newberg, Ore: Wild Flower Press.

Lecercle, Jean-Jacques. 1985. *Philosophy through the Looking-Glass: Language, Nonsense, Desire*. La Salle, Ill.: Open Court.

Lehmann, W. P. 1965. "Decoding of the Martian Language: Coordination of ILU and WGW." *Graduate Journal* 7 (1): 265–72.

Leinster, Murray. [1945] 1998. "First Contact." In *First Contacts: The Essential Murray Leinster*. Framingham, Mass.: NESFA Press. 85–108.

Lenain, Thierry. 1997. *Monkey Painting*. London: Reaktion.

Lepselter, Susan. 1997. "From the Earth Native's Point of View: The Earth, the Extraterrestrial, and the Natural Ground of Home." *Public Culture* 9:197–208.

———. 2005a. "The Flight of the Ordinary: Narrative, Poetics, Power, and UFOs in the American Uncanny." Ph.D. dissertation. University of Texas, Austin.

Lepselter, Susan. 2005b. "Why Rachel Isn't Buried at Her Grave: Ghosts, UFOs, and a Place in the West." In *Histories of the Future*, edited by Daniel Rosenberg and Susan Harding. Durham: Duke University Press. 255–79.

Leslie, Desmond, and George Adamski. 1953. *Flying Saucers Have Landed*. New York: British Book Centre.

Lester, Toby. 2002. "Oh, Gods." *Atlantic Monthly* 289 (2): 37–45.

Lévi-Strauss, Claude. [1955] 1984. *Tristes Tropique*. Translated by John Weightman and Doreen Weightman. New York: Atheneum.

Lewels, Joe. 1997. *The God Hypothesis: Extraterrestrial Life and Its Implications for Science and Religion*. Mill Spring, N.C.: Wild Flower.

Lewis, James, ed. 1995. *The Gods Have Landed: New Religions from Other Worlds*. Albany: State University of New York Press.

Lieb, Michael. 1998. *Children of Ezekiel: Aliens, UFOs, the Crisis of Race, and the Advent of End Time*. Durham: Duke University Press.

Lilly, John Cunningham. 1967. *The Mind of the Dolphin: A Nonhuman Intelligence*. Garden City, N.Y.: Doubleday.

Lindstrom, Lamont. 1993. *Cargo Cult: Strange Stories of Desire from Melanesia and Beyond*. Honolulu: University of Hawaii Press.

Lister, Martin, et al. 2003. *New Media: A Critical Introduction*. London: Routledge.

Lorenzen, Coral. 1969. "UFO Occupants in United States Reports." In *The Humanoids*, edited by Charles Bowen. Chicago: Regnery. 143–76.

Lorenzen, Coral, and Jim Lorenzen. 1976. *Encounters with UFO Occupants*. New York: Berkley.

Lowell, Percival. 1895. *Mars*. Boston: Houghton Mifflin.

———. 1906. *Mars and Its Canals*. New York: Macmillan.

———. 1909. *Mars as the Abode of Life*. New York: Macmillan.

Lyotard, Jean François. 1984. *The Postmodern Condition: A Report on Knowledge*. Minneapolis: University of Minnesota Press.

Ma, Sheng-Mei. 2000. *The Deathly Embrace: Orientalism and Asian American Identity*. Minneapolis: University of Minnesota Press.

Mack, John E. 1994. *Abduction: Human Encounters with Aliens*. New York: Charles Scribner's Sons.

———. 1999. *Passport to the Cosmos: Human Transformation and Alien Encounters*. New York: Crown.

Mandelker, Scott. 1995. *From Elsewhere: Being E.T. in America*. New York: Carol Publishing Group.

Marchetti, Gina. 1993. *Romance and the "Yellow Peril": Race, Sex, and Discursive Strategies in Hollywood Fiction*. Berkeley: University of California Press.

Marcus, George. 1998. *Ethnography through Thick and Thin*. Princeton: Princeton University Press.

———. 1999. *Paranoia within Reason*. Chicago: University of Chicago Press.

Marcus, George, ed. 1995. *Technoscientific Imaginaries: Conversations, Profiles, and Memoirs*. Chicago: University of Chicago Press.

Martin, Emily. 1997. "Anthropological Fieldwork and the Study of Science as Culture: From Citadels to String Figures." In *Anthropological Locations: Boundaries and Grounds of a Field Science*. Edited by Akhil Gupta and James Ferguson. Berkeley: University of California Press. 131–46.

Massumi, Brian. ed. 1993. *The Politics of Everyday Fear*. Minneapolis: University of Minnesota Press.

Matheson, Terry. 1998. *Alien Abductions: Creating a Modern Phenomenon*. Amherst, N.Y.: Prometheus.

Mazzarella, William. 2003. *Shoveling Smoke: Advertising and Globalization in Contemporary India*. Durham: Duke University Press.

McKay, David S., Everett K. Gibson, Jr., Kathie L. Thomas-Keprta, Hojatollah Vali, Christopher S. Romanek, Simon J. Clemett, Xavier D. F. Chillier, Claude R. Maechling, and Richard N. Zare. 1996. "Search for Past Life on Mars: Possible Relic Biogenic Activity in Martian Meteorite ALH84001." *Science* 273:924–30.

Melley, Timothy. 2000. *Empire of Conspiracy: The Culture of Paranoia in Postwar America*. Ithaca: Cornell University Press.

Melton, J. Gordon, and George M. Eberhart. 1995. "The Flying Saucer Contactee Movement, 1950–1994: A Bibliography." In *The Gods Have Landed: New Religions from Other Worlds*, edited by James R. Lewis. Albany: State University of New York Press. 250–332.

Melucci, Alberto. 1996a. *Challenging Codes: Collective Action in the Information Age*. Cambridge: Cambridge University Press.

———. 1996b. *The Playing Self: Person and Meaning in a Planetary Society*. Cambridge: Cambridge University Press.

Menzel, Donald. 1965. "An Earthling's View: Meet the Martians." *Graduate Journal* 7 (1): 220–34.

Meyers, Walter E. 1980. *Aliens and Linguists: Language Study and Science Fiction*. Athens: University of Georgia Press.

Michel, Aimé. 1969. "The Problem of Non-Contact." In *The Humanoids*, edited by Charles Bowen. Chicago: Regnery. 249–56.

Midgley, Mary. 1992. *Science as Salvation: A Modern Myth and Its Meaning*. London: Routledge.

Mitchell, W. J. Thomas. 1998. *The Last Dinosaur Book: The Life and Times of a Cultural Icon*. Chicago: University of Chicago Press.

Mitchell, William J. 2003. *Me++: The Cyborg Self and the Networked City*. Cambridge, Mass.: MIT Press.

Mithun, Marianne. 1999. *The Languages of Native North America*. New York: Cambridge University Press.

Montgomery, Ruth. 1979. *Strangers among Us: Enlightened Beings from a World to Come*. New York: Fawcett Crest.

Morgan, Lynn M., and Meredith W. Michaels, eds. 1999. *Fetal Subjects, Feminist Positions*. Philadelphia: University of Pennsylvania Press.

Moseley, James W. 1957. Untitled editorial. *Saucer News Newsletter* 4:1–2.

Moseley, James, and Michael G. Mann. 1959. "Screwing the Lid on 'Doctor' Williamson." *Saucer News* 6(2): 3–5.

Moseley, James, and Karl T. Pflock. 2002. *Shockingly Close to the Truth! Confessions of a Grave-Robbing Ufologist*. Amherst, N.Y.: Prometheus.

Mullis, Kary. [1998] 2000. *Dancing Naked in the Mind Field*. New York: Vintage.

Myerhoff, Barbara. 1986. "Life Not Death in Venice: Its Second Life." In *The Anthropology of Experience*, edited by Edward Bruner. Urbana: University of Illinois Press. 261–86.

Nader, Laura, ed. 1996a. "The Three-Cornered Constellation: Magic, Science, and Religion Revisited." In *Naked Science: Anthropological Inquiry into Boundaries, Power, and Knowledge*, edited by Laura Nader. New York: Routledge. 259–75.

———, ed. 1996b. *Naked Science: Anthropological Inquiry into Boundaries, Power, and Knowledge*. New York: Routledge.

Narby, Jeremy. 1999. *Cosmic Serpent: DNA and the Origins of Knowledge*. New York: Jeremy P. Tarcher/Putnam.

Nash, Susan Smith. 1996. *Channel-Surfing the Apocalypse: A Day in the Life of a Fin-de-Millennium Mind*. Penngrove, Calif.: Avec Books.

N. D. "Resist Enumeration." http://www.networkusa.org/fingerprint/page6/fp-resist.html. Web page part of larger website, "Fight the Fingerprint," http://www.networkusa.org/fingerprint.shtml.

Nelkin, Dorothy, and Laurence Tancredi. 1989. *Dangerous Diagnostics: The Social Power of Biological Information*. New York: Basic Books.

Okada, Toshio. 1996. *Otakugaku Nyuumon (Introduction to Otakuology)*. Tokyo: Ota Shuppan.

Okrand, Marc. 1992. *Klingon Dictionary*. New York: Pocket Books.

———. 1997. *Klingon for the Galactic Traveler*. New York: Pocket Books.

Ong. Aihwa. 1999. *Flexible Citizenship: The Cultural Logics of Transnationality*. Durham: Duke University Press.

Packard, Vance. 1957. *The Hidden Persuaders*. New York: McKay.

Palmer, Ray. 1975. *The Secret World*. Vol. 1: *The Diary of a Lifetime of Questioning the "Facts."* Amherst, Wisc.: Amherst Press.

Palmer, Susan J. 1994. *Moon Sisters, Krishna Mothers, Rajneesh Lovers: Women's Roles in New Religions*. Syracuse: Syracuse University Press.

———. 1995. "Women in the Raëlian Movement: New Religious Experiments in Gender and Authority." In *The Gods Have Landed: New Religions from Other Worlds*, edited by James R. Lewis. Albany: State University of New York Press. 105–36.

———. 1997a. *AIDS as an Apocalyptic Metaphor in North America*. Toronto: University of Toronto Press.

———. 1997b. "Woman as World Savior." In *Millennium, Messiahs, and Mayhem: Contemporary Apocalyptic Movements*, edited by Thomas Robbins and Susan J. Palmer. New York: Routledge. 159–74.

———. 2004. *Aliens Adored: Raël's UFO Religion*. New Brunswick, N.J.: Rutgers University Press.

Palmer, Susan J., and Charlotte E. Hardman. 1999. *Children in New Religions*. New Brunswick, N.J.: Rutgers University Press.

Partridge, Christopher, ed. 2003. *UFO Religions*. London: Routledge.

Patton, Phil. 1998. *Dreamland: Travels inside the Secret World of Roswell and Area 51*. New York: Villard.

Payne, Roger. 1970. Sound recording. *Songs of the Humpback Whale*. Los Angeles: Capitol Records.

Payne, Roger, ed. 1983. *Communication and Behavior of Whales*. Boulder: Westview.

Peirce, Charles Sanders. [1883] 1989. *The Writings of Charles S. Peirce*, edited by Max S. Fisch. Vol. 4. Bloomington: Indiana University Press.

Pelley, William Dudley. 1950. *Star Guests: Design for Mortality*. Noblesville, Ind.: Soulcraft Chapels.

Pemberton, John. 1994. *On the Subject of "Java."* Ithaca: Cornell University Press.

Penley, Constance. 1991. "Brownian Motion: Women, Tactics, and Technology." In *Technoculture*, edited by C. Penley and A. Ross. Minneapolis: University of Minnesota Press. 135–62.

Pennock, Robert T., ed. 2001. *Intelligent Design Creationism and Its Critics: Philosophical, Theological, and Scientific Perspectives*. Cambridge, Mass.: MIT Press.

Philo, Chris, and Chris Wilbert, eds. 2000. *Animal Spaces, Beastly Places: New Geographies of Human-Animal Relations*. London: Routledge.

Pickering, Andrew. 1999. "The Mangle of Practice: Agency and Emergence in the Sociology of Science." In *The Science Studies Reader*, edited by Mario Biagioli. New York: Routledge. 373–94.

Pinch, T. J., and H. M. Collins. 1984. "Private Science and Public Knowledge: The Committee for Scientific Investigation of the Claims of the Paranormal and Its Use of the Literature." *Social Studies of Science* 14(4): 521–46.

Pobst, Jim. 1989. *Shaver: The Early Years*. Stone Mountain, Ga.: Arcturus.

Poovey, Mary. 1998. *The History of the Modern Fact: Problems of Knowledge in the Sciences of Wealth and Society*. Chicago: University of Chicago Press.

Porges, Irwin. 1975. *Edgar Rice Burroughs: The Man Who Created Tarzan*. Provo, Utah: Brigham Young University Press.

Pranger, Burcht. 2001. "Images of Iron: Ignatius of Loyola and Joyce." In *Religion and Media*, edited by Hent de Vries and Samuel Weber. Stanford: Stanford University Press. 182–97.

Pritchard, Andrea, David E. Prichard, John E. Mack, Pam Kasey, and Claudia Yapp, eds. 1994. *Alien Discussions: Proceedings of the Abduction Study Conference*. Cambridge, Mass.: North Cambridge Press.

Prophet, Mark L. [1965] 1981. *The Soulless One: Cloning a Counterfeit Creation*. Los Angeles: Summit University Press.

Puccetti, Roland. 1969. *Persons: A Study of Possible Moral Agents in the Universe*. New York: Herder and Herder.

Punch. 1893. "1,000,000 A.D." *Punch* 105 (November 25): 250.

Rabinow, Paul. 1992. "Artificiality and Enlightenment: From Sociobiology to Biosociality." In *Incorporations*, edited by Jonathan Crary and Sandord Kwinter. New York: Zone. 234–52.

Raël. 1998a. *The Messages Given by Extraterrestrials*. Quebec: Raëlian Religion.

———. 1998b. *The True Face of God*. Quebec: Raëlian Religion.

———. 2001. *Yes to Human Cloning*. Quebec: Raëlian Foundation.

Ramet, Sabrina. 1998. "UFOs over Russia and Eastern Europe." *Journal of Popular Culture* 32 (winter): 81–87.

Ranciere, Jacques. 1995. "Politics, Identification, and Subjectivication." In *The Identity in Question*, edited by J. Rajchman,. New York: Routledge.

Reber, Grote. 1940. Cosmic Static. *Astrophysical Journal* 91:621.

Richardson, James. 1995. "Manufacturing Consent about Koresh: A Structural Analysis of the Role of Media in the Waco Tragedy." In *Armageddon in Waco: Critical Perspectives on the Branch Davidian Conflict*, edited by Stuart A. Wright. Chicago: University of Chicago Press. 153–76.

Robbins, Thomas, and Susan J. Palmer. 1997. *Millennium, Messiahs, and Mayhem: Contemporary Apocalyptic Movements*. New York: Routledge.

Robins, Kevin, and Frank Webster. 1999. *Times of the Technoculture*. London: Routledge.

Robinson, John J. 1963. "George Hunt Williamson Re-visited." *Saucer News* 10 (3): 9–10.

Robinson, Kim Stanley. 1994. "The Translator." In *Remaking History and Other Stories*. New York: Tom Doherty. 287–302.

Rodenborn, Marcy. 1997. *Antietam Redux*. Produced at Nine Holes—A Festival of Short Plays. Theater Babylon, Seattle.

Rojcewicz, Peter M. 1987. "The 'Men in Black' Experience and Tradition: Analogues with the Traditional Devil Hypothesis." *Journal of American Folklore* 100 (396): 148–60.

Roof, Wade Clark. 1993. *A Generation of Seekers: The Spiritual Journeys of the Baby Boom Generation*. New York: Harper San Francisco.

Roth, Christopher F. 1995. "UFO Abductions as Reverse Colonial Fantasy." Paper presented at the seventy-second annual meeting of the Central States Anthropological Society, Indianapolis.

Royal, Lyssa, and Keith Priest. 1992. *Visitors from Within*. Phoenix: Royal Priest Research Press.

Rushkoff, Douglas. 1996. *Media Virus! Hidden Agendas in Popular Culture*. New York: Ballantine.

Rutherford, Danilyn. 2003. *Raiding the Land of the Foreigners*. Princeton: Princeton University Press.

Sagan, Carl. 1978. "For Future Times and Beings." In Carl Sagan, F. D. Drake, J. Lomberg, L. S. Sagan, A. Druyan, and T. Ferris, *Murmurs of Earth: The Voyager Interstellar Record*. New York: Random House. 1–44.

———. 1985. *Contact*. New York: Simon and Schuster.

Sagan, Carl, and P. Fox. 1975. "The Canals of Mars: An Assessment after Mariner 9." *Icarus* 25:602–12.

Sagan, Carl, F. D. Drake, J. Lomberg, L. S. Sagan, A. Druyan, and T. Ferris. 1978. *Murmurs of Earth: The Voyager Interstellar Record*. New York: Random House.

Sagan, Linda Salzman. 1978. "A Voyager's Greetings." In Carl Sagan, F. D. Drake, J. Lomberg, L. S. Sagan, A. Druyan, and T. Ferris, *Murmurs of Earth: The Voyager Interstellar Record*. New York: Random House. 123–48.

Said, Edward W. 1978. *Orientalism*. New York: Random House.

Saler, Ziegler, and Charles B. Moore. 1997. *UFO Crash at Roswell: The Genesis of Modern Myth*. Washington, D.C.: Smithsonian Institution Press.

Sanders, Todd, and Harry G. West. 2003. "Power Revealed and Concealed in the New World Order." In *Transparency and Conspiracy: Ethnographies of Suspicion in the New World Order*, edited by Harry G. West and Todd Sanders. Durham: Duke University Press. 1–37.

Sanderson, Ivan T. 1967. *Uninvited Visitors: A Biologist Looks at UFO's*. New York: Cowles Education.

Sandoval-Sanchez, Alberto. 2003. "*Sirena Selena Vestida de Pena*: A Novel for the

New Millennium and for New Critical Practices in Puerto Rican Literary and Cultural Studies." *CENTRO Journal* 15:5–23.

Saussy, Haun. 2001. "In the Workshop of Equivalence: Translation, Institutions, and Media in the Jesuit Re-formation of China." In *Religion and Media*, edited by Hent de Vries and Samuel Weber. Stanford: Stanford University Press. 163–81.

Schodt, Frederik L. 1996. *Dreamland Japan: Writings on Modern Manga*. Berkeley, Calif.: Stonebridge.

Schwartz, Hillel. 1996. *The Culture of the Copy: Striking Likenesses, Unreasonable Facsimiles*. New York: Zone.

Scott-Elliot, W. [1925] 1962. *The Story of Atlantis; and, The Lost Lemuria*. Rev. ed. London: Theosophical Publishing House.

Scully, Frank. 1950. *Behind the Flying Saucers*. New York: Holt.

Sebeok, T. A., and Jean Umiker, eds. 1976. *Speech Surrogates: Drum and Whistle Systems*. The Hague: Mouton.

Sefton-Green, Julian. 2004. "Initiation Rites: A Small Boy in a Poké World. In *Pikachu's Global Adventures: The Rise and Fall of Pokémon*, edited by Joseph Tobin. Durham: Duke University Press. 141–64.

Seiter, Ellen. 1993. *Sold Separately: Parents and Children in Consumer Culture*. New Brunswick, N.J.: Rutgers University Press.

Shannon, C. E. 1948. "A Mathematical Theory of Communication." *Bell System Technical Journal* 27 (379–423): 623–56.

Shaver, Richard S. 1975. "The Ancient Earth, Its Story in Stone." In Ray Palmer, *The Secret World*. Vol. 1: *The Diary of a Lifetime of Questioning the "Facts."* Amherst, Wisc.: Amherst Press. 47–144.

Sheehan, William. 1996. *The Planet Mars: A History of Observation and Discovery*. Tucson: University of Arizona Press.

Shermer, Michael. 1997. *Why People Believe Weird Things: Pseudoscience, Superstition, and Other Confusions of Our Time*. New York: Freeman.

Sidky, H. 2004. *Perspectives on Culture: A Critical Introduction to Theory in Cultural Anthropology*. Upper Saddle River, N.J.: Pearson Education.

Singerman, Robert. 1986. "The Jew as Racial Alien: The Genetic Component of American Anti-Semitism." In *Anti-Semitism in American History*, edited by David A. Gerber. Urbana: University of Illinois Press. 103–28.

Sitchin, Zechariah. 1976. *The 12th Planet*. New York: Stein and Day.

Smith, Bruce A. 1990. "Fatherhood in the New Age: One Man's Story of Alien Abduction for Cross-Breeding Purposes." Manuscript.

Smith, Jonathan Z. 1994. "Close Encounters of Diverse Kinds." Nuveen Lecture, University of Chicago Divinity School. April 4.

Song, Hoon. Forthcoming. "Humanitarian Universalism and Its Figure of the Victim." *Cultural Anthropology.*
Stacey, Jackie. 2003. "She Is Not Herself: The Deviant Relations of *Alien Resurrection.*" *Screen* 44 (3): 251–76.
Stafford, Barbara Maria. 1999. *Visual Analogy: Consciousness as the Art of Connecting*. Cambridge, Mass.: MIT Press.
Starobinski, Jean. 1979. *Words upon Words: The Anagrams of Ferdinand de Saussure*. New Haven: Yale University Press.
Steedley, Mary 1993. *Hanging without a Rope: Narrative Experience in Colonial and Post-Colonial Karoland*. Princeton: Princeton University Press.
Steedman, Carolyn. 1986. *Landscape for a Good Woman: A Story of Two Lives*. London: Virago.
Steiger, Brad, and Francie Steiger. 1981. *The Star People*. New York: Berkley.
Steiger, Brad, and Sherry Hansen Steiger. 1992. *Starborn*. New York: Berkley.
Stephenson, Neal. 1992. *Snow Crash*. New York: Bantam.
Stevens, Wendelle C. 1989. *UFO Contact from the Pleiades: A Supplementary Investigation Report—the Report of an Ongoing Contact*. Tucson: UFO Photo Archives.
Stewart, Kathleen. 1995. *A Space on the Side of the Road: Cultural Poetics in an Other America*. Princeton: Princeton University Press.
Stock, Gregory. 2002. *Redesigning Humans: Our Inevitable Genetic Future*. Boston: Houghton Mifflin.
Stocking, George W., Jr. 1968. *Race, Culture, and Evolution: Essays in the History of Anthropology*. Chicago: University of Chicago Press.
———. 1987. *Victorian Anthropology*. New York: Free Press.
Stone, Idella Purnell, ed. 1969. *14 Great Tales of ESP*. London: Hodder Fawcett.
Strassman, Rick. 2001. *DMT, the Spirit Molecule: A Doctor's Revolutionary Research into the Biology of Near-Death and Mystical Experiences*. Rochester, Vt.: Inner Traditions.
Strathern, Marilyn. 1991. *Partial Connections*. Savage, Md.: Rowman and Littlefield.
———. 1995. *The Relation: Issues in Complexity and Scale*. Cambridge: Prickly Pear Press.
———. 1999. *Property, Substance, and Effect: Anthropological Essays on Persons and Things*. London: Athlone Press.
———. 2000. "Introduction: New Accountabilities." In *Audit Cultures: Anthropological Studies in Accountability, Ethics, and the Academy*, edited by M. Strathern. London: Routledge. 1–18.
———. 2003. "Emergent Relations." In *Scientific Authorship: Credit and Intellec-*

tual Property in Science, edited by Mario Biagioli and Peter Galison. London: Routledge. 165–94.

Strieber, Whitley. 1987. *Communion: A True Story*. New York: Beech Tree.

Strum, Shirley C., and Linda M. Fedigan, eds. 2000. *Primate Encounters: Models of Science, Gender, and Society*. Chicago: University of Chicago Press.

Swords, Michael D. 1985. "Ufonauts: Homo Sapiens of the Future?" *MUFON UFO Journal* 202 (February): 8–10.

———. 1991. "Modern Biology and the Extraterrestrial Hypothesis." In *MUFON International UFO Symposium Proceedings, 1991*. Seguin, Texas: Mutual UFO Network. 51–78.

Sykes, Karen. 2003. "My Aim Is True: Postnostalgic Reflections on the Future of Anthropological Science." *American Anthropologist* 30 (1): 156–68.

Szasz, Thomas Stephen. 1996. *The Meaning of Mind: Language, Morality, and Neuroscience*. Westport: Praeger.

Szwed, John F. 1997. *Space Is the Place: The Lives and Times of Sun Ra*. New York: Pantheon.

Taussig, Michael. 1993. *Mimesis and Alterity*. New York: Routledge.

———. 1997. *The Magic of the State*. New York: Routledge.

Taylor, Verta A. 1996. *Rock-a-By Baby: Feminism, Self-Help, and Postpartum Depression*. New York: Routledge.

Terrusse, Marcel. 2001. "Crop Circles." *Apocalypse* 124: 31–33.

Tesla, Nikola. 1901. "Talking with Planets." *Collier's*. February 9: 4–5.

———. 1907. "Signaling to Mars: A Problem in Electrical Engineering." *Harvard Illustrated*, March.

———. 1909. "How to Signal to Mars." *New York Times*, May 23.

———. 1919. "Signals to Mars Based on Hope of Life on Planet." *New York Herald Sunday Magazine*, October 12.

Thomas, Kenn. 1999. *Maury Island UFO: The Crisman Conspiracy*. Lilburn, Ga.: IllumiNet.

"Thorn." Report. http://lycaeum.org.

Tillett, Gregory. 1982. *The Elder Brother: A Biography of Charles Webster Leadbeater*. London: Routledge and Kegan Paul.

Tobin, Joseph, ed. 2004. *Pikachu's Global Adventure: The Rise and Fall of Pokémon*. Durham: Duke University Press.

Tobin, Samuel. 2004. "Masculinity, Maturity, and the End of Pokémon." In *Pikachu's Global Adventure: The Rise and Fall of Pokémon*, edited by Joseph Tobin. Durham: Duke University Press. 241–56.

Todorov, Tzvetan. 1975. *The Fantastic*. Ithaca: Cornell University Press.

———. 1982. *Theories of the Symbol*, translated by Catherine Porter. Oxford: Blackwell.

Tomlin, R. S. 1986. *Basic Word Order: Functional Principles*. London: Routledge.

Trachtenberg, Joshua. 1943. *The Devil and the Jews: The Medieval Concept of the Jew and Its Relation to Modern Antisemitism*. Cleveland: World.

Tsing, Anna Lowenhaupt. 1993. *In the Realm of the Diamond Queen: Marginality in an Out-of-the-Way Place*. Princeton: Princeton University Press.

Turkle, Sherry. 1984. *The Second Self: Computers and the Human Spirit*. New York: Simon and Schuster.

Turner, Victor. 1981. "Social Dramas and Stories about Them." *Critical Inquiry* 7 (1): 141–68.

———. 1982. *From Ritual to Theatre: The Human Seriousness of Play*. New York: Performing Arts Journal Publications.

Urban, Greg. 1996. *Metaphysical Community: The Interplay of the Senses and the Intellect*. Austin: University of Texas Press.

Vallee, Jacques. 1969a. *Passport to Magonia: On UFOs, Folklore, and Parallel Worlds*. Chicago: Regnery.

———. 1969b. "The Pattern behind the UFO Landings: Report on the Analysis of 200 Documented Observations Made in 1954." In *The Humanoids*, edited by Charles Bowen. Chicago: Regnery. 27–76.

———. 1979. *Messengers of Deception: UFO Contacts and Cults*. Berkeley, Calif.: And/Or Press.

Vincent, J. 1992. "Self-Help Groups and Health Care in Contemporary Britain." In *Alternative Medicine in Modern Britain*, edited by M. Saks. Oxford: Clarendon. 137–54.

Wagner, Roy. 2001. *An Anthropology of the Subject: Holographic Worldview in New Guinea and Its Meaning and Significance for the World of Anthropology*. Berkeley: University of California Press.

Wagner-Pacifici, Robin. 2000. *Theorizing the Standoff: Contingency in Action*. Cambridge: Cambridge University Press.

Walsh, Diana Chapman. 1987. *Corporate Physicians: Between Medicine and Management*. New Haven: Yale University Press.

Ware, Norma C., and Arthur Kleinman. 1992. "Culture and Somatic Experience: The Social Course of Illness in Neurasthenia and Chronic Fatigue Syndrome." *Psychosomatic Medicine* 54(5): 546–60.

Washington, Peter. 1993. *Madame Blavatsky's Baboon: Theosophy and the Emergence of the Modern Guru*. London: Secker and Warburg.

Wauchope, Robert. 1962. *Lost Tribes and Sunken Continents: Myth and Method in the Study of American Indians*. Chicago: University of Chicago Press.

Weatherford, Jack. 1988. *Indian Givers: How the Indians of the Americas Transformed the World*. New York: Fawcett Columbine.

Weber, Samuel. 2001. "Religion, Repetition, Media." In *Religion and Media*, edited by Hent de Vries and Samuel Weber. Stanford: Stanford University Press. 43–55.

Weinberg, Robert. "Of Clones and Clowns." *Atlantic Monthly* 280 (1997): 54–59.

Weldes, Jutta, et al. 1999. *Cultures of Insecurity: States, Communities, and the Production of Danger*. Minneapolis: University of Minnesota Press.

Wells, H. G. 1893. "The Man of the Year Million: A Scientific Forecast." *Pall Mall Budget*, November 16.

———. 1895. *The Time Machine: An Invention*. New York: Holt.

———. [1898] 1983. *The War of the Worlds*. Cutchogue, N.Y.: Buccaneer.

Werbner, Richard P. 1989. *Ritual Passage, Sacred Journey: The Process and Organization Religious Movement*. Washington, D.C.: Smithsonian Institution Press.

West, Harry G., and Todd Sander, eds. 2003. *Transparency and Conspiracy: Ethnographies of Suspicion in the New World Order*. Durham: Duke University Press.

White, Luise. 1994. "Alien Nation." *Transition* 63:24–33.

White, Merry. 1994. *The Material Child: Coming of Age in Japan and America*. Berkeley: University of California Press.

Whorf, Benjamin Lee. 1941. The Relation of Habitual Thought and Behavior to Language. In *Language, Culture, and Personality: Essays in Memory of Edward Sapir*, edited by Leslie Spier. Menasha, Wisc.: Sapir Memorial Publication Fund. 75–93.

———. 1950. An American Indian Model of the Universe. *International Journal of American Linguistics* 16:67–72.

———. N.d. "Ancient America and the Evolution of the Coming Race." Draft manuscript for an address delivered before the (Hartford, Conn.?) Theosophical Society (late 1930s?). Benjamin Lee Whorf Papers, Reel 3, frames 557–77.

Williams, Ben. 2001. "Black Secret Technology: Detroit Techno and the Information Age." In *Technicolor: Race, Technology, and Everyday Life*, edited by Alondra Nelson and Thuy N. Tu, with Alicia Headlam Hines. New York: New York University Press. 154–76.

Williams, Raymond. [1962] 1980. "Advertising: The Magic System." In *Problems in Materialism and Culture*, edited by Raymond Williams. London: New Left Books.

———. 1977. *Marxism and Literature*. Oxford: Oxford University Press.

Williamson, George Hunt. 1953. *Other Tongues—Other Flesh*. Amherst, Wisc.: Amherst Press.

———. 1959. *The Road in the Sky*. London: Neville Spearman.

Williamson, George Hunt, and Alfred C. Bailey. 1953. *The Saucers Speak! A Documentary Report of Interstellar Communication by Radiotelegraphy*. Los Angeles: New Age.

Willis, Roy. 1999. *Some Spirits Heal, Others Only Dance: A Journey into Human Selfhood in an African Village*. Oxford: Berg.

Willwerth, James. 1994. "The Man from Outer Space." *Time* 143 (17): 74–75.

Wilson, Robert A. and Miriam J. Hill. 1998. *Everything is under Control: Conspiracies, Cults, and Cover-Ups*. New York: HarperCollins.

Wolfram, Stephen. *A New Kind of Science*. Champaign, Ill.: Wolfram Media, 2002.

Wolstenholme, G., ed. 1963. *Man and His Future*. London: Churchill.

Wood, John, ed. 1998. *The Virtual Embodied: Presence/Practice/Technology*. New York: Routledge.

Woodman, Eric. 2000. "Information Generation: Berkeley Study Measures Gargantuan Information Boom." http://www.emc.com/news.

Wright, Dan. 1996. "Sexuality, Aliens, Hybrids and Abductions." MUFON UFO *Journal* 334:11–12.

Wright, Stuart A., ed. 1995. *Armageddon in Waco: Critical Perspectives on the Branch Davidian Conflict*. Chicago: University of Chicago Press.

Wu, William F. 1982. *The Yellow Peril: Chinese Americans in American B Fiction, 1850–1940*. Hamden: Archon.

Yaguello, Marina. 1991. *Lunatic Lovers of Language: Imaginary Languages and Their Inventors*, translated by Catherine Slater. London: Athlone Press.

Yano, Christine R. 2004. "Panic Attacks: Anti-Pokémon Voices in Global Markets." In *Pikachu's Global Adventure: The Rise and Fall of Pokémon*, edited by Joseph Tobin. Durham: Duke University Press. 108–38.

Young, Allan. 1995. *The Harmony of Illusions: Inventing Posttraumatic Stress Disorder*. Princeton: Princeton University Press.

Young, Robert. 1972. "The Anthropology of Science." *New Humanist* 88(3): 102–5.

Ziarek, Ewa Plonowska. 2001. *An Ethics of Dissensus: Postmodernity, Feminism, and the Politics of Radical Democracy*. Stanford: Stanford University Press.

Žižek, Slavoj. 2002. *Welcome to the Desert of the Real*. London: Verso.

CONTRIBUTORS

Debbora Battaglia is a cultural anthropologist specializing in personhood and creative social action. Most recently she has engaged the human cloning controversy, focusing on the contingency of self and identity in fluid faith-based communities. Her books include *On the Bones of the Serpent: Person, Memory, and Mortality in Sabarl Island Society* (Chicago) and *Rhetorics of Self-Making* (California). She is Professor of Anthropology at Mount Holyoke College.

Richard Doyle maps the rhetorical interfaces between information technology and the life sciences, those sites where living systems and information ecologies blur. Author of *Wetwares: Experiments in PostVital Living* (Minnesota) and *On Beyond Living: Rhetorical Transformations of the Life Sciences* (Stanford), Doyle currently serves as Expert, Wetwares and Human/Machine Interaction, for the International Electrotechnical Commission (IEC). He is Professor of Rhetoric and Science, Medicine, Technologies and Cultures at Pennsylvania State University.

Joseph Dumit is the Director of the Science and Technology Studies Program and Associate Professor of Anthropology at the University of California at Davis, and Associate Professor of Anthropology and Science and Technology Studies at the Massachusetts Institute of Technology. His books include *Picturing Personhood: Brain Scans and Biomedical Identity* (Princeton), *Cyborg Babies* (Routledge), and *Cyborgs and Citadels* (School of American Research).

Mizuko (Mimi) Ito is a cultural anthropologist of technology use, focusing on children's and youth's changing relationships to media and communications. She has been conducting ongoing research on Japanese technoculture, looking at how children in Japan and the United States engage with post-Pokémon media mixes. Her research on mobile phone use appears in *Personal, Portable, Pedestrian: Mobile Phones in Japanese Life* (MIT), which she coedited. She is a Research Scientist at the Annenberg Center for Communication, University of Southern California.

Susan Lepselter received her Ph.D. in social anthropology from the University of Texas at Austin in 2005. She has conducted ethnographic fieldwork, both on a UFO experiencers group in Texas and near Area 51, a major center of American UFO-based conspiracy discourse. Her articles include "Why Rachel Isn't Buried at Her Grave," in Daniel Rosenberg and Susan Harding, eds., *Histories of the Future* (Duke) and "From the Earth Native's Point of View," in *Public Culture*. She has taught anthropology and interdisciplinary studies at Brooklyn College, New York University, and Columbia University.

Christopher F. Roth received his Ph.D. in anthropology from the University of Chicago in 2000 and has taught at Lewis and Clark College, the University of Northern British Columbia, and the University of Wisconsin, Milwaukee. He is currently a visiting assistant professor in the Department of Anthropology, Northern Illinois University, DeKalb. Most of his research has focused on the aboriginal people of British Columbia and Alaska. He has published in *American Ethnologist*, *Northwest Anthropological Research Notes*, and *B.C. Studies*.

David Samuels is a linguistic anthropologist whose work on language, music, and popular culture has appeared in *American Ethnologist*, *Cultural Anthropology*, and the *Journal of American Folklore*. He is the author of *Putting a Song on Top of It: Expression and Identity on the San Carlos Apache Reservation* (Arizona). He is Associate Professor of Anthropology at the University of Massachusetts, Amherst.

INDEX

Debbora Battaglia is Professor of Anthropology at Mount Holyoke College. She is the author of *On the Bones of the Serpent: Person, Memory, and Mortality in Sabarl Island Society* and the editor of *Rhetorics of Self-Making*.

Library of Congress Cataloging-in-Publication Data
E.T. culture : anthropology in outerspaces / edited by Debbora Battaglia.
p. cm.
Includes bibliographical references and index.
ISBN 0-8223-3632-4 (cloth : alk. paper)
ISBN 0-8223-3621-9 (pbk. : alk. paper)
1. Human-alien encounters. I. Battaglia, Debbora.
BF2050.E8 2005
306'.1—dc22   2005025677